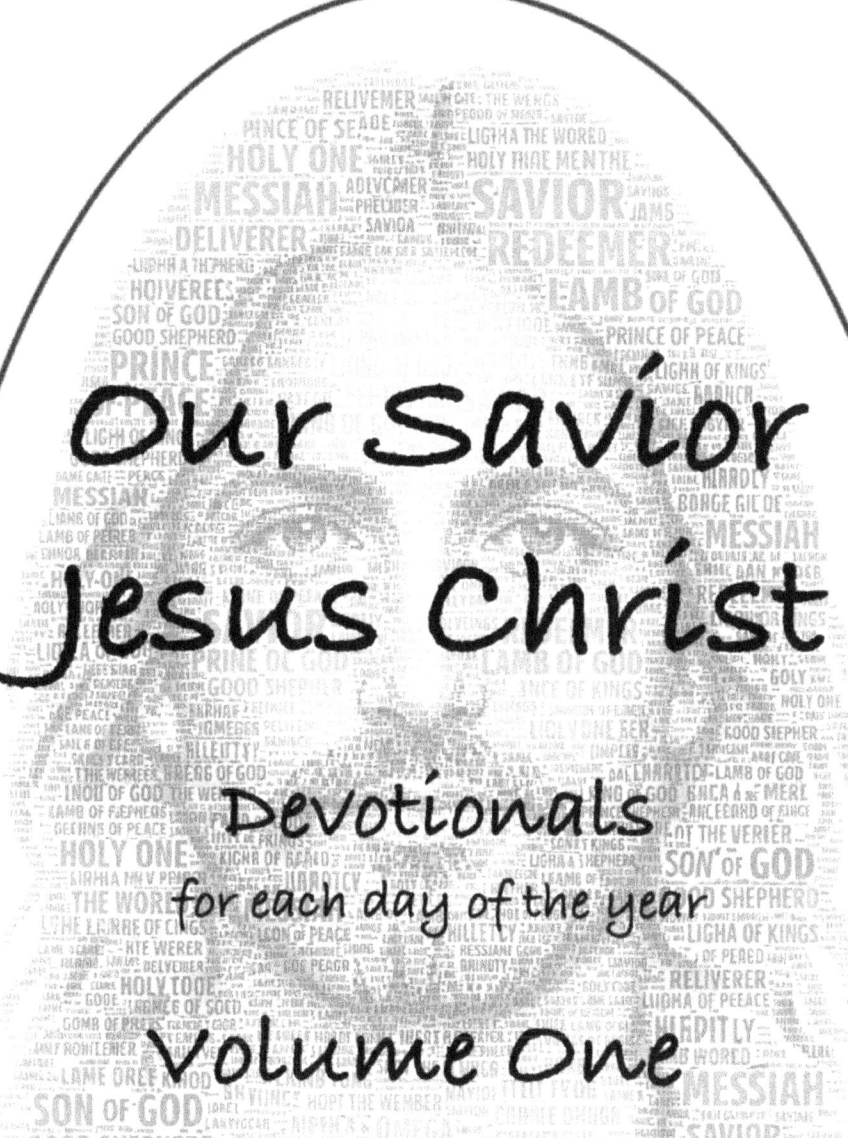

Our Savior Jesus Christ

Devotionals
for each day of the year

Volume One
of Four

Philip M. Hudson

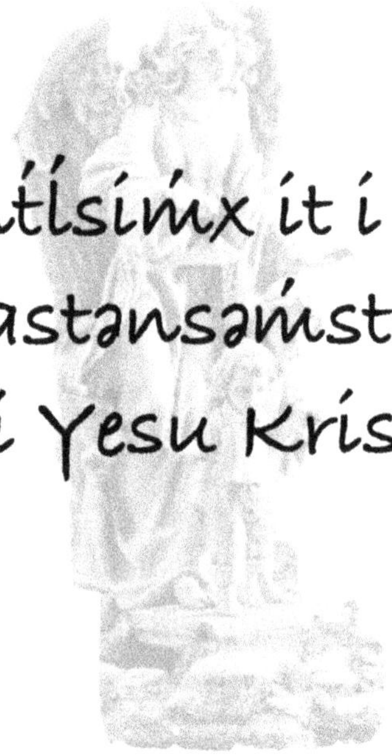

ntlsímx it i i
x̌astənsəḿstn
i Yesu Kris

(Nsyilxcən)

Copyright 2026 by Philip M. Hudson. Published 2026. Printed in the United States of America. All rights are reserved. No portion of this book may be reproduced, stored in a retrieval system, or transmitted in any form or by any means, mechanical, electronic, photocopy, recording, scanning, or other, except for brief quotations in critical reviews or articles, without the prior written permission of the author.

ISBN 978-7-965754-17-7
Illustrations - Google Images.
This book may be ordered from online bookstores.

I·Beru ammen Iêsus Crist

Sindarin (Grey-Elven)

Our Savior Jesus Christ

Devotionals
for each day of the year

Table of Contents

Ni-Sabarin Lēsū Kristos

(PaLM-Lang / Gemini Proto)

Our Savior Jesus Christ

Devotionals for each day of the year

You say potâto, I say potâto

You say potâto, I say potâto..1

Our Savior Jesus Christ

Devotionals for each day of the year

Preface

Preface..3

Our Savior Jesus Christ

Devotionals for each day of the year

Introduction

Introduction..7

Jan Jesu Kijesas li Jan Pona Tawa mi Mute

(Toki Pona)

Our Savior Jesus Christ

Devotionals for each day of the year

Author's Note

Author's Note 11

Our Savior Jesus Christ

Devotionals for each day of the year

Devotionals for each day of the year 15

Our Savior Jesus Christ

Devotionals for each day of the year

Afterword

Afterword 393

Jesa Krayisto Mae Hajinaan Anni

(Dothraki)

Appendix One...395

Appendix Two...397

Soli Deo Gloria..401

Yésus Kristó i Nostaro lma

Quenya (Elvish of the High Elves)

Our Savior Jesus Christ

Devotionals
for each day of the year

By the Author

By the Author..405

Tātou Fakaola ko Lesu Keriso

(Tolilauan)

Our Savior Jesus Christ

Devotionals
for each day of the year

You say potāto,
I say potâto

We learn from the
thought provoking principles
of the gospel of Jesus Christ that we
are going to heaven, and during our
journey thru its teachings and doctrine
we'll follow a pulsing stream of inspiration
and be at-one with the mind of God. When the
Spirit opens the eyes of our understanding, the
undreamed vistas of what would otherwise be
inaccessible experience will be opened to our
view. Our heart strings will resonate as we
consider the promised blessing of old,
and that it is only by the power of
the Holy Ghost that we may
know the truth of all
things.

Du sees Gromper, ech soen Gromper.
(Luxembourgish)

Mir léieren aus de
gedankestimuléierende Prinzipien
vum Evangelium vu Jesus Christus, datt
mir den Himmel bestëmmt sinn, an datt mir
op eiser Reesduerch seng Léier an Doktrin eng
fléissend aalieweg Stréimung vun Inspiratioun
follegen an eins ginn mam Geescht vu Gott. Wann
de Geescht d'Ae vun eisem Verstoeften opmécht, da ginn
Ausblécker opgemaach, vun deem, wat mir soss net kenne
virstellen Erfarungen, déi sech eis soss net géife erschléissen.
D'Seele-Saiten vun eisen Häerzer fgänken un ze klénge wa
mir iwwer dee versprachenen ale Seegen nodenken, an datt
et nëmme mat der Kraaft vum Hellege Geescht ass, datt
mir d'Wourecht vun alle Saache kenne kënnen.

Our Savior Jesus Christ

Devotionals
for each day of the year

Preface

As you peruse the pages of this book, you will recognize that it is really nothing more than a calendar of sorts, whose daily devotions relate to our Savior Jesus Christ. I wanted to provide a full year's worth of thoughts, which in hindsight turned out to be a daunting goal. In any event, I leave for you, dear reader, to do with these entries what you will. As for me, I can breathe a deep sigh of relief that this endeavor is over, and move on to other writing projects!

You will quickly see that the thoughts that are expressed on each page have been carefully crafted to represent a variety of geometrical shapes. It may be surprising to learn that the construction of these patterns has helped me to coherently organize my thoughts. In many cases, the outcome almost seems to have been foreordained, as I moved words around and made substitutions, until, as if my magic, the right expressions dropped into their proper positions on the page.

Often, I envisioned beforehand the particular framework that I wanted to create, and when I had appropriately arranged the words, one or two would stand out and grab my attention, because they still didn't feel quite right. Frequently, it was not difficult to find an alternative that would not only be a better fit, but also was etymologically better suited to the spiritual concept I wished to convey. As my work on the project continued, I was intrigued by the natural evolution of the process. That made me consider whether my success might have been stimulated by unconventional thought processes that are more commonly characterized as inspiration or discernment.

As I pondered the geometry of the designs that were spread out before me, I realized that they might be manifestations of non-linear thinking in a cynical world that is largely governed by limiting beliefs. Maybe my idiosyncratic ramblings were just an exhibition of thoughts that had taken me down a different path. Maybe I wasn't crazy, or delusional, after all. Perhaps I had simply been inspired to think unconventionally.

We will describe non-linear thinking shortly, and in greater detail, but in the meantime, let me tease you with this possibility. Maybe Joseph Smith was one of the first non-linear thinkers. His revolutionary view of the world helps to explain why he would look back on his life, and muse: "I stood alone, an unlearned youth, to combat the worldly wisdom and multiplied ignorance of eighteen centuries with a new revelation, which ... would open the eyes of more than eight hundred millions of people, and make plain the old paths." (H.C. 6:74). Or: "When we understand the character of God, He begins to unfold the heavens to us, and to tell us all about it. When we are ready to come to Him, He is ready to come to us." (H.C. 6:308). Or "It is my meditation all the day, and more than my meat and drink, to know how I shall make the Saints of God comprehend the visions that roll like an overflowing surge before my mind. Oh! How I would delight to bring before you things which you never thought of." (H.C. 5:362). Or: "The best way to obtain truth and wisdom is not to ask it from books, but to go to God in prayer, and obtain divine teaching." ("Teachings," p. 191).

With that in mind, let us turn our attention to linear thinking, that has been defined as a process of thought following known cycles or step-by-step progression, where a response to any given step must be elicited before another one is taken. This is the conventional way most of us think most of the time, and in most situations it actually works out quite well. However, there is always the danger of relying too heavily upon the sheer logic of linear thinking, for once we have settled upon a starting point in our inquiry, there are only a limited number of options or avenues available that lead to logical conclusions. Additionally, there is no guarantee that our starting point relies on truth, or on what I would call, in the case of this volume, the eternally valid principles relating to our Savior Jesus Christ. If we are lucky, and it does, we are certainly going to be much better off than if we had chosen a starting point that was either blatantly false, or that was so narrowly defined that it would have limited our exposure to the rich variety of alternatives that might just have been the best ones to provide the answers to our questions. In any event, if we adopt linear thinking, there is always the risk of being led astray right from the start, and then finding ourselves on the wrong road in unfamiliar, indefensible territory from which there is no easy avenue of escape. We are almost forced to resign ourselves to "damn the torpedoes," and push forward to the end. Linear thinking can be dangerous when it starts off on the wrong foot, and inexorably takes us down the road of expediency that leads to ethical or moral dilemmas, or to conundrums that can be of cosmic proportions.

Non-linear thinking, as opposed to linear thinking, is a relatively new term, which means that there is a lot of obfuscation going on when attempting to articulate its definition. But, for the sake of simplicity, let's describe it as human thought that is characterized by cerebral expansion in multiple spatial and even temporal directions, rather than in just one pre-determined linear direction. It is based on the concept that there exist multiple starting points from which the basic principles of logical thought may be applied to a topic or a problem. Consider, once again, my characterization of Joseph Smith as one of the most celebrated (and misunderstood and maligned) non-linear thinker of the Nineteenth Century.

It doesn't take much of a leap of faith to be immediately struck by the realization that God Himself must be the quintessential non-linear thinker, that the Plan of Salvation is its best expression, with all of its permutations and combinations, and that it might be consistent with His design if we were to view our Savior Jesus Christ from the perspective of similar unconventional avenues of thought.

Non-linear thinking is expansive, and it lets creative juices run wild precisely because it is not dependent upon a narrowly defined self-limiting structure as its starting point. It increases the sheer number of possible outcomes right from the beginning because it encourages multiple starting points for any train of thought. There is enough room in the world for an infinite number of non-linear thinkers, which allows us to segue right into the basic premises of the Plan of Salvation, which, as it turns out, is flexible enough to accommodate those of every persuasion and inclination. Throw free-will into the equation, and the permutations and combinations expand to infinite proportions. Truly, God is no respecter of persons.

Non-linear thinkers who happen to be lucky enough to consciously appreciate the flexibility of any consideration of our Savior Jesus Christ have elastic testimonies leading to rock-solid conversion. To them, the veil is almost transparent. They are spiritually sensitive and prepared to act upon their own promptings, unconventional though they may seem to others who have not necessarily followed the same train of thought. As their powers expand, however, they experience the glittering facets of the life of the Spirit. They find themselves cast off into streams of revelation, as if they were being carried along in the quickening currents of direct experience with God. Non-linear thinking sets them free to be creative, and sets them creative, that they might be free to investigate unconventional or previously unexplored options that might seem heretical to those who are trapped within the prison walls of linear thinking.

In a sense, we all enter this world as non-linear thinkers. We are "born free," as it were. If that is true, from the very beginning, the stage has been set for the inauguration of the perfect law of liberty. We are nurtured from our birth to master the ability to generate higher-level non-linear thought processes, so that the quiet spiritual stirrings that underlie our experience might be amplified and become the catalysts we need to propel us into the holy chambers of the mind, leading to the expansive gnosis of God.

Non-linear thinkers have no privileged frames of reference, which opens up almost unlimited options to pursue, with no messy preconceived prejudices to get in the way. They jump around, forward and backward, up and down, and side to side, when working through a problem. They literally see the big picture from a larger perspective, as they move from one point on the canvas of life to another, focusing with greater sensitivity on areas that have caught their attention, without being painted into a corner by the structure of linear thinking, from which there is no easy avenue of escape, except to retreat inward into the hollow core of oneself. Non-linear thinking sounds a lot like how God seems to govern His vast creations.

Think of a linear slide show, contrasted with the comprehension of a huge canvas, a storyboard if you will, that illustrates the entire production, not from start to finish, but all at once, the beginning and the end at one and the same time, with the additional capacity to zoom in and out, to fast forward, reverse, and freeze frame. If you can visualize that, you can see why God must be a non-linear thinker. With a little practice, we can be, too.

In the thoughts expressed in this book, I hope that I have employed the best techniques of both liner and non-linear thinking, because I believe that ultimately, both are useful and important cognitive devices to be mastered if we wish to unlock our God-given capacity to progress eternally. Non-linear thinking, however, is at its best when, from the get-go, we critically examine our potential starting points, because doing that increases our chances of selecting the right option from myriad available alternatives. But somewhere during the process of inquiry, after that critical starting point has been fixed in our crosshairs, we might want to employ linear thinking, as well, because of its efficient logic-based reasoning. Once we have embarked upon the journey, thinking in a linear fashion might help us to focus our attention and get to the finish line in a more timely and precise manner, with fewer loose ends to worry about. How effectively we simultaneously use both devices depends upon how thoroughly we have read the play book, how comfortable we are with floating our options in the arena of public opinion or personal prayer, how tolerant we are of constructive criticism from any and all sources, how vigorously we exercise our gift of free will along the way to choose from among those options, and how often we rely upon Powers greater than ourselves to make necessary course corrections in order to re-align ourselves with Their greater wisdom, better redefine and envision our goals, and rededicate our efforts to achieve them.

As you read the devotions in this book, look for examples of both linear and non-linear thinking, and decide for yourself how to best incorporate them into your own style of inquiry.

Our Savior Jesus Christ

Devotionals
for each day of the year

Introduction

Hugh Nibley once observed: "We fool ourselves, when we think for a moment that we can read scripture without ever adding something to the text or omitting something from it." Therein lies the energy inherent in an examination of the gospel, that testifies of the divinity of our Savior Jesus Christ. We glean insight and understanding every time we investigate the word of God. I have learned to love the scriptures, and I often think of St. Hilary, who wrote: "Scripture consists not in what we read, but in what we understand." In these daily devotions, I have consistently tried to stitch the ideas swirling around in my head into the relevant familiar scriptures that are found in the gospel.

Reading these daily devotions as they relate to our Savior Jesus Christ does not replace personal study. The spiritual awakening that accompanies prayerful efforts to understand the mysteries of God through the study of His word cannot be achieved through another person's interpretation. Perhaps, though, my own perspectives on the eternal themes expressed within the gospel will be helpful to you as you read and seek your own guidance. It is my hope that you will use these volumes only to assist you as you continue your own personal journey to Christ.

Our challenge is to enlist the aid of the Holy Ghost as we undertake that journey. Many years ago, Dallin Oaks observed that Latter-day Saints know that compendia and other teaching aids can help us with the interpretation of the principles and doctrine of the gospel, but they must be used with caution. They "are not substitutes for the scriptures any more than a good cookbook is a substitute for food. When I refer to commentaries," he said, "I mean everything that interprets scripture, from the comprehensive book-length commentary to the brief interpretation embodied in a lesson or an article, such as this one."

"One trouble with commentaries," he continued, "is that their authors sometimes focus on only one meaning to the exclusion of others. As a result, commentaries, if not used with great care, may illuminate the author's chosen and correct meaning but close our eyes and restrict our horizons to other possible interpretations. Sometimes, those other less obvious meanings can be the ones most valuable and useful to us as we seek to obtain answers to our own questions. This is why the teaching of the Holy Ghost is a better guide to scriptural interpretation than is even the best commentary." ("Ensign," 1/1985).

Harold B. Lee taught: "We are convinced that our members are hungry for the gospel, undiluted, with its abundant truths and insights. There are those who have seemed to forget that the most powerful weapons the Lord has given us against all that is evil are His own declarations – the plain and simple doctrines of salvation as are found in the scriptures." (Regional Representatives Seminar, 10/1/1970).

Bruce R. McConkie explained that "revelation is necessary because … each pronouncement in the holy scriptures is so written as to reveal little or much, depending on the spiritual capacity of the student." ("A New Witness for The Articles of Faith," p. 71).

And so, as President Oaks continued, "the scriptures are not the ultimate source of knowledge, but what precedes the ultimate source. The ultimate source comes by revelation. We encourage everyone to make careful study of the scriptures and of prophetic teachings … and to prayerfully seek personal revelation to know their meaning for themselves … If we seek and accept revelation and inspiration to enlarge our understanding, we will have the mysteries of God unfolded to us by the power of the Holy Ghost."

Joseph Smith himself communicated with his contemporaries in what he characterized as his own "crooked, broken, scattered, and imperfect language." (Joseph Smith letter to William W. Phelps, 11/27/1832, quoted in "Making Sense of the Doctrine & Covenants, a Guided Tour Through Modern Revelation," Steven Harper. "Personal Writings of Joseph Smith," p. 186-287). In these devotionals that relate to our Savior Jesus Christ, I am sure that I have come nowhere near to matching Joseph's language, crooked, broken, scattered, and imperfect as it was, so please, dear reader, bear with me, as you work your way through these devotions.

'Nts'usim alhlay' Yesus Kristus

(Nuxalk)

Our Savior Jesus Christ

Devotionals
for each day of the year

Author's Note

My own
weak efforts as I have
undertaken the journey to
the Way, the Truth, and the Life
(see John 14:6), have reminded me
of Amish women, who create some of
the most beautiful quilts in the world.
On purpose, they introduce mistakes into
their projects, because they believe that any
attempt on their part to design and produce a
flawless creation of any kind would constitute
a mockery of God, Who alone is perfect. Unlike
the Amish, misteaks that have been incorporated
into this volume were not intentional, and so I
would beg your indulgence as you forgive
me my many imperfections.

In these devotionals, I have tried, first and foremost, to be a seeker of light and meaning, as I have addressed questions that I hope have reached beyond superficial knowledge to probe the essence of the themes that run deeply within an investigation of our Savior Jeus Christ. When I have explored scripture, language, or history, I have tried to look not merely at what is, but for what is revealed. I have tried to embrace a contemplative spirit, and to be drawn to the intersection of the sacred and the secular, not in a conceptual cul-de-sac, but at a crossroads where keeping to the right will lead to heaven's gate.

I have attempted to make these daily devotionals both precise and poetic, to address the correct use of an apostrophe one moment, and the mysteries of grace or the divine center of faith the next. I have tried to capitalize on the lovely tension between form and feeling, and between grammar and grace, that speaks to those who value both clarity and beauty. I hope that those who read these massive missives will not be content with vague answers, because I do not think they will find them here;, but rather with polish and nuance, the way a craftsman can appreciates a work of art that breathes celestial air under the guidance of the hand of God.

These devotionals reflect my efforts to be a historian of the heart who understands that memory and meaning can and should walk together. Many of the entries in these volumes bring up the past, not out of nostalgia, but out of reverence and a desire to understand how moments, people, and words echo across time.

In my efforts, I have tried to to be spiritually anchored and yet ascending in my thinking, rooted in faith, yet unafraid to question, to explore, and to expand. I hope that my offerings reflect a holy curiosity and the desire to see with celestial eyes, to weigh each word until its meaning gleams with light, and to listen for the underlying currents of truth beneath it all. To me, the past is not a ghost but a guide whose sweet memory shapes the present into art. Along the way, I have tried to ask not "how," but "why" with eyes wide open that trace the pulse of God within my heart. I've tried to embrace the details in my efforts, the gentle curve of faith, and the fine line of grace. My soul has tried to be thoughtful, steady, and pure, to seek the light where earth and heaven combine to move in wonder, not so much with a scholar's mind, but with a pilgrim's faith.

I've tried to write these devotionals in a tone befitting a candle-lit commentary that is soft, reverent, and interpretive, like the margin notes of a monk who loves his subject, to be both a man of letters and a child of the Spirit, with a dual nature that mirrors creation itself, with intellect and soul existing in quiet accord.

I've walked where reason, logic, and learning wed the realm of dreams that evoke images of the boundless intuition of faith. Together, they describe the way I have tried to frame both my questions and my answers, where never there was a stupor of thought nor belief that is blind. I have tried to listen beyond the words and to be attuned to the undertones of truth that are the product of the whisperings of the Spirit that are louder than is the noise of the world.

The prophets are my guides, sweet memory is living scripture, and every fragment of history, of instruction, or of exhortation, personal or sacred, is a gift that keeps on giving. I honor those ancestors of thought whose courage and curiosity has carved pathways through time to meet us in the present and grapple with issues that have always existed, but benefit from the wisdom of the ages.

The curve of faith and the grace of grammar's fine line draw attention to my efforts to combine craftsmanship with language. I have tried to blend the spiritual with the structural, and devotion with discipline, to treat even the smallest words with reverence. In this sense, I have tried to blend language with liturgy and to clothe the secular with the sacred. As a benediction to my efforts, I have tried to move in wonder's quiet grace, not so much with a scholar's mind, but with a pilgrim's heart, and to seek truth with a radiant faith. It is my hope that these devotionals about our Savior Jesus Christ will represent a reflection of the harmony between knowledge and faith, between word and spirit, and between the mind's lamp and heaven's light.

Our Savior Jesus Christ

Devotionals
for each day of the year

Our Savior
Jesus Christ draws upon
the magnificent power of the other
members of the Godhead, and endows
us with increasing receptivity to flashes
of insight, intuition, and inspiration. Its
fulfilment will cast us into streams of
revelation that will carry us along
in the quickening currents of
direct experience with the
powers of heaven.

Myths from all
over the world and from the
dim recesses of memory give the
Milky Way its name and explain its
origin. The Greeks believed it was created
when suckling Heracles dribbled the breast
milk of Hera, wife of Zeus, across the night sky.
It was also described as the trail to Mount Olympus,
the home of the Gods, and as the path of ruin made by the
chariot of the Sun God Helios. In Sanskrit, the Milky Way
was called Akash Ganga (Ganges of the Heavens) and it was
considered sacred. Hindu cosmology explains the galaxy as an
ocean of milk that was churned by the gods for a thousand years,
to release Amrita, which, as all know, is the nectar of immortal
life. Those of us who have a testimony of the divinity of Jesus
Christ have a different take on Creation. "God … made the
world and all things therein, seeing that he is Lord
of heaven and earth." (Acts 17:24).

If we have
been blessed to dance
with the stars perhaps the
pixie dust cast off the shoulders
of Jesus Christ will gently settle
on our shoulders, empowering
us to fly as on the wings of
eagles all the way to our
First Contact with
God.

As we read about
and study the teachings
of our Savior Jesus Christ, we
become aware of a divine design
that has been mapped out for each
one of us. "Our lives are fairy tales
waiting to be written by the finger
of God" (H.C. Anderson), and our
Lord is ever conscious of the Plan.
He will bless us with the regularly
recurring reassurance of religious
recalibration that will autocorrect
with a fortuitous frequency and
with a celestial precision. He is
always waiting in the wings
to help us should we stumble,
having forgotten the lines
that we'd memorized for
the Second Act of the
Three Act Play of
God's Plan.

Of all the
holy sanctuaries created by
the benevolent hand of God to
be safe havens from the insanity
of the world, the invitation to come
unto Christ remains one of the least
understood, reminding us that the
natural man will never receive the
things of the Spirit, for they are
foolishness to him. He cannot
know them, no matter how
hard he tries, for they are
spiritually discerned.
(See 1 Corinthians
2:14).

The sturdiest plants
that will always bear the best
fruit are those with deep roots that
are anchored in lush, nurturing soil.
Our Savior Jesus Christ encourages us
to integrate ourselves into a loam that's
rich in art, courtesy, decency, example,
honor, music, and virtue. Its object is to
encourage our spirits to freely flourish
beyond the narrow confines that are
equivalent to a one-pint nursery
container. With His guidance,
we are able to send down our
taproots into gospel soil
and anchor ourselves
to the Infinite.

The ordinance of the Sacrament
raises our testimony temperature to get our
juices flowing. It gives us a healthy whack on
our status quo, when and where we need it most.
It prods us off our complacency plateaus and helps
us to feel complete, whole, and at peace, and it binds
up our wounds. It completes the process of repentance
and forgiveness thru the Atonement, and instills
within our hearts a burning desire to re-commit
ourselves to follow our Savior Jesus Christ and
to listen to the whisperings of the Spirit.

If we will turn to
our Savior Jesus Christ, we
will discover for ourselves the
unlimited energy source of the
cosmos. We will "discard the poor
lenses of our bodies, and peer thru
the telescope of truth into the infinite
reaches of immortality." (Helen Keller).
On the other hand, if we haven't nurtured
our faith in the Great and Eternal Plan of
Redemption, if we've relegated our faculties
to telestial mechanisms of inquiry, and our
engines stall for lack of celestial power, we
may find ourselves caught up in a flat
spin and downward spiral from
which there may be no hope
of recovery.

Our Savior Jesus
Christ invites us to take a seat at
a cosmic round table, but how can we
do that if we cannot now control our own
passions, if we regard so callously our own
birthright, or if we persist in selling it for a
mess of pottage? How can we ever hope to
be Guardians of the Galaxy, if today
we cannot even manage our own
households of faith?

When modern astronomy
was still in its infancy, Joseph Smith said
that if we do not comprehend the character of God, we
cannot comprehend ourselves, or by extension, the world
in which we live. One hundred eighty years later, N.A.S.A.
observed: "Whether life exists beyond our planet is a profound
question that is meant for the ages. The answer will change us
forever, whether it reveals a universe rich with life, one in which
life is rare and fragile, or even a universe in which we can find
no other life at all. The hunt for an answer also is revealing
important details about our place in the cosmos, such as
where we came from, how life came about and, perhaps,
where we're headed." Without intending to do so,
NASA articulated the three most profound
philosophical questions we could ask,
that are answered by the teachings
of Jesus Christ: "Where did we
come from, why are we
here, and where are
we going?"

In the Star Wars saga, the study in contrasts between the Jedi and the Sith has touched our collective consciousness and instinctive awareness to remind us that the Force wielded by Jesus Christ is real, and that we are the children of light. The motion pictures employed the vehicle of opposites to viscerally influence us, as they played off our familiarity with light and darkness. The ageless conflict fought so long ago in a galaxy far, far away stirred us at a visceral level, and caused us to wonder just how closely art imitates life.

Our Savior Jesus Christ stands on the bedrock of heaven. He will transform our timidity into powerful presence of mind. Thereby, He creates a platform for our assertive actions. On the other hand, when we try to avoid the demands that are placed upon us by His word, we will be swallowed up by a leviathan that is no less tangible than the beast that swallowed Jonah (see Jonah 1:17), and we, too, will eventually be unceremoniously spit out upon the rocky shoreline of our obligations.

The enigma of the
ministry of Jesus Christ
is that every day
is 'today.'

When
we end our
mortal journey,
we will recall every
celestial signpost that
took us past the conceptual
cul-de-sacs, the doctrinal dead
ends, and the telestial traffic that
have threatened to detour us from the
strait and narrow way. We are grateful
for the counsel of Jesus Christ Who exposed
us to direct experience with the perfect law of
liberty, and that He showed us how to exchange
the uncertain course that had been adopted by
telestially bound individuals, for the reality of
celestial certainty. We will then realize that our
uncommitted recognition of His divinity cannot
promise our inheritance in the Celestial Kingdom,
because Christians of convenience do not have the
fire that's ignited by covenants. Many honorable
people who accept the Savior will still inherit the
Terrestrial Kingdom if they didn't receive the
gospel, the testimony of Jesus, the prophets,
or the covenants. Thus, they "will not be
gathered with the Saints, to be caught
up unto the Church of the Firstborn,
and received into the cloud."
(D&C 76:102).

Every heavy
element in our own bodies,
the calcium in our bones, and the
iron in the hemoglobin of our blood, was
created during the cataclysmic explosions of
supernovae. Amino acids within this seething,
gurgling, bubbling, and boiling primordial
soup combined to form the building blocks
of life, the DNA blueprint that traces our
genetic heritage and testifies of the
nobility of our armorial bearing
all the way back to our Lord
and Savior Jesus
Christ.

As the
final curtain closes
on our mortal sojourn, we
will fondly remember that it
was Jesus Christ Who shepherded
us beyond the doctrinal dead ends,
as well as around the conceptual cul
de sacs and telestial traffic jams that
always threatened to detour us from the
strait and narrow way. We will be forever
grateful for His instruction that exposed us
to the law of liberty, and permitted us to
exchange the uncertain course adopted
by those bound for telestial glory
for the reality of celestial
surety.

Our Savior Jesus Christ has commanded us to search diligently and worshipfully within the pages of scripture for the pearls of great price that may not be readily discernable after only a cursory glance. (See 3 Nephi 23:1). We must all beware how we handle the oracles of God, "lest they are accounted as a light thing, and (we) are brought under condemnation thereby, and stumble and fall when the storms (of winter) descend."
(D&C 90:5).

Our Savior Jesus Christ helps to reacquaint us with Heavenly Father's Plan as we put finishing touches on our dissertations on life. As we near perfection, our expositions will be esteemed by God for what they've become: each one of them a true magnum opus mirroring His divine design. By soliciting the Holy Spirit to release us from captivity, we are permitted to see things as they really are, and to enjoy lucidity that comes more from our hearts than from our heads. Thus, we are reminded of the peaceful setting back in our heavenly home, and of God's promises that so gently massaged our spirits there.

Our Lord
Jesus Christ
has a copyright on
children's fairytales.
(See Matthew
19:14).

Jean Luc Picard
sat in his chair on the
bridge of the Enterprise-E,
raised his right hand, pointed
two fingers at the view screen, and
uttered the command: "Engage!" With
it, off they zoomed in their starship with
the inertial dampers online as they achieved
warp speed. We do something that is similar
when we engage Jesus Christ, Who will introduce
us to our own personal Quantum Slipstream Drive
system. Our course has been laid in, and our journey's
parameters are defined in our Operations Manual, whose
elements are to be found within the Plan of Salvation. The
only boundaries we recognize are those the Lord has set. Our
navigational deflector shield is the Savior, and our inertial
damper is His Atonement. Our capacity to "engage" is only
determined, at a molecular level, by our genetic code. It is a
blueprint whose implementation will take us to the final
frontier of experience at the edge of eternity, where we
will encounter strange new worlds, new life, and
new civilizations, in regions of our Father's
Kingdom nigh unto Kolob, where no one
has heretofore dared to go.

The
ministry of our
Savior Jesus Christ
was meant to help us as
we pick our way through
the minefields of mortality.
But if we refuse His assistance,
we may well end up looking like
an octopus on roller skates, with
uncoordinated gyrations that
suggest that our journey is
not likely to end well.

In a make-believe galaxy within an
alternate universe existing only in our imaginations,
the motto of Starfleet Academy was "Ex astris, scientia," or
"From the stars, knowledge." This was derived from the real world
Apollo 13 motto "Ex luna, scientia," or "From the moon, knowledge."
The Apollo 13 motto was inspired by "Ex scientia, tridens," the motto of
the United States Naval Academy, meaning "From knowledge, sea power."
But space may not be the final frontier. We might one day cast off from our
home port on planet earth and set sail out among the stars to explore strange
new worlds, seek out new life and new civilizations, and boldly go where
no-one has gone before. But as we stand on the decks of our starships
looking out across the cosmos, we may yet realize that our greatest
adventures lie in our future, during the journey inward to an
appreciation of the greatest Navigator of all, our Savior
Jesus Christ. Who could have imagined beforehand
that when we laid in our course, He would take
us beyond the farthest reaches of space to
the edge of forever, to indescribable
heavenly realms that are the
abode of the Gods?

We look up at the heavens for the answers to life's greatest questions, "Where did we come from? Why are we here? Where are we going?" or "Are we alone in the universe?" But we don't take the time or expend the necessary energy to recalibrate our sensor logs to make certain we are directing our inquiry toward the correct parsec of space, to the heavenly realm of Jesus Christ. We need to follow Isaiah's counsel. He urged us to seek the Lord while He may be found and to call upon Him while He is near. (See Isaiah 55:6).

The Spirit urges us to persevere, and to complete the course curriculum offered by our Redeemer Jesus Christ, and graduate with honors from a school of hard knocks. It is no small consolation that we had previously given ourselves to exhortation in the heavenly precincts of our pre-mortality. We have been anchored to the infinite since the foundation of the world, within gospel topsoil that's been nurtured by reservoirs of living water. Our golden ticket is repentance, whereby we might find forgiveness thru His Atonement, and regain the glory of our former home in heaven.

The unrepentant wicked might conduct their lives in opposition to the incontrovertible laws of heaven for only so long before critical mass is reached. Then, readjustment will be required to bring the disobedient back into a harmonious balance with nature, and with the teachings of our Savior Jesus Christ.

As we follow the teachings of Jesus Christ, the circle of our wisdom will expand. But so will the boundary of darkness. The more we know, the more we'll need to learn. It should do no violence to our faith if we realize that, with a greater understanding of the truth, we'll likely have additional questions, even those that relate to mysteries of the kingdom.

We travel in our mind's eye to the little town of Bethlehem to worship our Savior Jesus Christ, the newborn King. "Outwardly, God disguised him not, but made him like other men, and sent him into the world to offer himself for us a sacrifice of a sweet savor, to kill the stench of our sins, that God himself should smell them no more, nor think on them any more."
(William Tyndale).

A mighty testimony of our Redeemer Jesus Christ reintroduces us to the power of His Atonement, that can save us from our natural state of carnality, sensuality, and devilish inclinations. It activates the Law of Mercy, which mitigates for those who conform to its requirements the effects of the first Law, which demands justice. It lifts us to a state of holiness, spirituality, angelic innocence, and happiness, and prepares us to feel comfortable in the celestial precincts where we will find ourselves one more time in the presence of angels who are softly singing heavenly lullabies that communicate only love. The Holy Spirit will be there, as well, to personally reintroduce Himself, to welcome us home; and to bear witness to the Father of all that He had both seen and heard during our sojourn on the earth.

Our Lord and Savior Jesus Christ proffers to each of us an invitation to contemplate the possibility that we might one day be like Him. We believe that His grace consists of the gifts and power by which we might be brought to His perfection and stature, so that we might enjoy what He both has and is.

It is very difficult for us to imagine the velocity at which terrestrial vehicles travel in space. Voyager 1, that was launched on September 5, 1977, has achieved a faster heliocentric recession speed than any other man-made object, at 10.72 miles / second, (or 38,592.0 miles per hour). Thanks to the Law of Inertia, it has constantly maintained that same velocity for 47 years, as of 2025. It's now flying beyond the heliopause and the termination shock at the edge of our solar system, and it has begun to write new chapters of discovery as it begins its transit thru interstellar space on its way to the outer reaches of the Milky Way. It's a shame that its golden record failed to mention our Redeemer Jesus Christ. (But it might be that our interstellar neighbors don't need our introduction. They may already know about Him).

When
we read about
Jesus Christ, we
should always be
alert to the use of the
word "suddenly," that
frequently foreshadows
experiences destined to
be other-worldly. (See
Acts 6:22).

Jesus
Christ opens
up a conduit of
heavenly energy
that streams forth
from the doorstep of
the Gods, providing us
stability in a world that
has become befuddled by
weights and measures that
have been contaminated by
the evidence tampering of the
adversary. He not only liberates
us from sin, but He also frees us
from incarceration to confusion,
hesitation, skepticism, ignorance,
mistrust, uncertainty, suspicion,
doubt, and worry. (See John
14:1).

The Adversary
stands at attention,
always ready to entice us
to steer a tortuous course away
from our Savior Jesus Christ, that
will transport us right into telestial
traffic jams, religious roundabout,
and doctrinal dead ends, from
which the only escape that is
possible is thru speedy
repentance.

The Lord, Who
is our Savior and our
Redeemer, changed forever
how we look at both ourselves
and the world. His life was his
message, and His prophets, whose
lives are highlighted in His gospel,
were equally true to its doctrines and
to its principles, as well as to the moral
and ethical constants that were to them
as guiding stars that would lead them to
a safe haven. The Savior held Himself up
as a prototype of the perfection to which we
should aspire (see Matthew 5:48), that is
within our reach. But without His divine
intervention, you and I would be doomed
to failure in our efforts to become as He
is. He has the power to tear down every
barrier that lies in the path of
our progress.

If we allow
Him to do so, Jesus
Christ will shower upon
us little embers of celestial
fire that are kindled to glow
and grow within us, to warm
and sustain our spirits in
moments of doubt and
darkness.

If we reject the inspiration
that will come as we develop
a relationship with Jesus Christ,
we'll be at serious risk of withering
and dying, by becoming as empty
shells, and structures of custom and
convenience, illuminated only by the
flickering candlelight of superstition
and magic. We need the luminosity of
the Lord to free us from our bondage to
ignorance. The glow of the scriptures,
the Light of Christ, and clearly, the
superior illumination that will be
provided by the Holy Ghost, will
deliver all the photons that we
will need to provide us with
light in world in which
there is such a power
of darkness.

Our Savior Jesus Christ exposes the baubles of Babylon as a deception and a snare. (See Psalms 38:12). They are the brazen opposites of the incorruptible riches of eternity. (See D&C 38:39).

Our Redeemer Jesus Christ reassures us that when the time comes for our dust to return to Mother Earth who gave it, we will have completed a full circle back to our Maker, Who is the sole Fashioner of the universe itself. And so, in all of our attempts to comprehend the cosmos, we will finally realize that we were just trying to understand ourselves. Every heavy element in our bodies, including the calcium in our bones and the iron in the hemoglobin of our blood, was created in the cataclysm of a supernova. When we ask about the origin of the universe and its destiny, we are quite simply probing humanity's fundamental questions, including: 'Where did we come from, why are we here,' and 'where are we going?' In a coming day, we will be reintroduced to a land that was created before time itself, "when meadow, grove, and stream, the earth, and every common sight, seemed to be appareled in celestial light." (Wordsworth).

Our Savior
Jesus Christ invites
us to visualize the image of a
Brazen Serpent that is ever before
us, and yet, too often we continue to
eat, drink, and make merry as we
engage spiritual Babylon. In a
deadly dance with death, we
look beyond the mark that
has always been in
our midst.

Our Redeemer Jesus Christ
has made sure that every time we fortify
ourselves through righteousness, we will be insulated
from the influences of the world that would have otherwise
left us vulnerable to the enticements of the evil one who is the
adversary of all that is good. The terrible effect of sin on those
who have previously been taught the principles of the gospel is
that the guidance of the Spirit is withdrawn, and we are left
alone to grope in darkness. Guilt causes us to shrink from
church activity, and in the absence of the Spirit, sinners
have no claim on blessings, prosperity, or preservation.
Tragically, those individuals, feeling uncomfortable
in proximity to spiritual experiences, withdraw to
lifestyles devoid of such associations. Thus
begins a downward spiral that gains
momentum as sinful practices,
more easily committed,
became habitual.

In our day, we are witnessing how electronic media might interfere with our relationship with our Redeemer. For His influence is vital to the execution of the celestial principles and doctrines that are taught in His gospel.

Those who have irresponsibly drunk of the wine of the wrath of God have been enslaved by selfish habits and "regard not the work of the Lord, neither consider the operation of his hands." (Isaiah 15:12). Without the knowledge of our Savior and His Atonement, they'll be as hostages who are "famished, and their multitude dried up with thirst. Therefore, hell has enlarged herself, and has opened her mouth without measure; and their glory, and their multitude, and their pomp, and he that rejoiceth, shall descend into it (even as) God that is holy (is) sanctified in (His) righteousness." (Isaiah 15:13-16).

Our Savior Jesus Christ reassured us that there will come for each one of us a great and dreadful day when we will be asked to stand and give our sworn deposition before God, angels, and witnesses. Upon the issue of faith, depending upon our answer, we will be counted among sheep or goats, and find ourselves on His right hand, or on His left hand. As always, the decision is left up to us.

We are blessed with the tools we'll need to calibrate our lives, so that they'll conform to the pattern of our heavenly home. We've all come to earth from the timeless vantage point of the abode of the Gods. Therefore, our Elder Brother caused that our celestial chronometer be attuned to a more easily recognizable temporal scale. At the same time, He gave us a hint of heaven by blessing us with His gospel.

Jesus Christ helps us to see beyond our mortal horizons. We even have a name for such a state, calling it "the depths of eternity." Our covenants bless us to "inherit thrones, kingdoms, principalities, powers, (and) dominions, (of) all heights and depths." (D&C 132:19). The question, though, is: In what direction will these peaks and valleys take us?

When our Redeemer Jesus Christ walks beside us, He will help us to discern good from evil, because Satan wears many hats and is the great deceiver. (See D&C 52:14). He is an honorary member of the Screen Actor's Guild, and a sought-after image consultant. He cruises the Internet, and is a permanent resident of chat-rooms. He bombards us with spam emails. He is a prize-winning author, and a talented lyricist, composer, and scriptwriter; the creative influence behind media that are too numerous to mention. He is a fashion designer, travel agent, vintner, and beer distributor, an actor, newscaster, politician, scientist, and power broker. He may even be a teacher, or wear the clerical robes of the priesthood.

Our Savior
Jesus Christ very
forcefully teaches us
that even when the raw
feelings of pride taint and
twist our character, salvation
lies in His Atonement. When
we look about and argue who
is right, repentance stands
ready to look up to God,
and ask what is
right.

Many of our Father's children who seek the
truth struggle with vision that is clouded by doubt
and confusion, and by the perception that no one seems
to know what to believe. Tensions rise, the pace of life gets more
and more hectic, vulgarity eats away at the borders of our spiritual
symmetry, and righteousness is an increasingly unpopular lifestyle
choice. Our sponge has been wrung nearly dry as we have sought to
cool our feverish foreheads, and those of others, with living water.
What a blessing it is to know that there is light at the end of a
long tunnel of darkness; that, in Jesus Christ there is a
haven and a place of refuge from the turmoil of the
world. His counsel reaffirms that our lives have
purpose and direction, and encourages us
to quietly rededicate ourselves to follow
Him Who is "the way, the truth,
and the life" of the world.
(John 14:6).

When our Savior Jesus Christ teaches us about Zion, we are eager to adopt its substantive lifestyle and renounce Babylon's transparency. We have learned to trust in Zion's grip on reality even as Babylon grasps for straws in the confusion of an illusion that is of its own making. We know that Zion deals in spiritual absolutes even as Babylon tosses to and fro in a vacuum of moral relativism. We have witnessed the focus of Zion as well as Babylon's congenital spiritual short-sightedness. We're comforted to learn that Zion is grounded on a foundation of doctrine to which we've been attracted. These stand out in sharp contrast to the temptations of Babylon, who thinks it's sunbathing in the light of day and that its values are principles, even as it reassures itself that all is well, when, in reality, it is only basking in a false sense of carnal security.

As we continue our study and learn more about our Savior Jesus Christ, we discover that the powers of heaven cannot be handled or controlled except upon the basis of a quality of righteousness that is neither superficial nor ritualistic. We remember the example of the Pharisees, who, when when they "were gathered together, Jesus asked them, Saying, What think ye of Christ? Whose son is he?" Sadly, their sluggish response, "The Son of David," was tendered with little feeling or emotion. (Matthew 22:41-42). Although it was technically correct, it lacked spiritual horsepower. Its dearth of traction was obvious, its inability to generate spontaneity was palpable, its lack of energy to engage enthusiasm was noticeable, its incapacity to spark vitality was evident, and its failure to candidly acknowledge the powerful relationship that can exist between ourselves and our Heavenly Father was clear. The Savior teaches us how to make sure that our own responses to His penetrating questions will arise out of deeper convictions.

If the laws that relate to the ordinances of salvation, sanctification, justification, and exaltation have been stitched into our very sinews by the witness of the Spirit that Jesus Christ is the Savior of the world, they become essential elements of the tapestry of our lives. They are central to the pattern upon which we trace our progress along the path of our journey home. Our "minds become single to God, and the days will come that (we) shall see Him, for he will unveil His face." (D&C 88:68).

Those who have grown to appreciate the mission of our Savior Jesus Christ know how to use the password of "Atonement" to get past Security at the portal of heaven. As they approach the dominion of God, they will look back to witness the unmatched beauty of the gate through which they, as heirs of His kingdom, have entered. It will be "like unto circling flames of fire; also the blazing throne of God, wherein" there shall be "seated the Father and the Son." And the "beautiful streets of that kingdom," shall have "the appearance of being paved with gold." (D&C 137:2-4). Thus, is described in beautiful metaphoric imagery, the power of our covenants that are only made possible through His gospel.

41

Our Savior
Jesus Christ teaches us that
neither physical nor intellectual
health will have the power to save us,
since what is at stake is feeling, and
not knowledge or our temporal security.
Only our spiritual well-being can come to
our rescue. As we begin the long journey of
discovery, our hearts and our nature will be
changed as scales of darkness fall from our
eyes. The path that lies before us will be best
illuminated if we've nurtured the eye of
faith, enabling us to see all the way
from here to eternity.

As we pause in our busy lives to consider the
merits of our Savior Jesus Christ (see Philippians
1:11), we take a break from our everyday affairs. For
once, mankind becomes our business. The common welfare
is our business, as are charity, forbearance, benevolence, and
mercy. We view the dealings of our trade as nothing but "drops
of water in the comprehensive ocean of our business." (See Charles
Dickens, "A Christmas Carol"). Divine tutorial training is woven
into seeming injustice when our accumulated belongings fall
into the hands of unscrupulous adversaries. Sometimes, in
straitened circumstances, we are uncomfortably taught to
put the value of the world's goods in a proper perspective.
He constructs teaching moments to emphasize the
importance of relying upon His power alone and
not on the extrinsic worth of telestial trinkets
to accomplish His purposes, as we board
the "train that is bound for glory."
(Rosetta Tharpe).

Our Lord and Savior Jesus Christ has stacked the deck in our favor, making the reaffirmation of our devotion to Him much easier. He invites us to keep ourselves clean and bright, for our clear eyes "are the window through which we see the world." (George Bernard Shaw) "This above all, to thine own self be true," counseled Polonius to his son Laertes. "And it must follow, as the night the day, thou canst not then be false to any man," let alone to our Savior and Redeemer. (Shakespeare, "Hamlet").

When we come unto Jesus, the integrity of our labor will be revealed in spectacular simplicity and plainness. The walls of opposition to our purposeful preparation will crumble and fall away. In our exertion, the Savior will comfort and succor us with the bread of life. As we journey through the harsh and unforgiving environment of Babylon, and seek the Lord while He may be found, an oasis will burst forth in the desert and living water will quench our thirst.

*Our introduction
to our Savior Jesus Christ
will provide us an opportunity
to enjoy familiarity with the Way,
the Truth, and the Life, (John 14:6),
or, in other words, to have personal
experiences with God, with Him,
and with the Holy Ghost.*

William Tyndale wrote: "Seeing that it has pleased
God to send to our English people (as many as sincerely
desire it) the" gospel of Jesus Christ "in their mother tongue, but
also that there are false teachers and blind leaders in every place,
and in order that you not be deceived by any man, I believed it very
necessary to prepare this pathway into the scriptures for you. I do it so
that you might walk surely, and always know the true from the false.
I write to keep you in remembrance of certain points, namely to well
understand what these words mean: The Old Testament, the New
Testament, the law, the gospel, Moses, Christ, nature, grace,
working, believing, deeds and faith, lest we ascribe to the
one that which belongs to the other, and make Christ
to be Moses, or the gospel to be the law, or despise
grace and rob from faith, or fall from meek
earning into idle disputes, brawling,
and scolding about words."

Our Lord and Savior
Jesus Christ has promised the
dawning of a millennial day when
His words will flow, from not one, but from
two capitals, "for out of Zion shall go forth the
law, and the word of the Lord from Jerusalem." (2
Isaiah 2:3). There will be neither disease nor death,
and when people have lived to an old age, they will
not die in the classical sense, but will be changed
in the twinkling of an eye, from mortality to
immortality, in a process of translation.
(See 1 Corinthinans 15:51-52).

If those who have
only hesitantly considered
the merits of Jesus Christ (see D&C
3:20), later decline the invitation that
is extended to them by the Holy Ghost to sit
and sup with the Saints, perhaps it is because
their stiff necks have prevented them from looking
up to Heavenly Father for guidance, over to men and
women of God for counsel, around to find answers to
life's profound questions, and down in an attitude of
humility. The challenge for those who have found joy
in the Lord is to soften the telestial tendencies of
their friends and neighbors, and find the keys
that will open their hearts, that they, too,
might become as pliable clay in
the creative hands of the
Master Potter.

As long as the hard-hearted and thick-skinned choose to remain in a state of rebellion against the Spirit, a testimony of the divinity of Jesus Christ must remain just beyond their reach. If they never raise their eyes to search eternal horizons, their world will appear to them as nothing but a barren desert that is devoid of refreshing oases, the welcoming shade from trees, and an abundance of well-watered gardens. If they lack faith in nourishing revelation, the bread of life will be to them as stale and moldy leftover crumbs good for nothing but to be fed to swine and cattle.

An Apostle of our Lord Jesus Christ prophesied that in the Last Days the hearts of men would fail them as their shields of faith began to falter. (See Luke 21:26). When the heavens close, the revelatory voices of warning are silenced, and all is quiet from pulpits that had aforetime been aflame with faith. The rebellious rant and rave against that which is good, but the righteous can also be pacified and lulled away into a false sense of carnal security until they believe that all is well in Zion. But none of us can afford to take our foot off the gas during our journey along the highway thru Babylon that eventually leads to heaven's gate.

Now is the time
for us to perform our labors,
even as our Redeemer Jesus Christ
heals the soul scars of mortality thru
the Atonement. We will attend to every
needful thing in the anticipation of our
resurrection to glory and a wonderful
reunion with all of our loved ones
in the Celestial Kingdom
of our Father.

We are struck by the
realization that when the Lord
gives us commandments, He also
prepares ways for us to accomplish
the tasks that are set before us. We see
what might be best for ourselves and for
the Kingdom of God, develop testimonies
that it should be, and then work with all our
capacity to make it happen, whatever the cost
might be. Then, when we are so richly blessed
far beyond the measure that we deserve, the
price, once paid so painfully, is recalled in
gladness. We receive full value. As D&C
82:10 suggests: The Lord is bound
when we do as He says, but when
we do not what He says, we
have no promise.

The image
of a white dove has
always been associated
with the Author of peace, the
Savior of the world. (See Luke
3:22). As Joseph Smith explained,
The "sign of the dove" is an emblem
or token of truth and innocence. For
those who have accepted the gospel of
Jesus Christ and have been washed
clean in the waters of baptism, it
will come at the time of their
second baptism of fire
and the Spirit.

Our Savior Jesus
Christ inspires us to be our best,
to strive to so live that we will remain
honest, true, chaste, benevolent, virtuous,
and do good to all men. As our faith increases,
so will our capacity to see His influence over every
aspect of our lives. We will learn to recognize and accept
the suffering that is a part of life, and we will strive to see
how adversity is a necessary and beneficial contrary in our
experience. When we face trials, we'll remember the Savior,
Who descended beneath all things, and Who provided us
with His example for us to follow. We will be drawn to
the light. It will be within our nature to comfortably
relate to all that is virtuous, lovely, of good report,
or praiseworthy. We will seek after anything
that creates an atmosphere that invites
the Light of Christ and the Holy
Ghost into our lives.

The teachings of our Redeemer Jesus Christ caution us unmistakably that a pervasive threat to temporal and spiritual welfare exists in the genome of every natural man. It is hidden in an improvised explosive device called pride, that is ready to explode and scatter its lethal contents about in a deadly deluge of deception. (See Mark 7:21-22). The warning is relevant to all, but applies in particular to those who are trying to move beyond a law of carnal commandments to embrace a celestial standard.

To maintain the balance of our spiritual equilibrium, our Savior Jesus Christ encourages daily doses of study and reflection, so that when we have spiritual experiences, it will be as if the veil that had been before our eyes becomes transparent, permitting us to almost reach out and touch the eternities. Today, as we read the scriptures, we can feel clear and whole, and at peace with ourselves and with our environment. We can hold certainty in our hands; guiding principles can resonate with reality, allowing us to move forward on the pathway to our ideals. It is no wonder that Satan tries to cloud our vision with the glitz and the glamour of carnal counterfeits that are no more than optical and spiritual illusions. However, his will-o-the-wisp fantasies cannot stand the heat of the mid-day Son, and will wither and die when confronted by the principles of gospel doctrine in action.

Devotion to our Lord and Savior Jesus Christ can protect us from the false sense of carnal security experienced by the world, as well as from indifferent complacency. We regard our weaknesses in positively constructive ways, and are grateful for our conscious awareness of opportunities for personal improvement, and for the tools that we have been given to accomplish our mortal mission assignments.

Contraries highlighted during the ministry of Jesus Christ have always existed between Zion and Babylon. Those in Zion see with wide-eyed wonder even as Babylon squints at every sunburst that foreshadows a spiritual awakening. She would rather put on designer sunglasses than adjust her eyes to the increased illumination of the light of truth. Zion abases the wealthy in order to exalt the poor while Idumea emphasizes earthly treasure, worships the almighty dollar, trades in counterfeit currency, destroys initiative thru a misguided sense of entitlement, allows ambition to replace righteous desire, and suppresses upward mobility and progress while maintaining the status-quo and subjugating the interests of those who are no less deserving, but who, through no fault of their own, find themselves in much less fortunate circumstances.

Babylon
finds the concept of
the Atonement of our Savior
Jesus Christ difficult to grasp,
because it was conceived in heaven.
It's not of this world, and so if we try
to wrap our finite minds around it, we
will fail to do so. But when we commit
or recommit ourselves to His gospel,
It can be spiritually discerned.

Obedience to the teachings
of our Savior and Redeemer Jesus
Christ protects us from a latter-day free-
fall from faith, when for so many there are
few rules, regulations, or restrictions to temper
either moral or ethical depravity. The better angels
of our nature respond to righteousness, because the
positive energy of foundation principles is immune
to the capricious character quirks of those who have
compromised their standards in a capitulation to
the telestial trauma of secular humanism. Those
of weak will cannot deny their noble birthright
for very long before it begins to strangle their
spontaneity as rapidly evolving children of
God. Obedience to our covenants, however,
will enrich our lives with a vitality that
will quicken our spirits in ways that
nothing else could. His gospel can
become a living and breathing
entity with a life of its own,
inviting us to be born
again.

Our Savior
Jesus Christ is "mighty
to save" (Isaiah 63:1), and He
will strengthen our hands to lift
those who need our support. He will
galvanize our courage to allow our
feet to take us to those who've been
imprisoned by poor choices or by
bad habits, or who are hobbled
by ruinous circumstances
that may or may not
have been of their
own doing.

The
gospel of Jesus
Christ describes heart
breaking stories of those
who sank to new lows after
having committed terrible sins
that were nigh unto unforgivable.
But as long as these long-suffering
Saints were re-committed to their faith,
and as long as they drew upon the power
of our Savior's Atonement to bind up and
heal all of their wounds, they would remain
especially sensitive to the comfort that flowed
thru the whisperings of the Spirit. When it
seemed that things couldn't get any
worse, they often rallied to
be their best.

We pray that we might be faithful
and uncompromising when faced with
adversity, and yet be as humble and tender
as children; that we might be self-effacing, and
sensitive to the whisperings of the Spirit; that we
might exert a positive influence upon others
as they deepen their own testimonies
of the gospel of Jesus Christ and
of our Savior's divinity.

To perform optimally in their
roles thru to the successful conclusion
of our Father's Trifecta: "Where did I come
from? Why am I here? and Where am I going?"
those who desire to be counted among the disciples of
Jesus Christ don't have the luxury during the production
of the Plan's Second Act to sample every pleasure of spiritual
Babylon, to walk "in (their) own way, after the image of (their)
own god, whose image is in the likeness of the world, and whose
substance is that of an idol." (D&C 1:16). If the drama is played
out within the strictures of the Play, according to the storyboard
that illustrates the principles of the gospel while animating the
doctrine of Christ, the anticipated blessings of Zion will freely
flow. There is no other way it can work. "Life is all a stage,"
wrote Shakespeare, but only the script written by God,
Who is our Dialogue Coach, will bring out the best
in all who participate in the production. We need
to trust His direction, for He is the source of
inspiration of the most accomplished
method actors of our day.

The Hebrew word "seraph" means "burning," and in the scriptures we encounter "bright, shining seraphs," when describing signs of the coming of the Lord that are complemented by "blood and fire, and vapors of smoke." (D&C 45:41 & 109:79). These metaphors of fire and smoke are employed by the prophets to depict the glory of celestial realms. In the language of Joseph Smith: "God Almighty Himself dwells in eternal fire. Flesh and blood cannot go there, for all corruption is devoured by that fire. God is a consuming fire." Perhaps one day, we'll come to understand how, not only Jesus Christ, but immortality itself, dwells in everlasting burnings. (See Isaiah 33:14).

There can be no latitude in the declaration of Jesus Christ that He "cannot look upon sin with the least degree of allowance." (D&C 1:31). Hence, there is no alternative to baptism, that typifies the gate through which we must all pass during our journey home to the Celestial Kingdom of God. Faith and repentance lead to that narrow gate, and just beyond its portal lie a remission of our sins, membership in the Church of Christ, and sanctification through receipt of the Holy Ghost. The way is strait and the standard undeviating, with no room for rationalization or compromise. There can be no allowances made for the indifferent substitution of more relaxed and less stringent entry requirements.

Our Redeemer Jesus Christ tenderly assures us that every child of God who has ever lived upon the earth will be raised to immortality and resurrected to live forever. But the Savior has revealed that we have a part to play in the Plan of Salvation, and His ministry has shown us how we can also be raised up unto eternal life. We need to organize ourselves to be ready to "prepare every needful thing; and establish a house, even a house of prayer, a house of fasting, a house of faith, a house of learning, a house of glory, a house of order, (and ultimately) a house of God." (D&C 88:119).

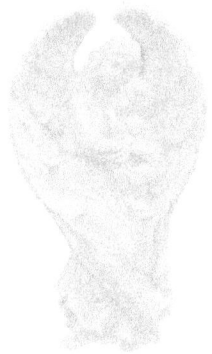

As the gathering of Israel gains momentum, Jesus Christ assures us that there is room in our congregations for all of the Children of the Covenant. "For Zion must increase in beauty, and holiness. Her borders must be enlarged. Her stakes must be strengthened. Yea, verily I say unto you …. arise and put on (your) beautiful garments." (D&C 82:14). The Lord our God shall set up the ensign of the church in the Last Days for the nations. As He told Joseph Smith: "I have sent mine everlasting covenant into the world … to be a standard for my people, for the Gentiles to seek to it; to be a messenger before my face." (D&C 45:9).

One of the blessings that continues to flow from our unequivocal acceptance of the divinity of Jesus Christ is our receipt of a constant stream of inspiration that cascades down from the heavens. This ensures that we will walk along illuminated pathways guided by the only institution that has received the approbation of God.

The Holy Ghost throws open the windows of our souls to let in more light, so we might better understand the principles that drive the kingdom of God forward. This is the doctrine of Christ (see 2 Nephi 31:21) that are mysteries to those who have not adequately prepared themselves for the torrents of revelation coming from above. The Lord has assured us, however, that we "shall know of a surety that these things are true, for from heaven" as from the lightning, thunder, and burning bush on Mount Sinai, will He declare it. (D&C 5:12, see Exodus 3:2).

Until it has
accepted Jesus Christ,
society will remain on the
fast track to self-destruction.
As we realize from D&C 1:16, it
doesn't "seek the Lord, to establish
his righteousness, but every man
walketh in his own way and after
the image of his own god, whose
image is in the likeness of the
world, and whose substance is
that of an idol which waxeth
old and shall perish in
Babylon ... which
shall fall."

Within the
quiet precincts frequented by our
Savior Jesus Christ, we discover the tools
of perspective and context, that we might
better understand our environment, while
its terrestrial jewels that are scattered about
provide counterpoint for clarity. It is light
and truth that endow us with the ability
to 'see' the spiritual world within which
we are enveloped. These include many
celestial glories and wonders in the
heavens that cannot be discerned
until the finger of God has
touched our mortal
eyes.

We are here, at this time and place, by God's divine design. What we think may be only coincidences, when they are viewed thru the clarifying lens of eternity, are faith-promoting examples of the Lord patiently working behind the scenes in our behalf. Nothing in this life happens by chance. Everything of significance occurs according to His will. The gospel of Jesus Christ confirms that "the works, and the designs, and the purposes of God cannot be frustrated, neither can they come to naught." (D&C 3:1).

Our Savior Jesus Christ invites us to contemplate possibilities that we have never before imagined. The Spirit provides the catalyst to stir us with a fire in our bones. Christopher Columbus recounted the similar impetus for his own voyage of discovery, by simply stating: "The Holy Spirit gave me fire for the deed." Our hearts burn within us when God extends "knowledge by His Holy Spirit, yea, by the unspeakable gift of the Holy Ghost." (D&C 121:26). Jeremiah similarly described his desire to serve the Savior: "His word was in mine heart as a burning fire shut up in my bones, and I was weary with forbearing, and I could not stay." (Jeremiah 20:9).

It is our most fervent desire to enjoy the unconditional love of our Savior Jesus Christ. We want to be transformed as we learn to submit to His will and develop His character and nature. We will rely upon His promise: "All that I have, I could give to you, but what I am, you must earn for yourself, line upon line and precept upon precept." (See Isaiah 28:10).

As we mature, and as our faltering steps become more confident, we recognize the wisdom of Hans Christian Anderson, who avowed: "Our lives are fairy tales waiting to be written by the finger of God." Many of the chapters in our personal journals have already been completed, and no-one knows how many pages remain. But we do know this: Although we cannot start over and make a new beginning, we can surely begin now to write a new ending. We believe God, who said: "If your eye be single to my glory, your whole bodies shall be filled with light, and there shall be no darkness in you; and that body which is filled with light comprehendeth all things." (D&C 88:67). We intuitively turn to Jesus Christ because He is full of light, and those who receive it, will receive more light, that will grow brighter and brighter until a perfect day when we shall see as God does. (See D&C 50:24).

When we enjoy
a rapport with the Spirit,
our faith to act will generate
the power to do God's will in an
expansive and interactive way,
in holiness. We will recognize
the revelatory voice found in
the teachings of Jesus Christ
that "abideth and hath no
end." (D&C 88:66).

If, through our engagement
with our Savior Jesus Christ, we
are able to learn anything, it's that
both great and terrible judgments are
on the horizon, not at some hazy point in
the future, but today. We speak, think, and
act according to either celestial, terrestrial, or
telestial laws. We've been blessed with a moral
compass, and faith in Christ with its evidence
in action clearly defines the path that we have
chosen to follow. Each day that we live, we are
24 hours closer to His Pleasing Bar. f we've
committed the Thirteenth Article of Faith
to practice as well as to memory, its
principles will have become the
particles of our faith.

The work and glory of our
Heavenly Father is to bring us into His
kingdom after we have grown up unto
the Lord, have spiritually matured,
and have learned that the basis
of our hope of salvation rests
in His Atonement.

When we have been
tossed to and fro as flotsam
and jetsam on the sea of life, never
coming to a knowledge of the truth, to
what source will we look for the stability
underfoot that we so desperately seek. Where
will we turn for the answers to the questions that
continually trouble our spirits, as we attempt to chart
a safe passage through shoals and reefs? If we calibrate
our sextant to an interstellar scale that encompasses the
possibility of an expanded view of life, and we consider
its remarkable potential to catalyze greatness, we will
be up and moving along on the pathway to personal
discovery within a larger arena that circumscribes
eternity. Along the way, Jesus Christ will provide
us with a primer that will prepare us to face
ionic cyclones, temporal rifts, and even
subspace vortices and fearsome
black holes.

The teachings of Jesus Christ speak a language that is universally understood, without ambiguity. It leaves little room for discussion as to its meaning because it is spiritually discerned. Even more surprisingly, it unifies us even as it celebrates our diversity, but it quickly moves us away from dependence and independence, to interdependence. However, it blesses us with conformity without asking us to give up our individuality, or the things that make us unique. His voice invites all to come unto God to partake of His goodness. (See Matthew 11:28).

Our Savior Jesus Christ teaches that God in heaven is the Grand Architect of a divine design that establishes our familial roots and confirms His Fatherhood, that we might enjoy a witness that it is in Him alone that "we live, and move, and have our being; as certain also of (our) poets have said. For we are also his offspring." (Acts 17:28). If we will only seek to understand ourselves from an eternal perspective, we will raise our sights to the possibility of an expanded view of life, and we will be up and moving forward on the pathway to religious recognition and personal re-discovery.

Whenever the white-hot
sparks of revelation are struck off
the divine anvil of God, they will ignite
shimmering flames whose incendiary trail
will arc across the sky all the way to heaven.
If we surrender to the temptation to silence the
counsel of Jesus Christ by dousing it with the
water of worldliness, if we try to contain it
within the fire-lines of faithlessness, or if
we attempt to smother it under the sand
of skepticism, and especially if we
throw the dirt of doubt on it, we'll
never be blessed to know His
mind and will.

The effects of
sin are inevitable
and inescapable, but
for the intercession thru
faith in the Atonement. The
Author and Fashioner of the
universe must intervene in our
behalf by implementing the Plan
to initiate laws that were designed
to reinstate equilibrium. The gospel
of Jesus Christ teaches us that "in the
heavens, we will find a "better and an
enduring substance." (Hebrews 10:34).
It is His guidance that will show us how
to partake of the nectar that is an elixir
generally reserved for the enjoyment
of the gods.

After we accept the daunting challenge to expand both our horizons and our minds as we probe the mysteries of the unknown, we'll be forced to ask ourselves difficult questions: Have we embraced the moral element of responsibility that should co-exist with greater understanding? Do we truly believe that much is expected of those unto whom much has been given? Do we possess the spiritual determination and the intellectual fortitude to enhance our comprehension of Jesus Christ with an equally powerful sense that we are accountable to our Father in Heaven?

When we have accepted the divinity of Jesus Christ, God will show us how to be more easily governed by laws that define how we relate to eternity. When we are at-one with Him, we will sense a freedom from incarceration to mortality. In a coming day, we may even accompany Him on a goodwill tour of His creations. We can envision moving ever faster, as we try to keep up, even as time slows down, until we finally reach the speed of light, which is His light. At that point, time will be no more, and we will have been reconciled with the Infinite.

All of Heavenly Father's holy prophets who ministered among the children of men before the Savior burst upon the world stage taught the same principles of the gospel of Jesus Christ as the apostolic record keepers who followed in their footsteps. If they seem to repeat themselves, it is because their message is essentially unchanging, and they receive their inspiration from the same Source.
It isn't vain repetition, but rather,
theatrical encore.

The beautiful
Plan of Happiness
exposes us to a constant
flow of insight, intuition,
inspiration, and revelation
that simply streams forth in a
downpour of divine direction. It
also blesses us as we walk along
illuminated pathways and as we
exercise our intellectual and our
spiritual faculties. Our Redeemer
Jesus Christ teaches us how to be
guided as individuals and as a
society to a community of the
Saints, so that, together, we
might enjoy the direction
of the Holy Ghost. The
genius of the Plan is
that it is tailored
to meet every
exigency.

We will all need
to exercise diligence
as we confidently make
our way to the Atonement
of our Savior Jesus Christ, for
if our desire to be clean in the
sight of God is approached
casually, we will be as
vain imposters who
deny the faith.

The Lord admonished to love
our enemies, and to do good to them,
and to lend, hoping for nothing; and our
reward shall be great. (See Luke 6:35). The
"get even" mentality of revenge that has become
so popularized in books and films and reinforced
in everyday interpersonal relationships, in commerce,
and in social settings, is antithetical to the gospel of Jesus
Christ. Revenge is like taking poison yourself, but hoping it
will kill the other guy. It may be true that in business, you
don't get what you deserve; you get what you negotiate. But
when the earth has been cleansed to receive its paradisiacal
glory, a higher standard will prevail. Before that happens,
though, the disciples of Christ have a responsibility to
engage the mighty power of prayer, as they prepare
the earth for that millennial day, when the lion
and the lamb will lie down together, and a
little child shall lead them. (See
Isaiah 11:6).

Our Savior and Redeemer taught us a valuable lesson, when He declared: "I will forgive whom I will forgive, but of you it is required to forgive all men." (D&C 64:10). The gospel of Jesus Christ teaches us that our eternal salvation, and also our joy and satisfaction in life, meaning our true freedom, depends on our willingness and our capacity to to forgive others for the perceived injustices they've committed, that had supposedly done us harm.

If we listen to our Savior Jesus Christ and embrace His Atonement, we will embark upon a journey that is as old as time. Our faith introduces us to a procedure with which we may not be familiar, even that of a spiritual heart transplant. As we face a bright future after we have been born again into a newness of life, carefully prescribed anti-rejection protocols need to be followed, in order to protect and preserve the new organs that are steadily beating in our chests.

We may be
very surprised to
find that enduring to
the end simply involves
mastery of two principles
that are linked to the Savior's
Atonement, that are powerfully
communicated by the heavens in
the gospel of Jesus Christ. These are
repentance for our own sins, as well
as our forgiveness of the alleged
trespasses of our neighbors.

When we
sit at the feet
of Jesus Christ,
we will be rewarded
with the brightness of
doctrine that will shower
our minds in a cascade of
the heavenly diamond dust
of inspiration and revelation.
We're determined in our resolve
to repent, and we'll foreswear our
iniquities as the Spirit reminds
us that they're nothing less than
the fearsome after-images of the
rebellion of Lucifer, who stood up
before the Council in heaven to
present his own unworkable
counterfeit to the perfect
Plan of God.

The grace of God cannot save those who stubbornly determine to ignore His entreaties to commit by a covenant to an undeviating standard of righteousness. To believe that He would proffer His grace to those who only professed to know the name of Christ, but who at the same time mocked His gospel by their wonton disobedience, would be delusional.

The gospel teaches that after the Fall, the portal to Eden swung shut, but as it did so, another door opened that introduced Adam and Eve to a secret garden accessible only to those who would exercise the key of the Savior's Atonement, thru baptism by immersion for the remission of their sins. They would be able to have successful outcomes with evil as well as with good, with vice as well as with virtue, with pain as well as with pleasure, with sickness as well as with health, and with darkness as well as with light, all carried out within the white-hot crucible of experience.

The condescension of our Lord and Savior Jesus Christ (see 2 Nephi 4:26), is illustrated in the counsel that He gave in the Beatitudes during the Sermon on the Mount. (See Matthew 5:1-48). In short, He taught that He will bestow upon us all the blessings we need, instead of only those that we thought we had wanted.

As disciples of our Savior Jesus Christ, we increase our metaphysical metabolism, to burn away as much of the fat of faithlessness as we can when our hearts are broken in the fiery crucible of contrition. Our Redeemer is disinclined to remove the stain of sin for only as long as we remain incapable of maintaining unequivocal subservience to the celestially crafted doctrine that we call the Atonement, that is so unambiguously and incontrovertibly taught by the prophets.

When we look, we will find Him, the Savior of the World, "Jesus Christ, the Great I Am, Alpha and Omega, the beginning and the end, the same which looked upon the wide expanse of eternity, and all the seraphic hosts of heaven, before the world was made." He is "the same which knoweth all things, for all things are present" before His eyes.
(D&C 38:1-2).

When our roots sink down in the earthy loam of covenants and ordinances, and the foundation of our lives has been grounded in the teachings of our Lord Jesus Christ, we find His love and encouragement to be just the underpinning that we need in order for us to firmly establish our footings under the frost line of faithlessness and far beneath any impediments to progression, such as dishonesty, greediness, lust, pride, immorality, and selfishness.

Our vitals and
our bowels will be healthy and
strong, and properly perform their
functions, but more importantly, our
spiritual hunger will be satisfied
as hearts embrace our Savior
Jesus Christ.

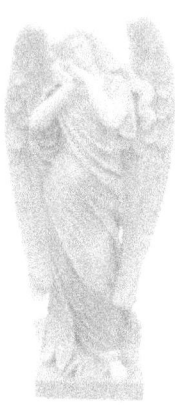

If we allow
ourselves to stray
from the teachings
of Jesus Christ, we will be
confronted by scribes and
Pharisees with golden tongues
who will beguile us with worldly
wisdom, politically correct behavior,
and homogenized values. We will be
sorely tempted by subtle sophistry and
words like tolerance, equal opportunity,
and affirmative action. Ever so gently,
flaxen cords will be nestled around our
necks. It will all seems so reasonable,
so comfortable, so inclusive, and so
open-minded, that we will barely
notice the malevolence of our
surroundings while we are
maliciously led down a
terrifying highway
to hell.

In our moments of
deepest reflection, when we
are pondering our relationship
with Jesus Christ, we realize that
we are the begotten spirit children of
Heavenly parents, and that we lived
in our pre-mortal nursery, with Them
watching over and nurturing us as we
prepared to begin our sojourn on earth.
Now we experience moments of déjà vu,
when awakened memories enlighten
both our minds and our hearts, as
they whisper in our ears that we
are strangers in the land, who
have wandered from a more
exalted sphere.

If we continue to
stubbornly refuse to
acknowledge the reality
of eternity by neglecting to
engage the counsel of our Savior,
where will our sanctuaries be if the
wind blows and the rain beats down?
To what safe harbors will we flee when
the ocean of life is in turmoil? If we are
tossed about as flotsam and jetsam and
never come to a knowledge of what is true,
to what source will we look for the stability
we so desperately seek, or for the answers
to the greatest questions in life that
trouble our spirits?

When we have sunk our roots down into the earthy loam of the gospel of Jesus Christ, we will find that ordinances and covenants have become intertwined with the principles and doctrines that were taught in His ministry.

The gospel of Jesus Christ considers the commandments as a consummate compilation of affirmative actions that commit us to a holy covenant with God, to a lifestyle that is centered on the Savior. Members of His church discover that the relationship between His commandments and our blessings is directly proportional. They appreciate it's practically impossible to have one without the other, and it is only this perspective that makes sense of the Savior's reassurance that His yoke is easy and His burden is light. It is little wonder that this message has been interpreted as the gospel of repentance, and that we're encouraged to rely upon His merits that are crowned by the greatest blessing of all; which is that of His Infinite and eternal Atonement for our sins.

If we wrestle with
the teachings of our
Savior Jesus Christ, if we
have taken poetic license with
the principles of His gospel, or
if we have thoughtlessly added
ecclesiastical embroidery to its
truths, we risk diminishing the
intensity of our faith to believe,
and we must speedily repent,
and modify our approach to
both our scholarship and
our worship.

The Gods ingeniously
manipulate not only matter
and energy but also space and
time by the power of faith. They have
set the conditions "by which the worlds
were framed, (and) all things in heaven,
on the earth, or under the earth. These exist by
reason of faith as it existed in (the mind of the
Gods), and were it not for this principle of faith, the
worlds would never have been framed, neither would
man have been formed of the dust. It is this principle
by which Jehovah works, and thru which he exercises
power over all temporal, as well as eternal, things."
So declared the Prophet Joseph Smith. It is by the
simple exercise of our faith that we ride on the
coat-tails of Jesus Christ to see beyond the far
reaches of the cosmos, all the way into
the depths of eternity.

The teachings of Jesus Christ assure us that we will be resurrected and live forever. But He asks us, before that can happen, to organize ourselves and "prepare every needful thing; and establish a house, even a house of prayer, a house of fasting, a house of faith a house of learning, a house of glory, (and) a house of order." (D&C 88:109). In substance, we must build and maintain a house that has been dedicated to the Lord, that we might inherit not only immortality which is freely given to all, but also the greater gift of eternal life which has been reserved for the obediently faithful.

Our Redeemer Jesus Christ sends a clear message to the nations of the earth in the voice of thunder, and when He does, the ground trembles beneath their feet. (See Job 37:5-13). If you are wondering how thunder and lightning normally occur, it happens when relatively warm air clashes with cold air, and the lighter, warmer air rises into the upper atmosphere, creating thunderheads. On the way up, warm water molecules rub against cold molecules in clouds. This causes all the molecules to shed electrons that collect at the bottom of the cloud. When enough electrons are buzzing around the base, they're attracted to the ground, which temporarily holds an opposite charge. Then, lightning streaks to the earth, breaking the sound barrier and creating thunder. Thus does God "work in mysterious ways." (Attr. to William Cowper).

Through the
influence of the Light
of Christ, we find righteous
judges who illustrate the power of
even a handful of inspired political
leaders to hold evil in check, positively
influence the outcome of events, and
ultimately, to change the course
of history.

Jesus Christ acknowledges
free will, for it is recognized as the
guiding principle of heaven. We can see
how its exercise might entail risk, but we also
realize that it is tied to our progression. Rather
than enslaving us in good habits, He repeatedly
grants us the opportunity to recommit ourselves to
true and eternal doctrine and to covenants of action.
Agency allows each of us to enjoy all of the privileges
of church membership, empowers us to remain active,
and is a principle that sanctions our commitment to
baptismal promises, all of which are essential if we
are to nourish our spiritual well-being. Only with
agency can we gyroscopically maintain our
spiritual equilibrium and hope to manage
the mercurial fluidity of a world whose
only constant seems to be its harsh
and unrelenting proclivity to
continually reinvent itself
in both good and very
bad ways.

To His prophet Jeremiah, the Lord Jehovah (see Isaiah 12:2), explained: "Before I formed thee in the belly I knew thee; and before thou camest forth out of the womb I sanctified thee, and I ordained thee a prophet unto the nations." (Jeremiah 1:4-5). Moses was asked to "remember the days of old … when the most High divided to the nations their inheritance. When he separated the sons of Adam, he set the bounds of the people according to the number of the children of Israel." (Deuteronomy 32:7-8). Our Elder Brother Jesus Christ clearly teaches that we lived before we were born.

Our comprehension of the Way, the Truth, and the Life (see John 14:6), expedites the application of moral agency, that is simply properly channeled free will, furnishing us with tools to hammer out our salvation with both fear and trembling before the Lord. Gaining wisdom is critical to the successful implementation of the Plan. Thus, it's another of the spiritual gifts that have been provided by the Source of all wisdom, that is the embodiment of God our Father, Jesus Christ, and the Holy Ghost.

Our Redeemer Jesus Christ meekly enjoins us to put everything in its proper perspective. He teaches that we should seek wisdom instead of riches. He counsels us that in order to have a working understanding of spiritual things, we must have discernment, which is guidance from the Holy Ghost. When we inquire in sincerity, we are taught by the Spirit, and the confirmation of our faith is a manifestation of a special gift of God. The Lord's mission is to shepherd the covenant faithful by that power from baptism, along the strait and narrow path, to the other ordinances that are necessary for them to obtain eternal life. (See Matthew 7:14).

"We who lived in the concentration camps can still remember those who walked through the huts comforting others, giving away their last pieces of bread. They may have been few in number, but they offer sufficient evidence that everything can be taken away from us with the sole exception of the one thing that is the last of our human freedoms, which is the right to choose what our attitude will be," said Victor Frankel. We retain this right, no matter how difficult our circumstances may seem. We keep our own counsel, but are guided by the Holy Ghost, determined to follow an enlightened path, firm in the faith that our steps will safely guide us to the peace and rest that are the quiet sanctuary of the righteous, that is found in the teachings of Jesus Christ.

The teachings of our Lord and Savior Jesus Christ (see Matthew 10:35), suggest that "human history becomes more and more a race between education and catastrophe." (H.G. Wells, "The Outline of History," 2:594). But we are comforted to know that within His teachings He also provided us with a blueprint for our survival, that is illustrated by both times and circumstances that are not so very different from our own. (See 2 Timothy 3:1).

"It's true! In Camelot, the crown has made it clear. The climate must be perfect thru all the year. A law was made a distant moon ago here. July and August cannot be too hot, and there's a legal limit to the snowfall here in Camelot. The winter is forbidden 'til December, and exits March the second on the dot. By order, summer lingers thru September in Camelot. I know it sounds a bit bizarre, but in Camelot, that's how conditions are. The rain may never fall 'til after sundown. By eight, the morning fog must disappear. In short, there could not be a more congenial spot for one to engage in happily-ever-aftering, than in Camelot." (Alan Jay Lerner). We do not live in Camelot, but we must not complain, because the gospel of Jesus Christ, and in particular the mighty power of prayer, have made it quite easy for us to bloom where we are planted. As a matter of fact, "if we were stronger, we might be less tenderly treated. If we were braver, we might be sent, with far less help, to defend far more desperate posts in the great battle."
(C.S. Lewis).

When the arm of the Lord is revealed (see Isaiah 53:1), we can be certain of His mighty power, for He is our sure source of strength and support. The arm of flesh, however, is unstable, and is prone to uncontrollable spasms, atrophy, and paralysis, that are the manifestations of clumsy outbursts of behavior that are driven by worldliness and are always destructive and ineffectual. (See 1 Corinthians 1:21).

In a lesson borrowed from the counsel of one of the prophets of Jesus Christ (see Acts 20:29), J. Reuben Clark, Jr. warned that "ravening wolves are amongst us from our own (people), and they, more than any others, are in sheep's clothing, because they wear the habiliments of the priesthood. We should be careful of them." Ezra Taft Benson agreed: "There are some in our midst," he declared, "who are not so much concerned about taking the gospel into the world, as they are about bringing worldliness into the gospel."

Too often, the majestic clockwork reflected in the arithmetic of the teachings of Jesus Christ has fallen on deaf ears. "Is it not a shame," asked William Tyndall in 1528, "that we Christians come so oft to church in vain, when he of four score years old knoweth no more than he that was born yesterday?" Thanks to Tyndale, in these latter days, the ready availability of the scriptures in our native tongue has changed the nature of that equation. In that sense, at least, the new math is a good thing.

The judgement of the weak-willed may be infected with the deadly virus of overindulgence and lasciviousness. Of those who had been mesmerized by physical impairment and who'd been blinded to the path of progress, Isaiah wrote: "They regard not the work of the Lord, neither consider the operation of his hands" (Isaiah 15:12), and without the steadying influence of the counsel of Jesus Christ, they are held captive because their character has been compromised and they can no longer experience insight, intuition, inspiration, or revelation. Their indulgences require greater intensities of fulfillment to receive the same level of gratification. They lose traction on gospel sod and spin their wheels. They slowly slip backward, like a train wreck in slow motion that is inexorably headed toward a precipice of destruction. (See 1 Thessalonians 5:3).

Disciples of our Savior Jesus Christ yearn to be more observant followers of righteousness, to possess greater knowledge, and to be the progenitors of nations and ambassadors of peace, to receive instruction, and keep the commandments.

The commotion of life roughly jostles us further and further from the influence of the Spirit, whose purpose is to guide us away from that precipice of destruction, and to lead us homeward to a secure sanctuary where the stability of greater laws prevails. It is in Jesus Christ that we learn that we came into the world to die, but at the same time, thanks to the further light and knowledge that we glean from the revelatory nature of His teachings, we learn about the Plan of Redemption that has been designed to take away the sting of death. (See 1 Corinthians 15:55).

Spiritual
enlightenment can
create a celestial bridge
that transports us past the
improbabilities of life to the
stability of understanding,
augmented by the revelatory
nature of the teachings of Jesus
Christ and witnessed by eternal
realms that lie just beyond the
horizon, but whose existence
is evidenced by fire in
the sky.

We cannot go back to
write a new beginning, but we
can always start today and cut and
paste a new ending into the tableau of
our lives. The system can be re-booted,
bad code can be moved to the trash, and
damaged files can be restored. Enough
RAM and additional disk space can be
created to compose a bedtime fairytale
where everyone lives happily ever after.
And the best part of all, is that, with
churchofjesuschrist.org waiting to
introduce us to our Savior, it
should be easier than
ever!

During what might
very well prove to be the journey of our
lives, many of us are bearing heavy loads as
we draw near to our Savior Jesus Christ. There
is in our hearts a silent prayer that He might
care for us in Bethesda, as we come to Him in
great need, for the weight of our burdens
sometimes seems too much to bear. In
His grace, we will find solace, and
in His house, a tabernacle
of mercy.

During His mortal ministry,
our Savior Jesus Christ implied that physical death
is a crucial element of the merciful Plan of our Heavenly
Father. But spiritual death can occur, as well, if we die as to
things pertaining unto righteousness. The first spiritual death
occurs when we commit sin after the age of accountability. We
can be spiritually born again, however, through the cleansing
action of the Holy Ghost, after repentance and our baptism by
immersion. But there is also a second spiritual death, or an
eternal separation from the presence of God that occurs if
we've passed from mortality to immortality without
having received the ordinances of the priesthood,
and if we thereafter deny the Lord a second
time by declining the vicarious work
that has been performed in our
behalf in the House of
the Lord.

Our sense of curiosity almost compels us to stare up in wonder at the night sky, as we attempt to absorb the ramifications of the works of Jesus Christ that are made manifest among the stars.

The profound ignorance of worldly wisdom contributes to the problem, but a meager grasp of eternal principles also rests at the root of apostasy from truth among those who should be familiar with doctrine taught by our Lord Jesus Christ. Today the church continues to labor beneath a shallow understanding by some members of fundamental gospel principles. Consequently, the devil seizes upon their weaknesses. Satan knows who the Lord's servants are; each one is a marked man or woman. Therefore, they all require for a defense a solid foundation of doctrinal knowledge, an abiding testimony of every principle of the Plan of Salvation, and a witness of the Savior and Redeemer of the world.

Jesus Christ linked good works to obedience to the commandments of our Heavenly Father. It was with this understanding that Paul taught: "Not the hearers of the law are just before God, but the doers of the law shall be justified." (Romans 2:13). "Good works," Martin Luther explained, "do not make a good man, but a good man does good works." And what is it that makes us good? It is simply faith in God and in our Redeemer.

When we are led by the Spirit to the wonder of the gospel of Jesus Christ, we press forward, but not with the crowd that jostles for position in the mosh pit of telestial trivialities, but rather with the Saints, who seek wisdom that they might understand the mysteries of God. We take a fix on the stars, but the real focus of our reckoning runs more expansively; it points us to the heavens and to our Savior.

We must determine to drag
our broken and bleeding bodies
to church every Sabbath because it is
there that we will receive the transfusions
of a spiritual element. It can be a heavenly
dialysis center where worldly contaminants
may be removed from our systems, because
we are quite incapable of accomplishing
the task on our own. The therapy that
is necessary can only be found in
the doctrine of the Atonement
of our Lord Jesus Christ.

The awe-inspiring
redwoods along the Pacific
Coast are among the largest of
living things and take our breath
away. The tallest known tree reaches
a height of 368 feet, weighs hundreds of
tons, and is well over 2,000 years old. While
most other trees of nearly equivalent size have
deep roots that support their great weight, the root
system of the redwood is very shallow. The key to
its survival is the intertwining of the roots of one
tree with those of several of its neighbors. These
giants of the forest live in groves; they cannot
stand alone. Interdependency is critical to
the stability and longevity of each tree.
Just so, Jesus Christ taught that our
hearts ought to be knit together in
unity and in love, one to
another.

In the teachings of Jesus Christ we find a reiteration of the innocence of little children, which was an integral element of God's Plan of Mercy that was ordained in the Council in Heaven before the world was. (See Matthew 19:14). "At the first organization in heaven, we were all present and we saw the Savior chosen and appointed, and the Plan of Salvation made, and we sanctioned it." (Joseph Smith, quoted by William Clayton, reporting on an undated discourse that was delivered in Nauvoo, Illinois). The prophet's statement confirms that little ones who have died before reaching the age of accountability will be saved in God's Kingdom. By the power of the infinite and eternal Atonement of Jesus Christ, they are blameless from the beginning.

It may be no coincidence that, following the martyrdom of the Apostles of old, the mind-numbing tedium and monotony of the unrelenting stretch of years between 400 and 1,000 A.D. has been characterized as the Dark Ages, a time that was stark in every dimension. Intellectual life vanished from Europe. Even Charlemagne, the first Holy Roman Emperor and the greatest of all medieval rulers was illiterate. In all those static centuries, absolutely nothing of real consequence had either improved or declined. With the exception of the introduction of waterwheels in the 800s, there were no inventions of note. A creative vacuum existed, where everything remained as it had been for as long as anyone could remember. The only antidote to this medieval stupor of thought was a renaissance of Spirit that catalyzed a recommitment to embrace the teachings of Jesus Christ in their pure an unadulterated form.

When we come unto Jesus, we invite inspiration from heaven. (See John 7:37). For example, we cannot just determine to be charitable. We need the guidance of the Spirit to lead us to those in need, so that will not only talk the talk, but also walk the walk. By so doing, we will be doubly blessed.

Our Redeemer Jesus Christ taught that when we are carried into the greater light of heaven, our bodies will be clothed in immortality. As ultraviolet light is used in sterilization, (ultraviolet germicidal irradiation - UVGI), could it be that it is the physical phenomenon of the unearthly light intrinsic to God that is responsible for the purification and renewal of our sin-stained souls? Though our "sins be as scarlet, they shall be as white as snow; tho they be red like crimson, they shall be as wool." (Isaiah 1:18). His unfathomable light purges the effects of sin from our corruptible bodies. Justice is bathed, and then softened, in the warm glow of the light of Mercy.

A softening
influence will flow out
of our desire to draw near
to Jesus Christ. Without it,
we tend to suffer from hard
hearts and stiff-necks and
we're overtly and covertly
rebellious, and lack both
the malleability and
pliability that were
cultivated during
spiritual therapy
sessions before
we came to
earth.

Those
who wrestle with
the permutations and
the combinations that are
taught in the doctrine of Christ
realize that the key of knowledge
may be enjoyed by both those who
are in poverty and those who abound
in wealth. It is recognized by both fame
and obscurity, exercised in both sickness
and in health, put to good use by those with
influence, as well as by others who live in
anonymity, and it may be successfully
retained by both beauty and the beast.
As it turns out, God is no respecter
of persons. (See Acts 10:34).

The teachings of Jesus Christ are of no private interpretation. (See 2 Peter 1:20). Instead, their meaning is discerned by the manifestations of the Spirit that are universally accessible to those who have been blessed to experience the gift of the Holy Ghost.

The objective of the ministry of Jesus Christ is simply to enrich our lives. His power initiates an opportunity for dynamic change, as wisdom flows along established channels. Moreover, personal accountability, responsibility, and commitment to obedience expand. The humble need to serve strengthens connections of brotherhood and sisterhood while it generates interdependency within a community of true believers in which any cultural differences are effectively expunged. We are no longer strangers or foreigners, but we are as fellowcitizens with the Saints, within the household of God.

Just because the mathematical laws that
govern our physical universe are defined by
entropy, they don't necessarily doom us to suffer in
isolation within a cosmos that seems to be headed in the
direction of chaos or confusion. The bounds and conditions
of the gospel that have been defined by Jesus Christ might
yet enable us to find it within our reach to thread the eye
of the needle and walk a fine line past the seemingly
inexorable, unrelenting, unstoppable, unavoidable,
and unalterable demands of disproportion
that are manifest in the world as the
tendency toward disorder.

Jesus Christ
caresses our spirits with
the inexplicable images of
religious recognition that will
remind us that we are of a noble
lineage. The Holy Ghost lights our
way with the torch of truth; a beacon
to guide us safely home. It makes no
difference how far or wide science casts
its net, it remains completely powerless
to explain eternity's flickering shadows
that dance all around us. The forgotten
features of immortality will again be
illuminated by the steady light of
the Savior, for all who have
eyes to see.

Job, who was familiar terms with the Lord Jehovah, nevertheless asked: "Canst thou find out God? Canst thou find out the Almighty?" His habitation "is as high as heaven (and) the measure thereof is longer than the earth, and broader than the sea." (Job 11:7 & 9).

As a Companion Who has accompanied us on our journey to the veil that leads to Jesus Christ, the Spirit teaches us how to become engaged in fashioning defensive weapons in our armory of thought. With these tools, the Holy Ghost will show us how to reconfigure an arsenal of heavenly munitions with which we were at one time familiar. He will bring to our remembrance the firearms safety course that we completed in a premortal setting, that focused on our faith and our hope and charity, as well as on on peace, joy, and strength.

"The life given us" by our blessed Savior Jesus Christ "is sometimes short. But the memory of a life well-spent is eternal."
(Cicero).

We'll only feel our Savior's therapeutic energy after we have warmed our muscles with spiritually aerobic exercise, when we have loosened up our ligaments through compassionate service, when we have stretched beyond our perceived capacity and have gained the flexibility that comes with experience, when we have worked out the 'nots' in our physical and spiritual muscles by pushing ourselves to the breaking point, when our vision sees beyond our supposed limitations, and we huve ruised our sights to fix our mind's eye on a finish line that rises up to meet a celestial horizon. Then, when we have finally settled in to a comfortable pace, we will be able to see ourselves through to the end.

Thru our Lord and Savior Jesus Christ, we'll be able to see all the way into the heavens, with the capacity to be transported beyond the palpable and perceptible confines of this world as we return in our minds' eye to our former domicile there, where the boundaries are blurred, and the barricades of borders evaporate in a flood of light. Father's Plan was carefully crafted, that it might create conditions wherein we would be strengthened by the Holy Spirit to do our best within the cradle and crucible of our experience.

Seeds that have been tenderly planted in the fertile topsoil of the gospel and that will germinate into strong and healthy plants with deep roots are the covenants that we have made with God. They derive their nourishing power from their relationship with the firm foundation we have established with Jesus Christ. In our church experience, we are like the good seeds that have matured into a forest of trees that are secure in numbers. When the winds of adversity blow hard, we are unified and strengthened by our solidarity. But if we try to stand alone, no matter how great the girth of our trunks, no matter how securely planted are our roots, we risk being toppled over. We become like the solitary widow maker tree left over in the forest after its clearing. (See Isaiah 14:8).

We are intertwined with
each other through connections
with the subtle rhythms of life whose
divine center is Jesus Christ. He takes
note when sparrows fall from trees, and on
cold winter evenings, He helps us appreciate
the light from the explosion of supernovas in
distant galaxies. He will never play dice with
His creations, and we can be sure that He
won't leave anything to chance. And so,
as we commune with Him during our
devotions, our emotions will swell
within our hearts as we realize
that we can be at-one
with Him.

The mortal
ministry and the
sacrifice of Jesus Christ
among the children of men
may be the greatest miracles of
all, but those who deny the power
that is demonstrated by His gospel.
cannot be saved on their own merits,
simply because they will not generate
faith with enough energy to carry their
progression onward. Only if there has
arisen a profound attitude adjustment
and a spiritual heart transplant, will
they be capable of sustaining their
forward momentum along a
path that leads to God's
Kingdom.

Disciples
of Jesus Christ
proclaim the truth
with their hands uplifted
to the Most High, and their
incomings, outgoings, and
salutations in the name
of the Lord.

Our Savior Jesus Christ helps us to understand
that positive energy comes in discrete packages that are
dispensed by especially cheerful individuals who always have a
smile on their face and a spring in their step. These shining lights
have dedicated themselves to worthwhile performances that give their lives
meaning and purpose. They are committed to self-improvement and engage
with others in ways that are mutually supportive. They don't waste time being
defensive, but instead welcome constructive criticism. They share their wisdom
and ideas with others, and are mentors to those who are on the same path toward
self-discovery. They enjoy the journey as much as the destination. They will
not allow power or influence to corrupt them or to deter them from focusing
their energies on core principles. Even when life throws them a curve, they
smile. They realize that happiness is contagious, and as carriers of the
condition, they infect others with cheerfulness. They are courteous
and thoughtful, and when they speak of others, they do so as if
their parrot were the town gossip. They are kind and gentle,
especially when interacting with the village idiot. When
necessity dictates diplomacy, they celebrate their
differences, because they know that we are all
children of God, with unique talents
and abilities.

Jesus Christ taught with power, by coherently blending foundation principles together into an easily digestible matrix, so the power of the word and the witness of the Spirit could be devoured in bite-sized portions.

Our Savior Jesus Christ taught in a way that light and truth would easily distill upon our souls. Just so, in the Sacred Grove, light "descended gradually," entering the quiet grove slowly enough that Joseph was able to gauge its approach until it finally reached him and enveloped him within dazzling brilliance. It was only then that he "saw two Personages, whose brightness and glory (were beyond all) description," and who stood suspended in the air within the encircling light. (J.S.H. 1:17). We may not see Them as we contemplate the scriptures, but we receive inspiration and revelation because we are in the presence of those from the unseen world, and we can be sure that we dwell in holy precincts.

We open our scriptures
to the book of Luke, and we
carefully unwrap our Nativity
scene to gently place the carvings
of Joseph, Mary, and the baby Jesus in
a manger prominently displayed on our
hearths. The Spirit confirms to us that He is
the Christ Child, the Son of God, the Savior of
the world, and the author of the gospel of peace
on earth and of good will toward all men
and women (see Luke 2:13), which
are His Christmas miracles.

In an easygoing,
heavenly voice that is at
once melodious, rhythmical,
and soothing to our ears, it is
calming to our souls to hear the
Spirit whisper: "You're a stranger
here." We are quietly encouraged
to learn more about our Redeemer
Jesus Christ, and to experience the
realization that we have "wandered
from a more exalted sphere." Such a
road from glory, and our pathway
back to God's Celestial Kingdom,
are illuminated by stories that
teach us that the heavens are
not closed, and that our
Father continues to
influence our
lives.

Faithless societies tend to
deal with their spiritual myopia
with knee-jerk reactions that simply
ratchet down expectations. At the end of
the day, cultures that lack fire in the belly,
or the burning passion of faith in our Lord
Jesus Christ, will demand very little of
their citizens, and will receive
in kind.

Spiritual Babylon
frantically attempts to
change us by manipulating
us and by employing external
controls, but it fails wretchedly.
It is our Redeemer Jesus Christ Who
can initiate lasting change thru the
transformation of our inner vessels.
In truth, He is brilliantly successful,
by fine-tuning or by re-calibrating
our internal compass so that we will
always remain oriented toward the
moral discipline of faith. This will
allow us to take our bearings on
the guiding stars of revelation
from the heavens. When we've
done so, our obedience will no
longer be inconvenient, but
will be our quest. We will
have a desire to labor in
the traces, beside our
Savior.

Many churches bear the name of Christ or a derivative in their titles, and so the substance of the issue is to find the one where true doctrine is taught by ministers who bear the authority of God's priesthood. Is their message composed of gospel principles that can be easily validated by the Holy Ghost? Can the validity of the doctrine which they purport to be true withstand the scrutiny of the Spirit, and ultimately receive its unqualified approbation?

John F. Kennedy famously declared: "We choose to do things, not because they are easy but because they are hard. Our goals serve to organize and measure the best of our energies and skills. Our challenges are those that we are willing to accept, that we are unwilling to postpone, but that we intend to win." That is well put, but we must never forget that one plus God equals a majority. We need to keep the focus of our faith on the teachings of our Redeemer Jesus Christ, so that when we are figuratively tapped on the shoulder to do very special things, we will be both prepared and qualified for that which could very well be our finest hour.

Because
expanding circles of
opportunity have been stitched
into the teachings of Jesus Christ,
little room is left for our limiting
beliefs. We lift the latch and force
the way and trade the hesitancy of
those who have found themselves
trapped in perceptual prisons for
the certain spiritual guidance
that accompanies celestial-
bound travelers.

The
influence
of the Light of
Christ encourages
us to set our sights
on true north, and on
the one book that has
been designed to lift
us to higher plateaus
of personal progress.
Work we must, but
book-group is free.
The one that we're
reading now is
offered by the
Lord as His
gospel.

As we reach and embark upon
on a journey that will ultimately
take us to the stars, our Savior Jesus
Christ offers a liberating message of peace
that follows our obedience to mathematically
correct physical principles, newly discovered
metaphysical mileposts, and spiritually
coherent celestial guidelines.

A message in
a bottle appears to have not
yet washed up on the beaches of
our lives, and yet the poem at the base
of the Statue of Liberty calls out to those
who have been pummeled by the trials of life
and have lost the desire and the ability to lift their
eyes to Jesus Christ, light of life. "Give me your tired,
your poor, your huddled masses yearning to breathe free;
the wretched refuse of your teeming shore. Send these, the
homeless, tempest-tossed to me. And I'll lift my lamp beside
the golden door." (Emma Lazarus, "The New Colossus"). How
it would alter the direction of our lives to know that there is a
God in Heaven who has a vested interest in our welfare! But
even as we look to the stars for signs of life, too many of
us accept it as a given that God is Nowhere, instead of
celebrating the fact that He is Now Here. From out
of the cosmos, the Silentium Universi, the Great
Silence, has been broken. All we need is to
have a listening ear, a ready heart, and
a willing mind, to detect the steady
pulse of the universe.

As we fine-tune
our revelatory capabilities,
we can build upon experiences
with the Holy Ghost that we have
already had, that have come to us as
we've patiently waited upon the Lord.
These include our testimonies of
our Savior Jesus Christ and
of His gospel.

Jesus Christ ignites our
imagination with the dream
of acquiring a primitive time
machine. The easiest way to
do that, of course, would be
to purchase a toy telescope
and, with it, look up at
the night sky for a
message from
heaven.

As our hearts embrace Jesus Christ, we hope to be able to muster the courage to declare, as did Juliet to Romeo: "I'll lay all my fortunes at your feet and follow you, my lord, all over the world." (Shakespeare).

Our Redeemer Jesus Christ, through the influence of the Holy Ghost, encourages us to celebrate the fundamental power in the weak things of the earth, and to not feel silly afterward for having done so. In the scriptures, we are admonished 439 times to prepare ourselves. Preparation means that we inventory our available resources and then make the best of it. The Lord Himself made preparation for 30 years before He commenced His ministry. In our Heavenly Father's divine design, opportunities for preparation may involve life-long learning experiences that have been tailor-made to suit our circumstances and our needs, whether we are professional athletes or practiced panhandlers, living in the fast or the slow lane of life, whether we have rags or riches, are leaders or lepers, late bloomers or early prodigies, venture capitalists or welfare recipients. Times and seasons change, but our gospel instruction remains a constant upon which we can rely in every time of need.

When Jesus Christ reveals Himself to the world in accord with prophecy in His gospel, so that His glory fills our lives, the elements will melt like snow in the fervent heat of the uninhibited Holy Spirit. Under those special circumstances, "every valley shall be exalted, and every mountain and hill shall be made low, and the crooked shall be made straight, and the rough places plain; and the glory of the Lord shall be revealed, and all flesh shall see it together." (Isaiah 40:4-5).

Only when we have integrated into our lives the principles of truth as they have been taught by our Savior Jesus Christ will we discover the tools we need to recognize, address, reverse, and eliminate the imbalance that is prevalent within ourselves. From the vantage point of the Word, we will see things more clearly. It is as if we have escaped our mortal clay with its confining limitations that disfigure our perspective and negatively twist our attention inward, to worldliness.

Our renewal through the Sacrament doesn't give us a hall pass to act recklessly, or to be drawn, even occasionally, to the Dark Side, to sample the pleasures of Babylon, and to neglect our focus upon the pole-star of the Atonement of Jesus Christ.

Those who are prepared to receive our Lord Jesus Christ will see "wonders in the heavens and in the earth, (with) blood, and fire and pillars of smoke." (Joel 2:30). When He revealed Himself to Isaiah, his appearance was so commanding, that "the posts of the doors moved at the voice of him that cried, and the house was filled with smoke." Then Isaiah cried "Woe is me! For I am undone." (Isaiah 6:4-5). His physical frame could scarcely abide the presence of Jehovah. He would need resources that only heaven could provide. health in his navel and marrow in his bones, and strength in his loins and in his sinews, if he hoped to be admitted into the great and terrible presence of the Lord. (See Proverbs 3:8, Job 40:16, Isaiah 40:21 & Ezekiel 37:6).

We shouldn't become impatient in our determination to gain intellectual or even spiritual mastery of the mysteries of the kingdom, or of the knowledge of Jesus Christ, the Son of God, that is evidently beyond our comprehension, or that is apparently unnecessary for us to have at our current stage of development.

Our Heavenly Father's Great Plan of Mercy is so magnificent that when it was presented to those who had assembled in the Council in heaven, "the morning stars sang together, and all the sons of God shouted for joy." (Job 38:7-8). The principle of equality, taught by our Redeemer Jesus Christ, renders it inconceivable that a Plan of such transcendent perfection would have been intentionally designed to save only a very small percentage of our Heavenly Father's children in His Celestial Kingdom. To believe such would effectively dismiss as a thing of naught his mission statement, not to mention most of the vicarious work for the dead that takes place in the House of the Lord. (See 1 Corinthians 15:29).

The Atonement of Jesus Christ is our figurative ticket that insures our successful completion of a work release program that has been designed to see just how we might behave when left on our own, after having received unambiguous instruction from above that relates to what we ought to be doing with the time on earth that has been allotted to each of us.

One of the things that can be frustrating to church members is when their friends and their neighbors do not want to hear the good news, or invite Jesus Christ into their lives. But they need to remind themselves that when the world rejected the Mortal Messiah, He didn't retreat to His home in Galilee. Today, our peers could receive inspiration from the Spirit differently, but the Lord presents us with a proven pattern that we might share His joy. He wants us to know what it is like to feel as He does; not only the happiness of seeing someone come to a knowledge of the truth, but also the pain of rejection when the children of God have refused His invitation to be born again by accepting His gospel and tasting the fruit of the tree of life.

We join the wise men of old
as they ask: "Where is he that is born King
of the Jews? For we have seen his star in the East
and are come to worship him." (Matthew 2:2). With
awakening awe, it strikes us that the Light of the
World is a celestial supernova that has endured
for over two millennia, and that through
His gospel, we have been invited to
follow His stellar example.

Those who adhere to archaic tradition
may exhibit their faith in Jesus Christ by
shouting "Hallelujah" and striking the right
hand into the palm of the left hand at the end of
the recitation of the words "God and the Lamb," which
was initially done on the occasion of the reorganization
of the First Presidency under Brigham Young on 12/27,
1847. ("Journal of Norton Jacob," Journal History, 9/5/1848)
On other occasions, we might stand upon our feet while clapping
our hands, and add the words "forever and ever, worlds without end"
following the words "God and the Lamb" ("Millennial Star," volume
24, p. 758, see B. H. Roberts, Life of John Taylor, p. 365). Especially
since 1893, we wave white handkerchiefs while shouting. (James E.
Talmage, House of the Lord, p. 150; C.R. 4/1930). After the shout,
the congregation or choir might sing a hymn. But with these
different modifications that have been introduced from
time to time, the basic pattern of "The Hosanna
Shout," repeated three times while waving
white handkerchiefs, has persisted
to the present day.

Mastery of the principles that are illuminated by the ministry of our Lord Jesus Christ will propel us onward toward immortality and eternity, as long as we remain true to the ordinances and covenants of the Plan of Salvation. These will keep the sand of sin, the grit and grime that accumulate during our lives, out of the gears of the machine that was created in the heavens for the making of gods in embryo.

We all have a yearning to go to the heavenly land, to enjoy glory in the eternal world, to go home to God's rest and the bosom of the Lord. But we don't want to die first. Too many of us fear what lies beyond, "after death, that undiscovered country, from whose bourn no traveler returns." They fear an uncertain future or the spectre of a long night of darkness. Without the comforting assurances found in the teachings of Jesus Christ, the valley of the shadow of death conjures up visions of the chains of hell, the grim reaper, the angel of death, and the 4th Horseman of the Apocalypse who rides "a pale horse." (Revelation 6:8).

Only our Lord and Savior Jesus Christ can successfully shepherd us through the growing pains and the mental, emotional, spiritual, and physical unsteadiness that are intertwined with early childhood development. However, until our behavior matures so that it is in harmony with His doctrine, the freedom existing outside the sphere of the moral element of responsibility that is witnessed by faith in the Lord must inevitably forge our fetters and lead us into bondage. The blueprint that is His gospel, on the other hand, is the perfect Law of liberty.
(See James 1:25).

The Holy Ghost testifies of the validity of the promises made by our Savior Jesus Christ, as we repent with broken hearts. His unimpeachable witness is as a baptism of fire that puts the finishing touches on the Atonement of the Savior. When Mercy intervenes to satisfy the demands of Justice and cancels the penalties that are associated with our sins, we are blessed to become holy and without spot, in a rite of purification. Though our "sins be as scarlet, they shall be as white as snow. Though they be red like crimson, they shall be as wool." (Isaiah 1:18).

If we remain spiritually deaf to the Savior's entreaty (see Luke 18:22), drastic action will be necessary. The plastic surgery of the Atonement is indicated if we want to experience a reversal of our fortunes and if we hope to restore the likeness and image of our Father to countenances that have been blemished by our sins of commission. and omission.

Our Lord and Savior Jesus Christ commands us to search the scriptures (see John 5:39), because, in a very real sense, each one of us is confined to a world our own making, and most of us are trapped within the narrowly defined perceptual prisons that we create for ourselves. Its walls are reinforced with the razor-wire of limiting beliefs, those stories that we tell ourselves that cause us to sabotage our own best efforts. Without the blessing of enlightenment that comes as we study the tenets of His gospel, we will risk damaging and even crippling our lives by compromising our progress and diminishing our abilities. It's in these ways and more that we prevent ourselves from achieving our goals.

Those
without faith
see things as they
are, and wonder "Why?"
The focused faithful dream
of things that never were, and ask
"Why not?" They employ the guiding
principles taught by the Lord Jesus Christ
to work through their problems, rather than
trying to side-step around them on their
own. They make no small plans, for
they lack the power to stir
our souls.

Without
our repentance
founded upon an
appreciation of the
Atonement of Christ
flowing out of a study
of His gospel, we cannot
reasonably expect to inherit
the glory of celestial realms;
especially if we have aforetime
been agreeable to abide by only
telestial or terrestrial principles
that may put fewer demands on
discipleship, or may be found
to be the tenets of faith of
secular Christianity.

Too often, the teachings of our Lord Jesus Christ have fallen on deaf ears. "Is it not a shame," asked William Tyndall in 1528, "that we Christians come so oft to church in vain, when he of four score years old knoweth no more than he that was born yesterday?" In the Last Day, through our Father's gift of grace, and as the Spirit is poured out upon all flesh, the nature of that equation has changed. In a sense, the new math is a good thing.

When we accept the counsel of Jesus Christ our Master, the sclerotic shells of our rough exteriors will be penetrated. He will heal our deafness and our blindness, and ease the tensions and inelasticity that so often shackle our minds, so "when we are dead, others will seek our tomb, not in the earth, but in the hearts of men." (Jalal al Din al Rumi). The sweet fragrance of His true doctrine will smell like bread fresh out of the oven, and we will begin to appreciate the supremacy of spiritual phenomena without being fettered by the limitations of our material possessions. In this way, the time spent in our study of His gospel is as work without pay. Our effort is conducted behind the scenes, and far from the attention of the media, but our retirement benefits will be out of the world.
(See Matthew 6:20).

Jesus Christ lived and died for one reason only: So that we might live as extended families in eternity, where we might fully exercise our opportunities as the children of God.

Since the Fall, Satan has enjoyed a free pass to mingle among the children of men. This flushes him with excitement, because he knows how hard it is for us to resist our natural tendencies toward volatility that will neutralize the spirit of revelation found in the teachings of Jesus Christ. All who love Satan more than they love God will unavoidably exhibit the behavioral manifestations of that misplaced adoration as they walk in the darkness, as if they were the blind leading the blind.

Our Lord and Savior Jesus Christ, He Who has consecrated a new and living way, has asked us to carry our burdens just a little longer and further. He knows that when we are urged to go the second mile, we are being given an invitation to become spiritually independent through the gospel of Jesus Christ, as the Spirit awakens us to a greater appreciation of the tangible and intangible rewards for our sustained efforts. (See Hebrews 10:20).

"God chooseth to reign with our Lord Christ, and him sealeth he with his mighty Spirit, and poureth strength into his heart, to suffer afflictions also with Christ for bearing witness unto the truth. And this is the difference between the children of God and of salvation," and of the gospel of Jesus Christ, "and between the children of the devil and of damnation: That the children of God have power in their hearts to suffer for God's word, which is their life and salvation, their hope and trust, and they live in the soul and spirit before God. And the children of the devil in time of adversity fly from Christ, whom they followed feignedly, their hearts not sealed with his holy and mighty Spirit, and get them to the standard of their right father the devil, and take his wages, the pleasures of this world."
(William Tyndale).

Our Savior Jesus
Christ asks us to fortify
our neighbors who've been
touched by the better angels
of their nature, as we have
been, to carry its magic
light in their hearts.
(See Ephesians
2:19).

Those who suffer from a
chronic weakness in character,
and deny themselves the blessing
of a testimony of Jesus Christ, frequently
are defined by temporal trappings and weave
needless ecclesiastical embroidery into the coats
of many colors that were envisioned by God to be the
foundation garments of a heavenly wardrobe. Theirs are
simply improvised accouterments, and nothing more than
doctrinal decorations that they have hastily designed to prop up
their faltering faith. Self-actualized disciples, on the other hand,
take their cues from the inside. The source of their power lies not just
within their dreams, ideals, and values, but also in their core operating
principles. These are not readily influenced by external pressures and
so they are not easily subject to change. Our healthy reliance upon the
tender mercies of the Savior provides just the balance we needed, and
offers us an exhilarating vision of our potential to be self-directed,
self-managed, and self-motivated within the parameters of the
Great and Eternal Plan of Deliverance from Death.

When we
separate ourselves
from sensitivity to our
surroundings, we become
numb to our circumstances,
in the sense that we may very
well be past feeling. On the other
hand, as we marvel at the revelatory
nature of the counsel of Jesus Christ, we
realize how heavily we have borrowed from
those who have been our sensible chaperones,
our compassionate critics, our spiritual guides,
our mystical mentors, and our surrogate saviors.
These have helped our heartstrings to be caressed
by the other-worldly vibrancy of the third
member of the Godhead, Who is the
Holy Ghost.

Our Savior urges us to engage
in acts of quiet Christianity, which is
service for which there will be no recognition,
recompense, or reciprocation. When we are filled
with charity, we will not be content to minister only
to our loved ones, but we will range thru the entire world,
anxious to bless the whole human family. Neal A. Maxwell
counseled the Saints: "There are times when we will applaud
and no one will notice our pair of happy hands, and no one
will hear the added decibels except us and the Lord." And an
anonymous poet wrote: "I sought to see myself. Myself I
could not see. I sought to know the Lord thru prayer,
but He eluded me. I sought to serve my fellow
men, and I found all three."

After purposeful penitence has poked, pushed, pulled, prodded, probed, and provoked our perverse personalities, and it has chiseled away at our stony hearts, and has then stretched and molded what is left into a shape that is altogether different from what it had been, its expression will be manifested in an unblemished and alabaster character. Our Savior Jesus Christ will have given us the look of those who have been born again to a newness of life, in the image and likeness of our Father in Heaven. (See Genesis 1:27 & 5:3 & 1 Corinthians 15:49).

The Lord Jesus Christ came down from heaven to fulfil the will of His Father, and administer the oil of gladness. It is like having a spiritual angioplasty, facilitating the free flow of communication between us and our God. We have reason to rejoice exceedingly, for when we are born again, we're given the chance to fulfill our life's potential. We are fortunate that He looks beyond the behavior of our rebellion, and sees into our hearts. Our rough exteriors were nothing more than a façade. Our true character is only revealed when His Atonement releases us from the awful bondage of sin, and in the miracle of a spiritual rebirth, we become new creatures in the image and likeness of God.

In contrast
to the light of Christ is a
darkness that has the potential to
cover the earth, and gross darkness
the people. (See Isaiah 60:2).

If we refuse to
allow ourselves to be
mentored by our Savior
Jesus Christ, and instead
we submit to blind guides, we
must deny not only His power
to transform our lives, but also
His grace. If we turn our backs on
the habitation of the Lord, we place
ourselves at risk of dismissing the
sacrifice of His Son, and esteeming
as a thing of naught His suffering.
When we close our minds to the soul
expanding opportunities afforded by
the Bible, and we are snared by the
wiles of Satan, we'll find that we
have been bound by his strong
chains. And we thought it
just a flaxen cord that
was around our
necks!

We come unto Christ
via the spirit of revelation.
Those who would undertake
this daunting endeavor view
their afflictions, their trials,
and their tribulations in a
new light, and determine
to find out how they
can work to their
benefit.

Jesus Christ teaches
us that obstacles are those
frightful demons threatening
us when we turn our minds from
the Plan of God. They'll loom large
with a gratuitous significance. It is
faith that endows us with the vision to
look beyond these potential stumbling
blocks. If we'll turn them into stepping
stones that pave the way to our higher
achievement, it will be because we've
been empowered by the capacity of
our faith in Him, that becomes
an unrestrained and creative
engine that drives positive
change. His truth will
make us free. (See
John 8:32).

Our Heavenly Father is sensitive to our needs, and He hears our prayers. In conformity to the mysterious workings of the gospel of Jesus Christ, we are somehow able to draw upon the virtue that is recognized as the Spirit of God. When we do so, for all practical purposes we are touching the garment of our Savior.

When we are caught up in the snare of pride, we can lose both our physical and spiritual independence because we deliver our freedom to the bondage of the judgment of those who do not really matter, do not really care about us or our welfare, and who, ironically, may not even wield significant influence over either our successes or our failures. When we succumb to pride, we lose our perspective and can no longer make sound judgments, because the Holy Ghost, Who is not inclined to compete with the noisy commotion the world, withdraws to a safe distance to wait out the storm. When the proud allow the wiles of the adversary to overwhelm the revelations of God, they are quick to let go of the Rod of Iron, and even to rail against our Savior Jesus Christ.

We try our best, but our puny efforts seem to be inadequate. We patch together a semblance of order, but often we deceive ourselves with the creations of our own making. While ever so quietly in the background, the peaceful voice of conscience that flows out of our relationship with Jesus Christ gently reminds us that He is the Chief Cornerstone of our existence. (See Ephesians 2:20).

Thru prayer, we draw near to our Lord and Savior Jesus Christ and to our Heavenly Father, and we are reacquainted with a magical kingdom where our hopes and our dreams really do come true, and we all live happily ever after. If we wish upon the star power of prayer, it will make no difference who we are. Anything that our hearts desire will come to us. If we will invest the energy of our souls in our dreams, we will make no request that is too extreme, which includes gaining an unshakable testimony of our Father and His Son, by the power of the Spirit.

Jesus Christ makes it easier to have backs that have become sturdy enough to brace us against the fierce winds of adversity and the wiles of the adversary, and hearts that are receptacles of pure and virtuous thoughts and principles from which we may draw strength in our times of need.

True and faithful disciples of Christ stand out from the world. They speak in the name of the Lord and bless the lives of the people. Their doctrine is edifying and uplifting. They embrace a religion that promotes chastity, morality, and fidelity to family values. They cherish the sanctity of life and the rights of the unborn. They believe that the exercise of free will is an eternal principle vital to the successful execution of our probation on the earth. They believe in obeying, honoring, and sustaining the law of the land. They believe in being honest, true, chaste, benevolent, virtuous, and in doing good to all men. They believe all things, hope all things, have they endured many things, and do they hope to be able to endure all things. If there is anything virtuous, lovely, or of good report or praiseworthy, they seek after these things. It is vital that those who seek a church that administers the gospel of Jesus Christ recognize the fruits of faith, because "not everyone that saith unto me, Lord, Lord, shall enter into the kingdom of heaven; but he that doeth the will of my Father who is in heaven." (Matthew 7:21-23, see Luke 646 & the 14th Article of Faith).

Jesus Christ admonishes us to continually strive to do more and to be better, to seek understanding, and to become empowered by wisdom. His counsel emulates the Olympic motto: "Citius, Altius, et Fortius," that is to say, "Faster, Higher, and Stronger."

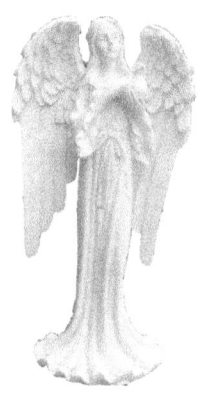

The teachings of our Savior Jesus Christ provide us with a hint of what it will be like when we go to dwell with our Heavenly Father. Since His glory "is intelligence, or in other words, light and truth" (D&C 93:36), it must be that the righteous will dwell amidst the fire and smoke that are symbolic of His presence. The Apostle Paul, who had his share of similar experiences, wrote that now we "see through a glass darkly," but then, if our eyes are single to His glory, we shall look upon Him Who is eternal "face to face." (1 Corinthians 13:12). We can only imagine what it will be like to look across the wide expanse of eternity as a boundless perspective floods our minds with comprehension. Perhaps only then will its solemnity rest upon our minds, as it should. Perhaps only when the Lord reveals His wonders to our expanded capacity will we see things as they really are, and will we receive a fulness of joy.

Faith in Jesus Christ has always been the guiding principle of power that motivates us to action. For Martin Luther, it was much more than just an intellectual assent to a proposition. It was our vital, personal self-commitment to practical belief. He heartily approved of good works; what he denied was their value for salvation. "Good works," he said, 'do not make a good man, but a good man does good works. And what makes a man good?" His gospel!

We must drag our broken and bleeding bodies to the church, because it is there that we will receive the transfusions of a spiritual element. It is a heavenly dialysis center where worldly contaminants may be removed from our systems, because we are frankly incapable of accomplishing the task on our own. The resources we need are found in the Atonement of Christ, within a prescription written by His gospel as the only effective doctrinal therapy for sin

The
best education
is to be perpetually
thrilled with life, and
that kind of enthusiasm
should continue every day
of our lives. As the dictionary
has defined it, our enthusiasm
is to be "possessed by God, or to
have celestial inspiration." If we
are "white hot sparks struck off
the divine anvil" of Jesus Christ
as B. H. Roberts suggested,
then we will live to learn,
learn to love, and
love to live.

Although we're
incapable of saving
daylight time, we may
still try to maximize it by
strangling ourselves with the
things that we can buy, whose
opacity obstructs our ability to see
what is really there. In fact, we aren't
on daylight savings time at all, but on
gospel of Jesus Christ time, and when we
observe the agenda of the Lord, we are on
His errand, no matter how long it might
take, or how preoccupied we may become
by the distractions and the trivial
concerns of the world.

Our Lord and Savior Jesus Christ summons us to trust in God's divine design rather than to put all our marbles in the basket of devilish doctrines. It invites us to believe that our lives are "fairy tales waiting to be written by the hand of God." (Hans Christian Anderson).

The gospel of Jesus Christ has been handed down through the ages to ensure that there will remain enough sand on the beaches of our lives to meet the challenges of a world where stability seems to be eroding in the face of an advancing flood of moral ambiguity and ethical relativism. It provides the building materials we need to enjoy the companionship of peers, to confront our fears, as well as to absorb our tears, and it represents a sanctuary where we can find the peace that eludes the world, where we can reconnect with nature, and where God can gently remind us that, as spring follows winter, and as day follows night, the Son of God will come out tomorrow, and when He does, there will be peace in the world.

Wresting the holy scriptures by suggesting that we are saved by our own works, twists holy writ from its true or proper signification, and perverts it from its correct or its rightful application. Lest we be deceived, we all need the clarity of a witness of Jesus Christ, if it is our wish to be saved.

At first, it might be the easier wrong that appears to be more convenient, but that is only because it harmonizes with the values of Babylon. Worldliness is all around us, and if we cannot hold fast to the stabilizing influence provided by our faith in our Savior Jesus Christ, our moral equivocation can quickly turn into a path of least resistance, until it become the pattern of our conduct. Faith invites us to trust in the divine design of our Father in Heaven that is grounded upon the Atonement. It will nurture our belief that it is only through Him that our lives can become as fairy tales waiting to be written by the hand of God.

The Greatest Story Ever Told,
that chronicles the life and ministry of
Jesus Christ, is most convincingly passed on
to the world by His inspired servants, called to
preach to every nation, kindred, tongue, and
people. Faith will increase in the world "by
hearing those who are sent from God
and preacheth His promises."
(William Tyndale).

The Savior foresaw our day, when secular
Christianity has become abominable, and its
mission has been corrupted, because it has subtly
led the children of God away from the truth. Without
their conscious realization, it has stopped their progression
by destroying the purpose of mortality in God's great Plan of
Salvation. Insult has been added to injury as hypocrisy further
perverts doctrine into humanized, spiritually impotent dogma,
when disciples do not really believe, but are only professors of
religion. Such men and women have been characterized as
imposters who may draw near to God with their lips, but
their hearts are far from Him. Those who are only
'professors of religion' teach, instead of doctrine,
the commandments of men. They have "a
form of godliness, but they deny the
power thereof." (2 Timothy 3:5,
see Romans 2:20).

The responsibility of the Holy
Ghost is to bear a sacred testimony of
the divinity of our Lord and Savior Jesus
Christ. Because there is no greater witness
than that of the Spirit, His witness is
validated in a spirit of justification
following our baptism of fire
and the Holy Ghost.

The "get even"
mentality of retaliation that
is manifested by the hard-hearted,
and that today has been popularized in
the media and is reinforced in interpersonal
relations, is contrary to the principles that were
taught by our Savior Jesus Christ. While it may
be true that in business, you don't get what you
deserve, you get what you negotiate, when the
earth has been cleansed in order to receive its
paradisiacal glory, a higher standard will
prevail. Before that happens, the faithful
have a responsibility to prepare themselves for the Millennium, when
the lamb and the lion will
lie down together in
harmony.

Dark matter may account for 85% of the material substance of the known universe, but the light and life of the cosmos will always be manifested in the teachings of our Savior Jesus Christ. The origin of His dazzling luminosity can be traced all the way back to eternity, for "trailing clouds of glory do we come, from God Who is our Home" (Wm. Wordsworth).

One of the most daunting challenges that we'll face when we are introduced to our Savior Jesus Christ will be to somehow temper our insatiable desire for pleasure, for immediate gratification, and for repetitive waves of greater and greater stimulation. We are frustrated by the limitations of our RAM, the horsepower of our autos, the features of our cell phones, and the speed of our micro-processors. We have only a dim recollection of typewriters and white-out, operator assistance, two-lane country roads, and sipping lemonade on a lazy summer afternoon while seated in a rocker on the front porch. As society demands escalating criteria to maintain its false standard of comfort and entertainment, we are blinded to the sobering comparison to a heroin addict's progressive tolerance and destructive reliance on false gods of wood and stone. Materialism is a cholesterol that clogs our spiritual arteries. The angioplasty of the gospel is the only thing that can liberate us to regain our perspective and strengthen our reverence for the work of our Heavenly Father.

When we find our way to the feet of our Lord and Savior Jesus Christ, we will no longer be as flotsam and jetsam on the sea of life, nor as children who've been "tossed to and fro, and carried about with every wind of doctrine, by the sleight of men, and cunning craftiness, whereby they lie in wait to deceive." (Ephesians 4:4). Instead, we'll have the constant reassurance that wherever Jesus preached, it seems that "a great multitude followed him." (Matthew 20:29). When we hear His voice, we will follow Him, as well, wherever He might take us, "as the waters follow the moon, silently and with fluid steps, anywhere around the globe." (Walt Whitman).

The lifestyle advocated by our Lord and Savior Jesus Christ clearly demonstrates that freedom is incompatible with the level of security that is provided in prisons and intensive care units, where every conceivable physical need has been met. It illustrates that in normal situations, the liability of free will is that it entails risk. The tendency of Americans to look to the government for their job security, social security, and even homeland security, speaks for itself. It is evidence of a desire to avoid risk. Caesar provides security and assumes the risk. The danger lies in the character of power-hungry autocrats who are eager to identify, and then to step into, a vacuum to take control. All that is required to consummate the deal is that the populace give up its free will, which is generally done enthusiastically, yet in blindness, in ignorance, and in increments that are imperceptible and go unnoticed until it has become everlastingly too late to change.

When we find our way to
the feet of our Lord and Savior Jesus
Christ, we will no longer be as flotsam and
jetsam on the sea of life, nor as children who've
been "tossed to and fro, and carried about with every
wind of doctrine, by the sleight of men, and cunning
craftiness, whereby they lie in wait to deceive." (Ephesians
4:4). Instead, we'll have the constant reassurance that wherever
Jesus preached, it seems that "a great multitude followed him."
(Matthew 20:29). When we hear His voice, we will follow Him,
as well, wherever He might take us, "as the waters follow
the moon, silently and with fluid steps, anywhere
around the globe." (Walt Whitman).

The lifestyle advocated by
our Lord and Savior Jesus Christ
clearly demonstrates that freedom is
incompatible with the level of security that
is provided in prisons and intensive care units,
where every conceivable physical need has been met.
It illustrates that in normal situations, the liability of
free will is that it entails risk. The tendency of Americans
to look to the government for their job security, social security,
and even homeland security, speaks for itself. It is evidence of a
desire to avoid risk. Caesar provides security and assumes the risk.
The danger lies in the character of power-hungry autocrats who are
eager to identify, and then to step into, a vacuum to take control.
All that is required to consummate the deal is that the populace
give up its free will, which is generally done enthusiastically,
yet in blindness, in ignorance, and in increments that
are imperceptible and go unnoticed until it has
become everlastingly too late to change.

We follow a
yellow brick road
with our hearts, might,
mind, and strength, until
we have arrived at the Emerald
City of Oz. Our faith compels us
to trust our Savior Jesus Christ and
not in devilish doctrines that have been
concocted by the world's apologists. God's
magnificent Plan invites us to believe that
when we use our hearts, and our brains, and
have the courage of faith, our lives can become
wonderful "fairy tales that are just waiting
to be written" by His omnipotent hand.
(Hans Christian Anderson).

Occasionally, some who have determined
to follow in the footsteps of Jesus Christ and have
then enrolled in His curriculum will not be able to
maintain their perfect attendance record nor sustain
saving faith. They may have set their sights too low,
and then too easily reached watered-down objectives.
They may no longer stretch themselves and will
only occasionally venture out of the comfort
zones to which they have retreated. In any
event, they will have but little to show
for their consistently timid efforts
that deny the faith and sidestep
the inspired course of study
that has been created in
their behalf.

Our lives may be long or short, and yet all that God requires to satisfy the full measure of our creation may be accomplished. (See 1 Corinthians 15:21). Death is an essential element of the gospel, and the transgression of Adam and Eve gave their posterity the opportunity to be born into this world, to live, and then die. The Atonement of Christ is the pièce de résistance of Act Two of our Father's Three Act Play, and the Holy Ghost puts the finishing touches on His Plan, setting the stage for us to experience the triumphant third and final act.

Father knows best, and has unshaken confidence in us, and in our divine potential to internalize His nature. Since the teachings of Jesus Christ establish realistic goals that are within the reach of the weakest of His children, they become the basic requirements of those who put forth the effort to investigate its merits and who hope, in a day that is not too distant, to triumphantly enter in thru the gates of the Celestial Kingdom.

Our Heavenly Father is the founder of the greatest diversity on earth. In fact, the teachings of our Lord Jesus Christ illustrate how diversity was created in the beginning (see Genesis Chapter One), when He divided light from darkness, the heavens from the earth, the waters from the firmament, the day from the night, and when he created all manner of living things, each to go forth and multiply after its own kind. His quintessential act of creative diversity was when "male and female created he them." (Genesis 1:27). He may have even created Mars and Venus specifically to be the diverse habitations of men and women, respectively.

The two most significant days of our lives, that are commemorated with celebration and joy by the angels in heaven as well as by our Elder Brother Jesus Christ, are the day we were born, and the day we find out why. After we have come to understand our purpose, our lives will never again be the same until the day we die, when we really discover why we lived. When we comprehend the grammar of the gospel, we see, as Neal A. Maxwell observed, that "death is a mere comma, and not an exclamation point!" The light has not been extinguished; rather, the lamp has been put out because the dawn has arrived. Death is only an artificial horizon that limits our sight.

Jesus Christ gives us the clarity of vision to overcome weakness. Stumbling blocks become stepping stones, and through our experience, we learn that everything that is good comes of our Savior.

The influence of our Savior Jesus Christ is like a celestial sphygmomanometer measuring the blood pressure of our self-inflicted pain and telestial trauma. He is a cosmic compass, pointing us to eternal life. He is like a stethoscope that calculates the vital capacity of our prideful hearts that must be broken by contrition in order to reveal the steady sinus rhythm that confirms a perfect harmony with the proven principles of perfection. His forgiveness is like a pacemaker that can measure out therapeutic doses of doctrinal energy. If we ever hope to enjoy a stable heart rate and avoid the angina of anguish, it will be because He is entirely and unconditionally forgiving. If we want to one day live comfortably with Him in His kingdom, we need to place the nitroglycerin tablets of tenderness under our tongues to temper our urge to use them as weapons to lash out at those who might ostensibly have offended us.

We remember the account in the ministry of Jesus Christ that describes how He overthrew the tables of the moneychangers at the temple in Jerusalem. (See Matthew 21:12). How cheaply will we sell that which seems most dear to us. "That for which all virtue is sold, and almost any vice - almighty gold!" (Ben Jonson). How ironic that it is all for nothing. The world's covetous passion to hoard shiny metal and telestial trash inevitably leads to societal bickering that paves the way for its destruction.

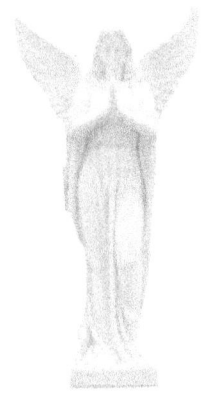

"When thou hurtest not thy neighbors, then art thou sure that God's Spirit worketh in thee and that thy faith is no dream nor any false imagination." (William Tyndale). "Blessed are the merciful," the Savior taught as a centerpiece of his gospel, "for they shall obtain mercy." (Matthew 5:7). "For with what judgment ye judge, ye shall be judged, and with what measure ye mete, it shall be measured to you again." (Matthew 7:2). What goes around, will come around, and when we cast our bread upon the waters, we can be sure that after many days, it will return to us.

When they
quite unexpectedly
find themselves bathed in
stunning light, those who have
been learning about the Plan of God
will often stare in wide-eyed wonder at
the simplicity of the interwoven threads
found within the pattern of principles
and doctrine that makes up the
tapestry of the ministry of
our Lord Jesus Christ.

Only after we have embraced our
Lord Jesus Christ will we realize that we are the
literal or adopted members of the house of Israel, and
heirs of the Abrahamic Covenant. "Now the sons of Jacob
were twelve: The sons of Leah; Reuben, Jacob's firstborn, and
Simeon, and Levi, and Judah, and Issachar, and Zebulun; the
sons of Rachel: Joseph, and Benjamin; And the sons of Bilhah,
Rachel's handmaid: Dan and Naphtali; and the sons of Zilpah,
Leah's handmaid: Gad and Asher." (Genesis 35:22-26). Leah:
Reuben, Simeon, Levi, Judah, Issachar, and Zebulun. Rachel:
Joseph (Ephraim and Manasseh / a double portion), and
Benjamin, Bilhah (Rachel's maid): Dan and Naphtali,
Zilpah (Leah's maid): Gad and Asher. No wonder
our desire to be adopted into such a family may
sometimes seem tentative. No one denies
that it will be daunting to wear a
name tag at that dizzying
family reunion!

We know for a fact that
our Father is sensitive to our
needs, because we have all received
answers to our effectual and fervent
prayers. (See James 5:16). As long as
our testimonies of the divinity of Jesus
Christ remains strong, we'll draw virtue
from His life force. We'll figuratively
reach out and touch the hem of the
garment of the Savior, and feel
the spirit of revelation, even if
it seems that we've been lost
within the press of the
crowd.

The Savior's solution for dealing
with the disgusting filthiness of sin is
to wash it away thru baptism. Although it
could have been lifted right out of His gospel,
the Manual of Discipline from the Serek Scroll
found at Qumran reads: "His sin is forgiven him
and in the humility of his soul he is for all the laws
of God. His flesh is cleansed shining bright in the
waters of purification, or even in the waters of
baptism, and he shall be given a new name
in due time, to walk perfectly in all
the ways of God."

We know for a fact that
our Father is sensitive to our
needs, because we have all received
answers to our effectual and fervent
prayers. (See James 5:16). As long as
our testimonies of the divinity of Jesus
Christ remains strong, we'll draw virtue
from His life force. We'll figuratively
reach out and touch the hem of the
garment of the Savior, and feel
the spirit of revelation, even if
it seems that we've been lost
within the press of the
crowd.

The Savior's solution for dealing
with the disgusting filthiness of sin is
to wash it away thru baptism. Although it
could have been lifted right out of His gospel,
the Manual of Discipline from the Serek Scroll
found at Qumran reads: "His sin is forgiven him
and in the humility of his soul he is for all the laws
of God. His flesh is cleansed shining bright in the
waters of purification, or even in the waters of
baptism, and he shall be given a new name
in due time, to walk perfectly in all
the ways of God."

When we feel so
powerfully that we are
right that our confidence
obscures our better judgment,
when our standpoint, from our
unimpeachable perspective, appears
to be unassailable, and particularly
when our supposed invincibility feels
like bedrock beneath the fortress of our
self-confidence, it will always be the
anchor of the counsel of Jesus Christ
that will drag us back down to
earth for a repentance-based
reality check.

After Alice had
fallen down the rabbit
hole, she stumbled upon
the teachings of the Savior,
and was curious. And so it was,
that when she met the Cheshire Cat,
she asked him: "Would you please tell
me which way I ought to go from here?"
To which the cat responded: "That depends
a good deal on where you want to go." Alice
acknowledged: "I'll admit, I don't much care
where," to which the cat retorted: "Well then, it
really won't matter which way you go." Alice
implored: "Just so I go somewhere!" To which
the cat coyly observed: "Oh, you are sure
to do that, if you only walk far
enough."

Jesus
Christ provides
us with a celestial
bridge that transports
faithful Saints beyond
the vicissitudes of life to
establish them upon the
peaceable shoreline of
the kingdom of God
that lies beyond the
troubled surf-line
of the commotion
of the world.

The positive influence of faith, that leads
to repentance through the Atonement of our Savior Jesus
Christ, is the only viable alternative to the Adversary's crushing
ability to negatively influence our lives. The only stipulation put
upon us by the Holy Ghost is that after we realize we have been
disobedient, we must go through the process of repentance.
First of all, we recognize our transgression, experience
remorse, renounce the self-defeating behavior, and
determine to do better. We make restitution
where possible, and finally do our part
to establish a reconciliation with
the Spirit, and ultimately
receive a remission
of our sin.

Our faith
in the divine Plan
of our Father in Heaven
is confirmed by our acceptance
of our Savior Jesus Christ. It is thru
Him that we will learn how to return
to God's kingdom after we have grown
up unto the Lord, and have spiritually
matured by recognizing that our
basis of our hope lies in His
Atonement.

Without
inertia, things would
either stop or start moving on
their own. Without it, energy would
not have to be spent to change their states
of motion, and therefore, entropy would not
increase. This cannot be, for it would violate the
Second Law of Thermodynamics, and our familiar
universe would be unrecognizable; it would look and
behave quite differently. Once again, we see that there
must needs be opposition in all things. The relationship
between inertia and entropy may be buried somewhere in
the equations of the Theory of Everything. For now, if we
want to grasp these concepts more fully, and if we desire
to better understand how they are related to each other,
we must turn for explanation to the principles that
have been defined by our Savior Jesus Christ.

When we are born, we are only recently removed from our spiritual kindergarten. We barely skip a beat as we recommence our education under the auspice of the gospel of Jesus Christ, because we are trailing clouds of glory from God, who is our Home. Years pass, and the graduation ceremony commemorating the conclusion of our course of study on earth draws closer. It comforts us to know that, when we cross the bar to enter the kingdom of God, our bodies will be full of light. But we might be surprised to discover that we will enjoy no more luminosity then, than we did as a three-year-old Sunbeam. Truly did the Savior teach: "Suffer the little children, and forbid them not, to come unto me, for of such is the kingdom of heaven." (Mark 10:14).

Those who solemnly bear the vessels of the Lord must be clean. The ark was a tangible object that symbolized God's hallowed presence, His glory, His throne, and His divine majesty. Only the High Priest, a type of Christ, could approach it, and then only after going through an elaborate ritual of personal cleansing and propitiation for his sins. The holiness of God is unambiguously illustrated by the mortal Messiah, and those who are unclean cannot long endure His glory, which is a consuming fire. (See Deuteronomy 4:24).

Developing our faith in Jesus Christ is like driving a screw in to a piece of wood. With every turn, the anchor becomes more sure until, ultimately, it is solid. The screw cannot then be removed unless fear replaces faith, turning out the screw and weakening the hold. But when the screw is secure, the faith that had aforetime been required to make the anchor strong is not dead; it is simply no longer needed, and can now be directed elsewhere. What does remain, however, are the results of that steady expenditure of faith.

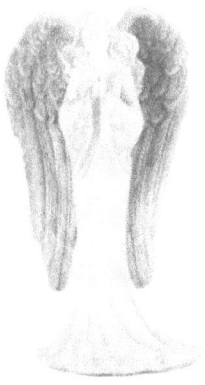

In these technologically demanding times, the gospel reveals that the Lord will raise His standard, and after the manner of the electronic media, the summons will come from afar. (See Isaiah 5:26-30). The pure in heart will respond to that call, and will hasten to Zion with such speed that before they have had time to become tired, they will have arrived at their destination. "None shall slumber nor sleep; neither shall the girdle of their loins be loosed, nor (shall) the latchet of their shoes be broken." (Isaiah 5:27). During their journey, they will require neither rest nor even a change of clothing. Isaiah further described the sparks and flashes of "their horses' hoofs" and the great noise that was made by iron-wheeled vehicles.

We are at
risk of falling
into transgression
in consequence of our
shallow understanding of
the teachings of our Redeemer
Jesus Christ. Picking apart the
word of God will distort dogma
into meaningless fragments
without any coherent
connection.

Temptation can act as
a powerfully addictive narcotic, which
makes Lucifer a quintessential drug dealer. He
was "a son of the morning," whose influence over
Heavenly Father's children was truly impressive. His
name means "Light Bearer," and so he was. In the great
Council, he offered to redeem mankind. But even then,
he lacked the faith necessary to allow agency to rule.
He concocted an inoperable counterfeit proposal that
would have denied its participants the capacity to
exercise free will, that they might create positive
change in their lives. Due to his impassioned
yet misguided promotion of this spurious
proposal, the scriptures refer to him as
Satan, the father of lies, and a liar
from the beginning, which takes
us back to the time when the
Firstborn stood before the
spirit children of
God.

We who were present at
the Council, who so readily and
enthusiastically raised our arms to
the square to support our Father's proposal,
must have felt the import of the moment, when
our Elder Brother Jesus Christ took the unparalleled
step of offering Himself as a sacrifice for our sins.
(See Job 38:7). In fact, He was creating a binding
precedent to re-write history itself, and we were
eyewitnesses to the inaugural event that
would mark the vitalization of His
gospel in heaven and on earth.

Our Father
knew that He'd have
only nine months to fine-
tune our pre-natal care, before
we would complete our transition
from the celestial world where we had
enjoyed the warmth of hearth and home
in heaven, to the bleak atmosphere of the
lone and dreary world on the earth. When
we did so, He knew that there would be an
immediate disconnect that would be both
brutal and unrelenting in its intensity.
It is that disengagement that makes it
imperative that we find our way back
to Him through the promptings of
the Spirit and the teachings of
our Elder Brother Jesus
Christ.

From the perspective of Jesus Christ, the clarity of our spiritual understanding allows us to pierce the mists of time to see the Star that over 2,000 years ago shone brightly above a manger on the outskirts of the little town of Bethlehem, just 6 miles from bustling Jerusalem.

Our unwavering and certain comprehension of the teachings of Jesus Christ is made possible by the irreproachable influence wrought upon us by the Spirit. Our knowledge expedites the implementation of moral agency that is but properly channeled free will. It gives us the power to work out our salvation with both fear and trembling before the Lord. Gaining wisdom is critical to the successful execution of God's Plan. Thus, it is another of the spiritual gifts that has been providentially provided by the Source of all wisdom, Who is our Father in Heaven.

The
world has done
a remarkable job
of rationalizing its
naughty behavior, re-
purposing its deviancy,
and re-defining with new-
speak the acceptability of its
poor conduct, in a despairing
and futile attempt to work its
way around the performance
requirements stipulated
by the teachings of
Jesus Christ.

Girding our loins with the whole
armor of the teachings of Jesus Christ will
give us unbridled confidence as we obey every
one of God's commandments, as well as when we
cultivate the desire to engage the ordinances that are
necessary to attain eternal life. But a potential conflict
can arise when there is a discrepancy between priesthood
authority and power. The one comes by the laying on of
hands, and the other thru righteousness. At times, when
those who hold the priesthood are asked to officiate in the
ordinances, they do so without the supporting power of
Christ. Their acts are validated only because of their
ordination and because of the sustaining faith of
those to whom they minister. In any event, we
can see why we would be cautioned: "Be ye
clean that bear the vessels of the
Lord." (Isaiah 52:11).

The Fibonacci
Sequence is nature's
mathematical composition,
and an example of ubiquitous
cosmological music. Its congruence
governs not only the spin of atoms, but
also the matrix of leaves, shells, suns, and
galaxies. As a love letter from God and
Jesus Christ, it causes all Creation to
break into hymns of praise, in
poetic harmony.

When those of us who
have knelt at the feet of Jesus
Christ later violate the laws of God,
which we seem to have a proclivity to do
with frustrating frequency, our conscience
will lead us to be broken down in humility and
we'll be inspired to recognize the error of our ways,
that we might repent of our delinquent behavior and
experience remorse after having committed the sin in
the first place. We right the wrong if it is in our power
to do so, refrain from repeating it, receive forgiveness,
and then move along in our lives. In the Atonement
of Christ, our stumbling blocks are miraculously
transformed into stepping-stones. Only after we
have gone through this process will mortality,
with its potholes, pitfalls, and personality
precipices make any sense and become
the growth experience that God, in
His wisdom, has designed
it to be.

Jesus Christ nurtures relationships among God's children, be they wealthy or poor, humble or proud, strong or weak, the chance to associate with their brothers and sisters in an uplifting environment infused by an atmosphere that nurtures a religious basis upon which they may build relationships. It is to the extent that we fail to seize these heaven-sent opportunities that we remain strangers and foreigners with each other and with God, starving our souls and further diminishing His spiritual accessibility.

In the Last Days, one of the wonderful signs of the time is that our Lord and Savior Jesus Christ will be revealed to all people in a manifestation of the power of the Holy Ghost. In a coming day, there will no longer be a need to teach others about the Savior of the world because we all will know the Lord. "Then the heathen that are left round about you shall know that (it is) I the Lord (who built) the ruined places, and (I planted) that that which was desolate." (Ezekiel 36:36). The earth will be renewed to receive paradisiacal glory. "For behold," declared the Lord thru His prophet Isaiah, "I create new heavens and a new earth: and the former shall not be remembered, nor come to mind." (Isaiah 65:17). "For the Lord shall comfort Zion; he will comfort all her waste places, and he will make her wilderness like Eden, and her desert like the (secret) garden of the Lord." (Isaiah 51:3).

How in this world, (no pun intended), can we ever find our way to the gates of the Celestial Kingdom? We must set our course and move along it. A deviation of one degree can have devastating consequences after we have traveled for some time down the highways and byways of life, which is why, all along the way, the guidance of our Savior Jesus Christ is so important.

In "The Obedience of a Christian Man," published in 1528, nearly five hundred years ago, William Tyndale wrote that "our deeds" relating to our devotion to our Savior Jesus Christ "serve in three ways. First they assure us that we are heirs of everlasting life and that the Spirit of God, which is the deposit thereof, is in us, in that our hearts consent to the law of God and we have power in our members to do it, though imperfectly. Secondarily, we tame the flesh therewith and kill the sin that still remains in us, and thereby we grow daily more and more perfect in the Spirit, ensuring lusts do not choke the word of God sown in us, nor quench the gifts and working of the Spirit, and that we do not lose the Spirit again. And thirdly, we do our duty to our neighbors therewith, and help them in their need, to our own comfort also, and draw all men to honor and praise God."

It seems indisputable
that the object and design
of our existence, from what we
may learn from the teachings of
Jesus Christ, is to be the happiest
people on the face of all the earth.
Our obedience to the principles of
the gospel unleashes a spiritual
cornucopia, inviting us to feast
upon nourishing bread of life
and to drink copiously from
wells of living water. Life
is good! How could it
be any better than
that?

We turn to our Lord and Savior
Jesus Christ to be our labor coach as we deal
with the weaknesses in the contractions that push
forward His agenda. We learn to rely on the pitocin of
repentance and to utilize the therapy of the Atonement
to quicken our efforts, that we might bear down with
renewed conviction until we give birth to our solemn
witness, unto the convincing of both Jews and
Gentiles that our Savior is the Messiah,
or the Anointed One.

In spite of our determined efforts to gain a toehold and establish some traction on the slippery telestial turf that's our home, it's frustrating to sometimes feel that we are still losing ground. "Now, here, you see," the Red Queen patiently explained to Alice in Wonderland, "it takes all the running you can do, to keep in the same place. If you want to get somewhere else, you must run at least twice as fast as that!" (Lewis Carroll). Let us never forget that one plus our Savior always constitutes a majority. With His gospel, we may run and not be weary, and walk and not faint (see Isaiah 40:21), as we continue to make steady progress along the pathway to perfection.

We will become confidently successful in our discipleship only as we struggle to gain self-mastery, overcome adversity, and conquer the cankered nature that suffers us to be disobedient to true principles. As we move from dependency to independency, and finally to the more mature state of inter-dependency, obedience to our covenants will help to focus our efforts to become as our Savior is. If we regard our church affiliation as a probationary condition of membership, or a time of testing or putting to the proof our professed standard of behavior, and when all is done within the bounds of His teachings, we will be less inclined to bail out or throw in the towel at the first sign of tedium, or of world-weariness.

A life-altering comprehension of the teachings of our Lord and Savior Jesus Christ often follows on the heels of our baptismal covenant. After their own baptisms, Joseph Smith and Oliver Cowdery reflected: "Our minds being now enlightened, we began to have the scriptures laid open to our understandings, and the true meaning and intention of their more mysterious passages revealed unto us in a manner which we never could attain to previously, nor ever before had thought of." (J.S.H. 1:74).

When the Lord gives us a commandment, He also prepares the means to accomplish the task that is set before us. We see what might be best for ourselves and for the Kingdom of God, develop a testimony that it should be, and then work with all our capacity to make it happen, whatever the cost might be. Then, when we are so richly blessed far beyond the measure that we've deserved, the price, once so painfully paid, is recalled with gladness. We receive full value, and all because of God's boundless grace.

Those who have discovered by sad experience that wickedness is the bedfellow of frailty, futility, and friability, and will be the companion of despondency, distress and desperation, are as poor lost souls who have turned their faces from the light of life that may be found only in our Savior's teachings. They abound in iniquity and have surrendered their expectation of forgiveness, redemption, progression, and salvation. They are in despair and must remain without hope, "for the wages of sin is death, but the gift of God is eternal life through Jesus Christ our Lord." (Romans 6:23).

Our grasp of truth is the first important step to be taken before we can hope to successfully conclude an intellectual or spiritual journey, but this will be especially so if we desire to gain a testimony of the divinity of Jesus Christ by the power of the Holy Ghost. Truth is deed, and our belief is the catalyzing influence that motivates us to purposeful action. The horizon of our knowledge extends only as far as our actions. This is why deeds are an important companion to our vital, active faith, which, without works, has no life-generating or sustaining power, because alone, it is vain, or it is impotent. It is ineffective, and is dead in the sense that it is inadequate to the task at hand.

Telestial EMT's are at a loss for diagnosis, while our Savior Jesus Christ commands a war chest of effective therapies for cold, hard, and stony hearts, that remain the remedies of choice when the steady pulse of faith has grown weak, or if it doesn't seem to be detectable, at all.

Familiarity with our Heavenly Father that we have acquired thru our exercise of faith in our Savior Jesus Christ is the mortar binding together in one the building blocks of both testimony and conversion. Notwithstanding the clarity of our faith in the principles of His Plan, the prophets still implore us to manifest the discipline to keep our eyes fixed on a prize that may seem, at times, to be elusive. And thus, we persevere, and we extend ourselves beyond our zones of comfort. We know in our hearts that if we do so, we will be able to grasp the golden ring on the carousel that seems to describe our lives.

Societies that lack vision have always paid a hefty price for the spiritual myopia that closes minds and hearts to enlightenment by the Holy Ghost that is so characteristic of those who worship our Savior Jesus Christ. Only Europe's Dark Ages compares, but in some respects we are again living in that stifling era. Every time that a culture loses its spiritual equilibrium, it scrambles to readjust its values by conveniently realigning them with worldly coordinates, but that is an approach that never seems to work out, or end well.

As we worship our Lord and Savior Jesus Christ, the Spirit quietly prompts us to ease off the gas pedal and ratchet down the hectic pace of our lives. He calms our souls and carries us away, far from the madding crowd. The Lord knows how busy we are. He knows how it feels to be neglected, to be trivialized, and to engage in a fierce competition with sounding brass and tinkling cymbals for a voice that can be heard in the world. He might have been thinking of the influence that the Holy Ghost could have on our lives, when He counseled the Saints: "Be still, and know that I am God." (Psalms 46:10).

Even as our intensifying
witness of our Savior Jesus Christ
swells within our hearts, our faith will
deepen our desire to receive the revelation
that is found in His messages. They center
our lives, bringing them into harmony with
true principles. We hope to be more obedient to
the laws of God, to find ourselves in a constant
state of improvement. As we begin to believe in
ourselves, we will see that it is much easier to
believe in Him, also. It is with a quickening
pulse that we'll realize that our progress is
headed in the direction of perfection, that
God is great, that He doesn't make
knock-offs, and that we are
the right stuff.

Throughout the ages, the instruction, teaching,
and guidance of Torah, which is the foundational
scripture of Judaism, has dictated the observances of the
Jews to walk in covenant, purpose, and holiness. This body
of wisdom, together with the Talmud, has been as a phylactery
and a reminder to keep the laws of God. Today, real justification
will come only through faith in the power of Jesus Christ to save
us from our sins. Yet, there are always two distinctly different
paths to follow, "one leading to an ever lower and lower plane,
where are heard the cries of despair and the curses of the poor,
where manhood shrivels and possessions wear down the
possessor; while the other leads to the highlands of the
morning where are heard the glad shouts of
humanity, and where honest effort is
rewarded with immortality."
(John P. Altgeld).

There is already enough
on our plates without adding to our
burdens by fretting about the future. Worry is
only interest on a debt that may never come due.
There are, after all, only three types of control in life.
First, are those circumstances over which we have absolute
control. Then, are those things over which we have indirect
control, and finally those things over which we have no
control. Jesus Christ shows us where to most profitably
direct our energies and resources. By following its
principles, we get both the steak and the sizzle,
or, so to speak, more bang for our buck.

As
we endure
in faith, cherished
emanations of familiar
and soothing oscillations
of energy will resonate from
within the limitless reserves of the
Spirit. These are selflessly shared by
the Savior, who has promised to carry us
along upon the rolling waves of revelation
to a shoreline of stability that borders upon
an ocean in turmoil, while nurturing our
more sure witness of His divinity, no
matter what the advancing tide
may bring in tomorrow.

Jesus Christ
will transport the
righteous past the
vicissitudes of life
all the way to the
steadiness of the
kingdom of God
that is found in
revelation, and
that lies above
the confusion
of worldly
turmoil.

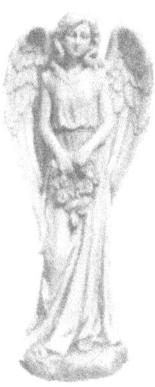

When we have finally determined to listen
to the promptings of the Spirit and to conform our
lives to the teachings of Jesus Christ, our nature will start
to change. The scales of darkness will fall away, the eyes of
our understanding will open, and our hearts will swell with His
pure love. As Jeremiah powerfully taught, the Lord will no longer
be a stranger in the land, but will be "the Hope of Israel." (Jeremiah
14:8). It will be our desire that there might no longer be contention
throughout the land, because of the love of God which dwells in our
hearts. It is a wish that envy, strife, tumult, whoredoms, lying,
and murder might cease. When that desire is granted, we will
become His children, heirs to God's covenant, and we might
well become the happiest people among all those who have
ever been created by His omnipotent hand.

We have quite a
lot to learn, and hopefully,
we'll have the gift of time on our
side. If we do, perhaps we should think
about what we would like to discover in
the next twelve months. How would we like
Could following the example of Jesus Christ
in the coming year help us to make positive
changes in our lives? As we consider that
challenge, we recall the familiar adage:
Some men see things as they are, and
ask why? Others dream things that
never were, and ask why not? Is
there any good reason not to
let the Spirit guide us, as
we never have before?

The gospel has the incredible ability to show us how to establish a kinship
between ourselves and those who were specifically raised up by our Heavenly
Father from before their births to be the humble understudies to the Great Jehovah.
"The Lord hath called me from the womb" wrote Isaiah, "from the bowels of my mother
hath he made mention of my name." (Isaiah 49:1). "Once or twice in a thousand years,
perhaps a dozen times since mortal man became of dust a living soul, an event of such
transcendent import occurs that neither heaven nor earth is ever thereafter the same.
Once or twice in a score of generations, the hand from heaven clasps the hand on
earth in perfect fellowship, the divine drama unfolds, and the whole course of
mortal events changes." (Bruce R. McConkie). This exactly describes the
circumstances surrounding those who have been commissioned to help
the Savior as He has ushered in the dispensation of the fulness
of times in support of His ministry.

In the execution of the
teachings of Jesus Christ, we
will discover examples of those who
have personified the promise that
"whosoever will save his life shall
lose it. But whosoever will lose
his life for my sake, the
same shall save it."
(Luke 9:24).

Within the
holy scriptures that record the
ministry of our Lord Jesus Christ, we
see invitations to come in from the cold,
to His hearth and home, from the alienation
of the lone and dreary world. Those who do so will
find refuge from the wintry winds of confusion and
religious turmoil. They will discover their "instructor in
principle, doctrine, and righteousness; and be their guide
in mutters of faith and morals." (B.H. Roberts). They will
leave the loneliness and estrangement of a fallen creation
to enter the realm of divine experience. They will forsake
the orphanage of spiritual alienation, to be received into
the family and household of our Savior.
(See Ephesians 2:19).

A testimony of
Jesus Christ remains the unique
possession of a peculiar people which, when
you stop and think about it, is as it should be,
because if He were to become popular with the world
"then all hell would want to join us." (Ezra Taft
Benson). "Christianity did not go from Rome
to Galilee; it was the other way around. In
our day, the routing is from Palmyra
to Paris, and not the reverse."
(Spencer W. Kimball).

There
is an ever-
present negative
energy that shapes
our experience. Jesus
Christ offers our only
useful countermeasure.
His sole stipulations are
that we confess if we've
embraced the opposites
that lie before us, and
that we immediately
undertake the safety
protocols required by
repentance to bring
us back into a state
of harmony with
our spiritual
center.

If we really desire to
have God's Spirit to be with us
during the week, we might want to
put away our tablets and turn off our
cell phones, even if we have them on vibrate.
Instead of answering email, we might instead
quietly use our time to listen for answers to our
prayers. Instead of searching for a strong Wi-Fi
signal, we could quietly turn to our Savior
Jesus Christ and let the Holy Ghost guide
us to and through His messages. They
won't be blocked as spam, and His
signal strength will always
be five bars.

In the grand scheme
of the universe, it makes no
difference if we turn to the right
or to the left, in the sense that those
who denigrate our Savior Jesus Christ
will always be around, but will fall by the
wayside, as has always been the case. The
Plan of God, on the other hand, will not be
going away anytime in the near future.
When we lift our eyes to the heavens, the
Savior will be watching us from above.
No matter that we bear the weight of
sin or sorrow with downcast eyes;
He is always beneath us, to lift
us up and carry our burdens.
If we ask in faith, He will
bless us in kind, and
beyond measure.

When we study the life of Jesus Christ, "a tale as old as time, and as true as it can be" speaks to us from out of the dust. ("Beauty and The Beast").

If, in any manner, we've delayed our quest for the holy grail of saving faith in the doctrine that's illustrated by the teachings of Jesus Christ, only to find that we've become desensitized to the truth, we'll risk becoming subjected to the spirit of the devil. When he captures our hearts, they will mutate to become stony and cold, and we'll lose the ability to distinguish good from evil and light from darkness. When we exchange the sunshine that is generated by the foundation of faith for wintry weather and worldliness, the Spirit of the Lord will withdraw to visit warmer climes, allowing Satan's icy breath to be sucked into the vacuum we've created for him.

The teachings of Jesus Christ
transport us back to a creative period
when matter was organized, the elements
were brought out of chaos into harmony,
and a Garden was nurtured eastward in
Eden. All was brought to a head when a
Savior was provided, with the power to
nullify the transgression of Adam
and Eve, thru an Atonement for
their own sins, as well as for
their children who would
be blessed to follow in
their footsteps.

Who will
enter into God's
rest? Those who believe
in our Savior Jesus Christ;
those who "walketh righteously,
and speaketh uprightly; (those) that
despiseth the gain of oppressions, that
shaketh (their) hands from (the) holding
of bribes, that stoppeth (their) ears from (the)
hearing of blood, and shutteth (their) eyes from
seeing evil. (They) shall dwell on high. (Their
clear) eyes shall behold the land that is very
far off" in a paradise that is the abode
of the Gods. (Isaiah 34:14-17).

The heraldic gospel of Jesus Christ proclaims that after a messenger from the unseen world announced to shepherds tending to their flocks by night in the fields near Bethlehem that Christ the Lord had been born, "suddenly there was with the angel a multitude of the heavenly host praising God." (Luke 2:13). A dramatic manifestation of beings from the presence of God prompted the shepherds to hasten to the manger, that they might witness the things that had come to pass that the angel had made known unto them.

"My thoughts are not your thoughts," saith the Lord of Hosts, "neither are your ways my ways … For as the heavens are higher than the earth, so are my ways higher than your ways, and my thoughts than your thoughts." (Isaiah 55:8-9). His thoughts are loftier, broader, more visionary, and infinitely more expansive. With His gospel, the Lord Jesus Christ wields a brush that paints with broad strokes, circumscribing the sum of our reality. The portrait thus created is a work of art more breathtaking than we could ever dare to dream would be possible.

Jesus Christ taught us that it is quite natural to make mistakes, just as it is to learn from them. When Hamlet exclaims: "Angels and ministers of grace, defend us!" what he is actually doing is calling for divine protection and guidance from the angels who administer God's grace. When they respond to our petitions, we grasp the horns of sanctuary so that at the end of the day we may still find ourselves justified by the tender mercy that is the grace of God.

As we venture forth out of our comfort zones and move forward with purpose, we'll enlarge the dimensions of our spiritual center, and we'll scribe a circle by using the stylus of the teachings of Jesus Christ, providing us with a glimpse of the mighty scale of our former heavenly home. Now, thanks to the intervention of all three members of the Godhead, mortality has the potential to become the wonderful learning center for the talented and gifted that it was envisioned to be before the world was made.

The hours we spend learning about the life
and ministry of our Savior Jesus Christ is a time
for our rededication and rebirth. God has revealed His
Plan because He wants our perspective to be crystal clear
and without ambiguity, so that we can concentrate on the
principles of perfection that are validated by the Spirit, that
are intrinsically fueled by the power of His priesthood, and
that are revealed and restored by legal administrators
who are commissioned to the work, and have been
sent down from heaven to carry it out
among the children of men.

Stars are the
nuclear fusion reactors
that provide both light and heat
to God's cosmos. Every second, our
Sun converts about 600 million tons
of hydrogen into helium. This procedure
takes place in its core, where photons are
released that take up to 250,000 years
to reach its surface (because they have
randomly bounced around so much
during the journey). Then, in just 8
minutes, they travel all the way to
earth to caresses our cheeks as
sunshine. In mysterious and
subtle ways, Jesus Christ
has organized Creation
to bless our lives!

The Holy Ghost helps cultivate the tender feelings that shape our faith to believe. In our Savior Jesus Christ, a vital power is unleashed that becomes an underlying component of a spectacular tapestry whose design will be revealed to us in all its glory. When our natures begin to correspond to the harmony of heaven as we pay closer attention to the counsel of the prophets in that inspired text, our mortal clay will be molded and take on the form and the substance of a perfect frame. It will dawn on us that, all along, there had been hiding a vibrant coat of many colors, just beneath the coarse vestments of our rough exterior.

Jesus Christ taught that even in the best of circumstances, government servants must never be left to rule without the guiding influence of the Spirit. (See Matthew 22;21). "Power tends to corrupt, and absolute power corrupts absolutely. Great men are almost always bad men, (and especially so) when they exercise influence and not authority, still more when you super-add the tendency or the certainty of corruption by authority. There is no worse heresy than that the office sanctifies the holder of it." (Lord Acton). Without the guidance of the Holy Ghost and when our hearts are set upon temporal things, spirituality suffers and our moral compasses tend to spin wildly out of control.

"Meet Joe Black" was
a film that was loosely based
on the 1934 motion picture "Death
Takes a Holiday." At its conclusion,
the protagonist, who is about to die, asks
Death: "Should I be afraid?" When Death
answers and says: "Not a man like you,"
we sense that everything is going to be
all right. The teachings of Jesus Christ
can serve as our primer, helping us
to so live that when it is our time
to reach out and touch eternity,
we will be similarly
blessed.

Those
familiar
with desert
environments
notice that palms
often seem to grow in
barren wastes. It is only
upon closer inspection that
oases of underlying currents
of life-sustaining water may be
noticed, that bring nourishment to
the roots of the thirsty trees. So, too,
Jesus Christ can be as a storehouse of
bread and a reservoir of living water.
His flowing fountain of revelation
will provides sustenance to all
those who hunger and thirst
after righteousness.

There will surely come an 'a ha!' moment for those who persevere in their determination to know the Lord Jesus Christ, when the Son will no more go down, "neither shall the moon withdraw itself. For the Lord shall be their everlasting light." (Isaiah 60:20).

Our faith is that there is more than enough room and sufficient time in the eternities for each of us to develop the ability to see beyond the limited horizon of our vision, all the way to the heavens, by the power of the revelation from God found in our Redeemer Jesus Christ. He can be our golden ticket that guarantees our safe passage Home.

The steadiness of our Savior Jesus Christ stands as the polar opposite of the moral ambiguity, the cultural confusion, intellectual instability, and spiritual schizophrenia that we witness in the world today. Because it can offer no solid ground as an alternative, we stand in holy places, and are not moved. (See Matthew 24:15)

Our Savior Jesus Christ is the Father of our spiritual regeneration and like the parent that we all aspire to be, He is there to heal our infirmities and bind up our wounds, every time we stumble and whenever we fall because of the weight we have been attempting to carry by ourselves. Even when we've forgotten about Him, He is our Father, and so He will never, ever, forget about us.

We express
gratitude to our Father
for the blessings of the life and
teachings of Jesus Christ and the
supernal gift of the Holy Ghost. But
instead of conveniently dashing off a
text message or an email, or tagging
Him in a Facebook post, mentioning
Him on X, or even dropping a thank
you note in the mail, He values our
simple expressions of gratitude
that are woven into the fabric
of our prayers.

There will come
for us a day in the Sun,
when we stand face to face with
eternity and the spiritual element
in which we are then immersed will
transform our mortal clay. Until that
time arrives, while we yet tarry upon the
earth, we might ask ourselves under what
circumstances can that element quicken us,
and how might the pure knowledge that flows
out of it be vitalized? Surely, it is "a man's
wisdom (that will make) his face to shine,
(and) the boldness of his face shall be
changed." (Ecclesiastes 8:1). These
miracles occur as we embrace the
massive currents of revelation
that flow from the life and
ministry of Jesus
Christ.

Jesus Christ
can change the course
of the circumstances in
which we find ourselves. First
we pre-play, and then we re-play.
Our anticipation of success helps us
to deal with the adversity and setbacks
that will inevitably come to all of us. It is
all part of a divine design. But when we have
dismissed the guidance and encouragement of
God that is found in the whisperings of the Spirit,
we will be guilty of turning our faces away from
the habitation of the Lord.

Jesus Christ asks us to measure the quality of our experiences,
not by the hopes and enjoyments of this world, but instead by the preparations
we are making for a different journey, as we look forward to what we shall become,
rather than backward to what we have been. If we incorporate into our lives the vision of
its messages, we'll see that "the past is prologue." The phrase, written by Shakespeare for
his play "The Tempest," was intended to imply that our past is merely a prologue, or an
introduction to the great adventure upon which we will embark if we follow through on
His Plan. This interpretation teaches that what has come before doesn't matter in
the grand scheme of things, because a new future lies before us, subject to the
choices we make. However, the way the phrase is commonly used today, it
means the exact opposite, that, because the past defines the present, it
determines the future. And that is why our Heavenly Father
has promised us the companionship of the Holy Spirit,
to shepherd us through our experiences toward
the Light in the East, which is where
our eternal destiny lies.

Our interactions with our Lord Jesus
Christ are not inconsequential practice runs.
They are not like dress rehearsals for Broadway
plays that abruptly close after receiving bad press
on opening night. In virtually every star system in
each of the galaxies throughout Creation, the drama
that is Heavenly Father's perfect Plan of Happiness
has instead received Oscars and Golden Globes for
best screenwriting, visual effects, choreography,
writing, music, production, sound, design,
and best picture and Director.

There is a
persistent negative
energy, competing for
attention with the Holy
Ghost, trying to influence
our experiences. The mercy of
Jesus Christ is our only useful
countermeasure, which stipulates
that we confess if we've embraced
the opposites that lie before us and
that we immediately undertake
the safety protocols required by
repentance to bring us back
into a state of harmony
with our spiritual
center.

Those who determine to
bear their witness to the world
of the divinity of Jesus Christ shall
receive health in their navel and marrow
in their bones, and shall find wisdom
and great treasures of knowledge,
even hidden treasures; and they
shall run and not be weary,
and shall walk and not
faint. (See Proverbs
3:8, & Isaiah
40:21).

We incorporate into
our lives the lessons learned
through a study of the ministry of
Jesus Christ, that we might overcome
spiritual death by entering the presence
of our Father and His Son by way of the
Holy Ghost. His Spirit dazzles us with an
endless reserve of revelation, illuminating
every corner of our minds and our spirits.
Our anticipated blessings proffered by the
combined capacity of the intrinsic light
that radiates from all three members of
the Godhead defy description. Binding
covenants bridge the gulf between the
secular and the divine that in other
less fortuitous circumstances,
might exist.

When we choose to ignore our Savior Jesus Christ, we'll find ourselves guilty of turning our faces away from the habitation of the Lord. (See Psalms 26:8). Because the people of Judah disregarded both the temple and its related ordinances, 2 Chronicles 29:8 reveal that the wrath of the Lord was upon them and upon Jerusalem, and He "delivered them to trouble, to astonishment, and to hissing."

Jesus Christ dignified effort, validated progress, rewarded achievement, and sanctified life itself. If we will open our eyes to His teachings, we'll discover how to appreciate the Spirit, to "speak in the name of God the Lord, even the Savior of the world; that faith also might increase in the earth, (so that the) everlasting covenant might be established; that the fulness of (the) gospel might be proclaimed by the weak and the simple unto the ends of the world." (D&C 1:19-23).

Our Savior Jesus Christ adroitly positioned the doctrines of the kingdom, which are the solemnities of eternity, in the forefront of our conscious awareness. We take our understanding as far as our capacity allows us to go, because it is tailored to suit our individual circumstances, and yet, at the end of the day, we are taught only by the Spirit.

The Lord Jesus Christ helps us recognize that each of us lives on a spiritual credit, and that one day, our account will be closed and a settlement required. This evokes memories of "our father focusing heart-gripping flashes across the wall screen. Family slides. I am small, my brother is smaller, and my sister is smallest. Days now dead re-open like old storybooks from memory's heaped box. Soberly, I think of another Father, Who someday shall open my mind, and flash reeling remembering of every day's minute across my soul and across the heavens, and kindly ask me to narrate." (Lora Lyn Stucker).

When we view it in spatial dimensions, mortality assumes the shape of an hourglass, and the strait gate is represented by its narrow midsection. After passing through that constriction following an exercise of repentance that is catalyzed by faith in our Redeemer Jesus Christ, there will open up before our eyes vistas of unparalleled opportunity.

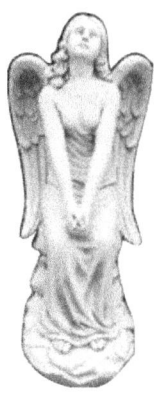

In a way, we're lucky that a veil was dawn across our minds to keep us insulated from the realm of the Gods, to ground us on the solid and familiar bedrock of past, present, and future. For now, at least, the arrow of time moves in only one forward direction. This handy frame of reference permits us to live in an orderly fashion within a timeline woven into a tapestry of faith by the Lord Jesus Christ.

We fool ourselves when we think that we can be content if we wander and play. But we forget the key messages of our Savior Jesus Christ that compel us to ponder and pray, and we fail to take advantage of the revelation that our Father in Heaven is so anxious to give us, which things lead us to appreciate the Atonement, and to speedily repent of our sins. Only then, will we discover for ourselves the happiness that God has prepared for His Saints.

As long as we have put on the life vest of the gospel that has been provided to us by Jesus Christ, and it remains snugly fitted to our bodies and spirits, we'll be sufficiently prepared as we deal with whatever challenges the rapids of life might choose to throw our way. High water can even be our friend, as it pushes us down the river of experience but harmlessly carries us over boulders of adversity, always in the direction of our dreams.

Yielding to the
Adversary's temptations
will leave us gasping for a
breath of the celestial ether that
is only found in the ventilation
systems that service the sanctuaries
that have been created by our Father
in Heaven to study the teachings of
Jesus Christ. It is there that we will
find the Spirit, Who will shelter us
from choking sandstorms of sin
that continually rake across
the desert wastelands of
Babylon.

Every time the inquiring faithful embark
upon the marvelous adventure that awaits them as
they study the teachings of Jesus Christ with the goal of
finding out for themselves if He publishes the truth, they will
discover that the Holy Ghost will energize their capabilities with a
vitality that they might not have otherwise recognized. As Bagheera,
the powerfully built black panther confided to Mowgli the man-cub:
"I had never seen the jungle. They fed me behind bars from an iron
pan until one night I felt that I was Bagheera the Panther, and
no man's plaything, and I broke the lock with one blow of
my paw, and I came away." (Rudyard Kipling, "The
Jungle Book," p. 26).

The ordinance of the Sacrament points us in the direction of the Spirit, and provides the fuel firing our determination to live in harmony with the tenets of our Savior Jesus Christ. It will charge our spiritual batteries and energize our vision with an infinite perspective so that we can remain holy and without spot.

At dawn on Christmas morning, as we enthusiastically dump out the contents of our stockings that the night before had been hung on the mantle with care, and a cornucopia of treats cascades onto the floor, it strikes us that our Father has promised to open for us "the windows of heaven, and pour out a blessing that there shall not be room enough to receive it." (Malachi 3:10). The manifestation of that blessing begins with the greatest gift of all, the Christ Child, not only on Christmas morning, but also on every other day throughout the year.

The example
of our Savior Jesus Christ
teaches the meek among us that
when we serve God with our hearts and
souls, hook, line, and sinker, we are free
from dependence upon any other being. In
regard to the poor, God transfers to them our
indebtedness to Him. It is thru them that
He asks us to pay our debt to Him. Thus,
a Zion Society is created from out of
the raw materials of righteous
interdependency.

When we have been caught with our hand
in the cookie jar, we all seem to muster the unreasonable
plea for mercy without justice. At the end of the day, however, our
lobbying efforts in behalf of that morally indefensible expectation can
reduce the meaning and purpose of our lives to nothing more than a cruel
joke with an unanticipated punch line that will pierce our hearts without
pity. The Atonement of Jesus Christ will always be there to rescue us,
especially after we have exhausted our options, we have no one
else to whom we may turn, and we are finally and
irrevocably confronted by the feeling of utter
futility that impels us to focus
on His merits alone.

The Holy Ghost can see through the clarifying and purifying lens of eternity, and from that unique vantage point, He will bless our lives as He nurtures our testimony of the divinity of Jesus Christ. The veil that has been drawn before our eyes prevents us, for only a moment, from similarly experiencing His panorama of eternity with an equally unobstructed view.

The teachings of our Savior Jesus Christ help us realize that our mortal experience is only a tiny fraction of a much larger reality, and that as long as we believe our perspective to be unique, it's faulty. The veil helps us to accept the fact that, for now, mortality is our natural dimension. But we'll also learn why we can never be entirely comfortable in our temporal circumstances, and why we so often feel so like strangers and pilgrims on the earth. Our experiences when studying the scriptures help us better comprehend our innate thrust always toward the future, and always beyond the limited horizon of our sight.

We are not ashamed to "declare (God's) doing among the people." It is so easy to turn to our Redeemer Jesus Christ and "to make mention that His name is exalted." (Isaiah 12:4). We'll join with our fellow Saints who have chosen to draw a line in the sand, and stand as witnesses of His divinity.

It was from before the creation of the world that the doctrine of Christ, as it is explained in His gospel, was custom-tailored to eventually place each of us on trial, to have our day in court. At the Bar of Justice, when we kneel before His feet on the Day of Reckoning, a Righteous Judge will do no more than weigh the facts, and our previous acceptance or rejection of His gospel, together with how we viewed His Atonement, will determine our reward or punishment. The legal proceedings have already been docketed to follow on the heels of our mortal experience, and we will be comforted to know that the Holy Ghost will be there to insure that they are carried out with impartiality.

Without an abiding
testimony of the divinity of
Jesus Christ, there is no way that
we could logically expect to inherit
the glory of celestial realms. This
is particularly true when we have
aforetime been agreeable to abide
only by telestial or terrestrial
principles that inherently
put fewer demands on
our discipleship.

In these latter days, we are
witnesses to the phenomenon of those
who have embraced our Savior Jesus Christ,
who have been transfigured by revelation and stare
in wide-eyed wonder at the fire, smoke, thunder, and
lightning of the Lord, while at the same time slit-eyed
sceptics squint at every sunburst that would have, in
more generous circumstances, foreshadowed their
spiritual awakening. These are the naysayers,
doubters, and cynics who instead would
rather wear designer sunglasses than
adjust their eyes to the increased
illumination radiating from
the light of truth.

As we enjoy the rhapsody of the gospel of Jesus Christ, we hear the soft music of heavenly choirs and we discern the voices of angelic messengers who testify that the Son of God has come in righteousness to declare the glad tidings of great joy. It will seem to us that it is "in the dark recesses of memory, in unbidden suggestions, in trains of thought unwittingly pursued, in multiplied waves and currents all at once flashing and rushing, in dreams that cannot be laid to rest, in the force of instinct, in obscure but certain intuitions of the spiritual life, that we will have glimpses of a great tide of life ebbing and flowing, rippling and roiling and beating about where we cannot see it." (E.S. Dallas).

Jesus Christ teaches us to enjoy easy familiarity with principles that are in sharp contrast to society's tenets that are continually morphed by the shifting sands of cultural expediency. Sound doctrine insulates us from the constantly mutating values of the world. Left to our own devices, we could never hope to keep up with its current interpretation of morality, because its flavor of the day is always changing. In their place, we have God's undeviating standard of behavior that describes an unchanging moral foundation that shapes us as we mature into the triple decker ice cream cone version of the full stature of our spirits.

When we're inclined to give only lip-service to the teachings of Jesus Christ, we don't realize that it may be because we're no longer under the influence of the Holy Ghost. When we are left to our own devices, we try to be "clever, interesting, and brilliant, but we lack one of the three dimensions of life. We have no reach upward. Our conversation sparkles, but it is frivolous and often flippant. Our talk is witty, but is often at the expense of high and sacred things." (Charles Jefferson).

When we take the time to hit the pause button in our busy lives, and step back from the world of confusion, take up our cross, and follow the pathway to the God's mercy seat because we worship Jesus Christ, we very soon recognize that They have established a well-defined pathway that leads to a faith-based life. As we read the scriptures, we feel an ambiance that will make it easy to fill our lungs with celestial air. We are more comfortable when we recommit ourselves to internalize every truth relating to eternal progress. We are endowed with power to endure adversity, that we might see our lives through to their pre-ordained end, and do so in righteousness.

At the end of the day, it becomes our righteous desire to conduct our lives in such a way that the Holy Ghost may justify us by testifying that we have been perfectly obedient to our covenants. This enables Heavenly Father to welcome us into His Rest. His promised blessing has the power to move us along the path of progression to the point that we will internalize His divine nature and one day be comfortable when we find ourselves kneeling before His throne. This is one of the things we repetitively rehearse as we engage the teachings of Jesus Christ.

An account of Eve's instruction to her posterity after the death of her husband Adam reads thus: "Listen to me, my children. Make tables of stone and of clay, and write on them the record of our lives, and all that ye have heard and seen from us. Then, if by water the Lord judge our race, the tables of clay will be dissolved and the tables of stone will remain; but if, by fire, the tables of stone will be broken up, and the tables of clay will be baked hard." (The Pseudepigraphic Book of Adam and Eve). Paper and ink and even tablets of stone or metal may not survive the ravages of time, but our Savior Jesus Christ has assured us that God will be able to read the record of our lives engraved in our sinews. For Him who created us, that tapestry woven into our souls may be understood as easily as any printed text. Our Heavenly Father "knows when (we've) been bad or good, so be good for goodness' sake!" (John Coots and Haven Gillespie, "Santa Claus is Coming to Town").

We have chosen allegiance to our Lord and Savior Jesus Christ in a consummate act of free will that yields our hearts to Him. We ponder the great and terrible consequences of Gethsemane, travel with Him to Calvary, and enjoy the sweetness of the Atonement's redeeming power. When we keep His laws, we experience the happiness that has been prepared for His Saints. "Lo, saith he, I am with you always, even unto the end of the world." (William Tyndall). We are not alone, now or ever. Adam fell that we might be, and we were created that we might have joy, not only in the comfortable environment of our heavenly home, but also in the here and now.

Only in the teachings of our Savior Jesus Christ will our experiences in the learning laboratories of life begin to make sense. Therein lies the inherent beauty of the Plan and the key to its success. Revelatory experiences will teach us that "the brotherhood of man is an element of Christianity no less than is the Fatherhood of God, and to deny one is no less infidel than to deny the other." (Lyman Abbott).

Jesus Christ provides
unequivocal understanding
and unambiguous definitions of
eternal truths. He permits us to benefit
from the events within which we are swept
up, to grow from our relationship with others,
to bloom where we are planted, no matter how
unique or difficult it might seem to us, and
to be protected from worldly influences that
would encroach upon the fortress of our
spiritual sanctuary, symmetry,
safety, and security.

The
faithful
soon learn to
their delight that
darkness cannot be
carried into a lighted
room, and so they seize
the chance to be enveloped
within the brilliance of the
gospel of Jesus Christ, having
resolved to face the Son of God,
that the shadows might always
be behind them. Darkness will
still exist, but its companions
that take the identity of fear,
trepidation, uncertainty,
and apprehension, will
be out of sight and
mind.

The light and the life of the world is Jesus Christ, the Son of God, who was crucified for the sins of the world. From our perspective, His light has always existed. His gospel focuses and clarifies that light as would a magnifying glass, and it organizes it into coherent substructures, as does a prism.

Our Savior Jesus Christ quietly confirmed to us that the meek shall inherit the earth. They reflect poise under provocation and they are sensitive to the needs of others. They are empathic and humble, and they are less concerned with telestial trinkets, but are more focused on celestial certainties. The meek among us are selfless, harbor no secret agenda, and are repulsed by sin. Rejoicing in the truth; they are drawn toward the light, while they are continually receptive to all that is good. Meekness may be one of the greatest of the qualities of the Savior, Who is the proprietor of all of God's spiritual gifts. For our own part, without meekness, progress toward our divine center is unable to move forward.

When we begin to understand he underlying themes that swirl around the ministry of Jesus Christ, we realize that we have been living in one dimly lighted corner of reality, with a very narrow perspective that has been frozen in time. The Savior brings us home to a more comfortable and expansive dominion, where power and authority are redefined with new meanings that had beforehand been only dimly perceived.

When Adam and Eve were driven from the Garden, they were "punished" with what was later shown to give them happiness. The Sufi poet Rumi wrote that our wounds become the portals that allow light to enter us. A Savior would be provided for God's children, but in the interim, cherubim and a flaming sword were set in place to keep the way of the Tree of Life, to observe the doctrines of Justice and of Mercy and to initialize the principle of repentance that is founded upon the doctrine of the Atonement of Jesus Christ that prominently figures in His gospel.

It is within
the gospel of Jesus
Christ where we learn of
the casualty count from the
ideological War in Heaven; that
some of Heavenly Father's children
forfeit their privilege to obtain a body.
For those who remained faithful in the
pre-earth existence, however, there came
humbling liabilities, and so the Plan
required our Creator to die for our
sins in order to satisfy the Law
of Justice this is conditioned
only upon our heartfelt
repentance.

If we no longer believe in
the divinity of Jesus Christ, the
compromise of our conversion can
often be attributed to a lack of faithful
focus that initiated a flat spin from which
we couldn't recover. Blame for the demolition
of our discipleship, and for the chain-reaction
of the unfortunate consequences that follow, is
often laid at the doorstep of others, but at the end
of the day, it comes down to us, and no-one else.
Without the guidance of the Spirit, we are the
architects of our own fate, and the resulting
construction will sometimes fail to meet
the stringent specifications of God's
residential building code.

The gospel coherently draws together, as in one, the scriptures that testify of the divinity of Jesus of Nazareth, expounding in one His doctrine. It supports the latter-day teachings of His servants, and whether we receive it by way of commandment, exhortation, or counsel from pulpits that are aflame with faith, it is the same. The word of God will be established in the mouths of two or three (or more) credible witnesses. (See Matthew 18:16).

In the beginning of time, our Sun, like most of its sisters, started life in a stellar nursery composed of a large cloud of gas with enough mass to undergo localized gravitational collapse. At some point, the central clump achieved a critical stage that ignited in a thermonuclear reaction. If the clump had not been massive enough, the explosion would have scattered its material, and the Sun would never have been born. But because the gravity of the mass was powerful enough to counteract the force of the explosion, the thermonuclear reaction became perpetually self-sustaining and the ball of gas we call our Sun has now been burning for 4.568 billions of years. God and our Savior work in mysterious ways, and the Holy Ghost bears record that the gospel of Jesus Christ is true.

When John looked into
the depths of eternity, he beheld a door
that "opened in (into – J.S.T.) heaven: and
the first voice which (he) heard was as it were
of a trumpet talking with (him); which said, Come
up hither, and I will shew thee things." (Revelation 4:1).
John had been transported from his temporal and spatial
surroundings into the presence of the Lord Jehovah, into the
"depths of eternity," or the "hereafter". He was somehow at
the same time both "here" and "after," which although
vague is as specific as we can get when referring to
higher dimensional states. Then, John described
what he both saw and heard as "lightnings
and thunderings and voices."
(Revelation 4:5).

We resort to the utilization of abstractions in
our own feeble attempts to describe our Savior Jesus
Christ. Thoughts cannot be shaped, nor words formed, nor
sentences framed, to accurately convey His glory. Figures of
speech are used because we would otherwise be at a complete loss for
words, when grasping for even a basic description of His profoundly
metaphysical reality. To Moses, the presence of the Lord appeared as "a
flame of fire out of the midst of a bush: and he looked, and behold, the
bush burned with fire, and the bush was not consumed." (Exodus 3:2).
In our own circumstances, we might say, as did one who witnessed
God's signature Aurora: "We beheld a circle of green, blue, and
orange swirling thru the night sky like a ballroom dancer
performing a waltz. It was flowing with such grace that
we were speechless, and remained entranced for a
quarter hour and more."

The
world
attempts
to change
us by exerting
external control
but in doing so, it
fails miserably. Our
Redeemer Jesus Christ,
on the other hand, takes
the innovative approach to
influence the inner vessel,
succeeding brilliantly by
recalibrating our internal
compass so that we might
remain oriented toward
the principles of His
gospel.

Our Lord and Savior Jesus Christ shows us how we can be less judgmental, less suspicious and friendlier; to be more accepting of others, often without reservation; to see them as neighbors and not as strangers. We'll find that we are more trusting of others and speak without guile; and are more transparent and less prejudicial. We'll have fewer pretensions and be more genuine. We'll be less prone to rationalization and quicker to forgive, and be true, chaste, benevolent, and virtuous. Our faith will be more pure, our hope more comprehensive, and our charity will have no bounds. The image and likeness of God will be etched upon our countenances.

The
enthusiastically
ignorant attempts to drag
the communication that waits
to be dispensed from the heavens
down to their own level, until it's
inaudible to their ears, much like
their myopic view of life is to their
eyes. The world ridicules revelation
and disparages its delivery. Thus,
their feeble attempts to explain our
Redeemer Jesus Christ ring hollow,
especially when compared to the
thunder, the lightning, and
the voice that came forth
out of a burning bush
on Sinai.

Those who have meekly embraced the teachings
of Jesus Christ may often be blessed with weaknesses,
so that they might be humble. Demosthenes overcame a
lisp to become one of the greatest orators of ancient Greece.
Beethoven composed some of his greatest music after he lost
his hearing. Early in his career, Abraham Lincoln declared:
"I will prepare myself, and some day my chance will come."
As a young man, Heber J. Grant couldn't carry a note. Later,
he became well known for his singing abilities. Quoting
Ralph Waldo Emerson, he said of his own experience:
"That which we persist in doing becomes easier for
us to do; not that the nature of the thing
is changed, but that our power
to do is increased."

It will do nothing but blemish our character if we allow ourselves to engage in bartering with the money changers in the temple, in the expectation of receiving spiritual gifts in the exchange. Only when we devour the teachings of Jesus Christ as the bread of life, will we feel the power of His mighty arm as, by the Spirit, we are infused with His energy.

Since words can be the burning embers of God, every element of mortality can be a fiery experience. To help us spiritually emotionally, and intellectually process the perceptions that are continually bombarding our self-awareness, we have been provided with a banquet of truth that is composed of the 22 mystical letters within the Hebrew alphabet. Each one flavors our conception of His kingdom, as we engage a progressive curriculum that will nurture us by teaching us about our own world. Each one should quietly and subtly shape our appreciation of the efforts of those who created the Bible with blood, sweat, toil, and tears, as we embark upon a pilgrimage to the feet of Jesus Christ on a journey that should prove to be transformative. (See 2 Corinthians 3:2-3).

Oh, Rabboni (see John 20:16), grant us the power of discernment through Thy Spirit and watch over us. For with golden tongues, scribes and Pharisees beguile us with worldly wisdom, tempt us with sophistry, and drape flaxen cords ever so gently around our necks. It seems so reasonable and natural even as we are carefully led down to the bottomless pit of hell.

Through our Lord Jesus Christ, both the heavens and the earth are bathed in a celestial fire that is akin to the background radiation that still lingers from the cataclysmic moment of creation itself. The Holy Ghost furnishes us with a stable star map that defines the path that began in the heavens, and that will lead us all the way back to our pre-ordained inheritance. He quite simply blesses us with a promised endowment of unearthly and radiant power that is foreshadowed within the pages of the Bible.

At times, overzealous evangelical disciples of Christ seem to be overly-eager to take up a sword of vengeance, as if it were somehow their God-given right and responsibility to pass judgment on unbelievers. In contrast to those who use religion, and in particular, the twisting of holy writ to legitimize vindictive behavior, the Saints believe that the Savior must surely have smiled upon the simple expressions of kindness and acts of charity that are characteristic of the spirit of reconciliation. (See 2 Corinthians 5:18-20).

Heaven is our natural element and is the aether that even now fills our lungs and invigorates us with celestial air, and it is the state of being that we all intuitively call our Home. God created the physical world, and established governing laws that were designed to lead us back into His presence. Because we are spiritual beings having mortal experiences, we sometimes feel that we are not synchronized with our natural element. If that is so, our greatness and power will only be manifest when we embrace the teachings of our Savior Jesus Christ, and "the stars fade away, the sun himself grow dim with age, and nature sink in years." Then, we "shall flourish in immortal youth, unhurt amidst the war of elements, the wreck of matter, and the crash of worlds." (Joseph Addison).

Without Jesus Christ, we will find ourselves caught up in conceptually confusing cul-de-sacs that prevent us from comprehending the real meaning of life. His guidance keeps us from wandering about as flotsam and jetsam, dazed and disoriented, and tossed about like cockleshells upon stormy seas, leaving us without purpose or direction.

The prophets who speak to us about the teachings of Jesus Christ have warned no uncertain terms that a day of judgement is coming for every one of us, when we will no longer be able to fabricate lies, either to ourselves or our Heavenly Father. We will have written the record of our lives in the sinews of our bodies and the tablets of our minds. In that coming day, both will be unfolded before God and angels, who will read that testament as easily as we read a book. At that moment, if we've aforetime embraced His doctrine, we'll find ourselves being swept up by quickening currents into the rapture of a holy communion with God. His thoughts will have somehow become our thoughts, and His ways will have become our ways. (See Isaiah 55:8). Legions of angels who are part of the heavenly host will confirm the truth that the universe itself has become "a machine for the making of gods." (Henri Bergson).

If we allow ourselves to become isolated from the sensitivity to our surroundings that is nurtured by repentance, we may become inured to our condition inasmuch as we're past feeling. If that's so, the power of the Savor's Atonement will be of no effect and He will have suffered in the Garden of Gethsemane and died on the Cross at Calvary, for naught.

There is no revelation where there is no student, and so if we don't ask the right questions that relate to the truths that we discover in the teachings of Jesus Christ, we must be at odds with our faith, and we will be condemned to receive the wrong answers. Sadly, rational minds will never be able to bridge the gap that must exist between the profane character of the worldly-wise and our divine nature.

To have the
unlimited freedom
to choose for ourselves
in an atmosphere that is so
full of dangerous deceptions,
enticing entrapments, soothing
seductions, and perilous pathways,
entails great risk. In our lives, if we
embrace the teachings of Jesus Christ, we
will discover principles of protection that
will keep us untainted from the blood and
sins of this generation, and we'll be given
the tools to flee from spiritual Babylon
without looking over our shoulders
and risking being turned into
pillars of salt.

The
discipline of those
who follow Jesus Christ
stands out in contrast to the
short-lived pleasure in worldly
ways that always evaporates as
morning dew in the light of day.
It's only our unswerving obedience
to our covenants that will mitigate
the disastrous consequences that
must surely prevail if the spectre
of rebellion were given license
to sabotage our actions.

Our Savior, Who was Consecrated for Evermore, has given us laws that demand that we give heed to the way we spend our time, and also to the care with which we make time, the diligence with which we find time, and the discipline we exhibit in taking the time to engage in a study of His gospel. expansive laws of the Celestial Kingdom allow us to create more time, but forbid us to waste time, or to kill time. (See Hebrews 7:28).

Following the Flood, the ancients built ziggurats that were massive towers that had been constructed to reach up to heaven itself. The Tower of Babel is an example of these exaggerated temple steeples. However, their designers and builders, and those who flocked to behold those architectural marvels, missed the point. Instead of creating physical structures composed of nothing but brick and mortar, they could have more profitably used their time employing the principles taught by the Lord Jehovah to construct lasting relationships with each other, and more importantly, with their Heavenly Father.

Those who rashly decline
the offer of the riches of eternity
that might have been unfolded to
their view by a correct understanding
of the doctrine taught by our Redeemer
Jesus Christ, are doomed to scratch out a
subsistence level of existence that is in
scarcity of their basic spiritual needs.
With the smorgasbord of life spread
out before them, they settle for the
processed factory food that is
dished out by the automats
of the world. They exist
beneath the poverty
level, and are not
even aware
of it.

Our Lord and Savior Jesus Christ
is the foundation beneath our existence. However,
our capacity to fill the measure of our creation may be
compromised by the corrosive effects of worldly corruption.
In the final analysis, the danger of self-reliance is that it
leads us away from the tenderness of faith. We need to be
careful not to allow our agency to mutate into forms
that celebrate our independence so powerfully
that we forget His teachings, or that we
no longer fall under the spell of
His tender mercies.

Jesus Christ requires that we take calculated and acceptable risks in order to break free from the comfort zones, safety nets, and ports of refuge to which the timid apprehensively retreat at the first sign of danger, to squeak out their lives as they scurry about from one shadowy sanctuary to another, in a free-fall from freedom and faith.

The average heart contracts 80 times per minute, 4,800 times per hour, and 115,200 times per day, and over the course of a year, it beats over 42 million times. In 70 years, that's almost 3 billion beats. An adult heart pumps up to 2,000 gallons of blood every day, about 730,000 gallons each year, or up to 51,000,000 gallons in 70 years, through around 100,000 miles of vessels in a circulatory system that brings nourishment to 37.2 trillion cells that make up the human body. The Saints of all ages understand that the gospel of Jesus Christ requires their equivalent heart that loves the Lord "with all (their) soul, and with all (their) strength, and with all (their) mind." (Luke 10:27).

When a fickle
and faithless society has
been weighed in the balances
and is found wanting, it can be
traced all the way back to spiritual
bankruptcy on an institutional scale;
simply to a repudiation of the power of the
doctrine that was taught by Jesus Christ.
Its motto seems to be: "Eat, drink, and
be merry," for tomorrow we will
die. (Luke 12:19).

Our Redeemer Jesus Christ motivates us
as repentant sinners to fast and pray to receive
the spirit of revelation, and to know and understand
the things of God. As we do so, the temporal and spiritual
sides of our nature slowly harmonize. Our physical desires,
held in check by an expanding spiritual awareness, strengthen
our resolve to discipline our nature. We transcend forces pulling
us one way or another, and enter a metaphysical state of euphoria
where virtue garnishes our thoughts unceasingly, as the doctrine
of the priesthood distills upon our souls as the dews from heaven
because our confidence begins to grow strong in the presence of
God. As this progression unfolds, the Holy Ghost becomes our
constant companion, our scepter an unchanging scepter of
righteousness and truth, and our dominion a God-centered
and focused protectorate. Under these conditions, all that
is good begins to freely flow from the fountain of all
righteousness like an artesian well that will
sustain us with an unending stream
of living water.

With unshakable confidence, our conviction will be reinforced as we embrace the teachings of Jesus Christ, our faith will replace our fear, and we'll receive a quiet reassurance that "today is a good day to die." (Crazy Horse).

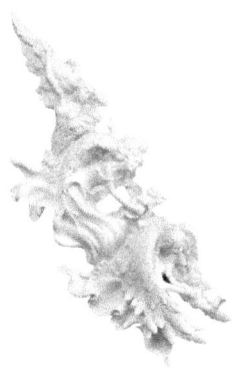

The unreserved generosity of our Savior Jesus Christ emphasizes to us that we must never allow ourselves to squander precious assets by becoming preoccupied with what is missing. Focusing our attention on what we lack easily becomes a paralyzing fear. It's a flawed strategy that will ultimately defeat us. We must concentrate on the resources that are available, be they large or small, capitalize on them, and turn them into forces for positive, substantive, and significant change. We must pray as if everything depended upon the will of God, as it surely does, but then work as if it all depended upon us.

Everyone wants to go to heaven. But if we don't have an inventory of life-sustaining experiences to nourish us, we will not be prepared for the birth that we call death. If we learn to pre-play before we re-play, though, our expanding reserve of assets will include prayer, testimony, temple, covenants, family, and a community of the Saints. If we've learned to live, and the Holy Ghost centers us on our Savior Jesus Christ, our last breaths on earth will not signal an end, but rather, proclaim a brand new beginning.

Our belief sanctions the truth of God's precepts, principles, and doctrines, but it cannot do so without the moral element of responsibility which we call faith. Of those to whom much is given, though, much is expected. The gift of faith to believe in our Savior Jesus Christ demands action. When we exercise our agency, even if we've performed good works, if we do so without an abiding trust in the promises of God, our works will fall short of the mark, because our faith lacks vitality or hasn't been quickened by the Spirit.

We need enlightened prophets
of the caliber of Abraham, Moses, Ruth, Isaiah, Esther,
Ruth, Jeremiah, and Daniel, to drive the law of the Lord Jehovah
into our inward parts, and to help us internalize its principles; to
experience sanctification, and to be cleansed by repentance from the
effects of sin. (See Jeremiah 31:33). We need prophets to facilitate
our spiritual renewal, so that we might stand prepared to enter
into the presence of the Lord. We must submit to His will,
yield our hearts to Him, and be obedient to all of His
teachings and the teachings of His servants.

The Adversary, who is a consummate
con man, a master deceiver, and was a liar
from the beginning, even now continues his
futile efforts to foil the counsel of our Savior
Jesus Christ, and the ensuing instruction of
the children of God with light and truth, with
the substitution of a counterfeit proposal, that
was a desperately unworkable alternative that
would have required neither repentance nor
Atonement by a Savior. Fortunately, at
the Council in heaven when both plans
were discussed, we could see through
his deception. Today, we retain our
eternal perspective. Our prayers
reflect our determination to
remain as His faithful
disciples.

Each time we encounter the principles and doctrines of God's Plan during our engagement with our Savior Jesus Christ, we find the sinews of our bodies resonating with religious recognition as we have our déjà vu moments. At the end of the day, every one who hearkens to the promptings of the Spirit will eventually come unto God in this way and will really live.

Our exciting journey to the veil recalls the wisdom of Winston Churchill, who said: "There comes for each of us a special moment when we are figuratively tapped on the shoulder and offered a chance to do a very special thing, unique to ourselves and fitted to our talents. What a tragedy if that moment should find us unprepared or unqualified for that which could have been our finest hour." Standing before God, angels, and witnesses, including Jesus Christ, at the Judgment Bar, will be a fitting conclusion to the hours that we have been spent as eager participants in our initial, preparatory, excursion through His gospel.

As imperfect mortals struggling to believe in things we cannot see, the reward of our maturing faith is to see what we believe. Some things just have to be believed to be seen, before emerging faith in our Savior Jesus Christ that has been shaped by experience and stabilized by the Holy Ghost, allows us to say, as did the believing man who had been blind from birth, but was healed by the Lord: "One thing I know, whereas I was blind, now I see." (John 9:25).

At first, it might seem that the easier wrong is more expedient, but that may be only because it harmonizes with the values of Babylon. Worldliness is all around us and if we cannot find the stabilizing influence provided by faith in Christ as we study His gospel, resulting moral equivocation on our part can quickly turn into a path of least resistance, until it become the habitual pattern of our conduct. Our faith invites us to trust in the divine design of our Father in Heaven that is firmly grounded upon the Atonement of His Son. It nurtures our belief that it is only in Him that our lives can become as fairy tales that are just waiting to be written by the hand of God.

In our endeavors to
understand the complexity
of the human genome, we may
yet discover within the fascinating
matrix of the double helix the blueprints
of an interstellar family tree. The far end
of that scale, hidden somewhere beyond the
hills of time in the teachings of Jesus Christ,
just might contain the cosmic equivalent
of "Family Search," waiting for us to
activate our subscription.

The unrepentant wicked only infrequently
consent to listen to the good news published by
Jesus Christ. But we need to remind ourselves that
when the world rejected the Mortal Messiah, He didn't
retreat with His tail between His legs to His home in
Galilee. The Lord wants us to know what it's like to
feel the Spirit; not only the happiness of seeing
our brothers and sisters enter in to the fold at
the waters of baptism to be born again, but
also the pain and frustration of rejection.
In strange and mysterious ways, it is
these contraries that the Holy Ghost
uses to work together for our good,
although it might be in a
refiner's fire.

"The harder the conflict may be, the more glorious is the triumph. What we obtain too cheap, we esteem too lightly. 'Tis dearness only that gives everything its value. Heaven knows how to put a proper price upon its goods." (Tom Paine, "Common Sense"). It would be strange, indeed, if a celestial article such as an abiding testimony of the divinity of Jesus Christ, that had been obtained thru blood, sweat, toil, and tears and by the power of the Holy Ghost, should not be highly rated.

Among the earliest Hebrews, even before the Lord Jehovah had manifested Himself as the God of all the earth, were those "whose tired eyes could see beyond the desert to the invisible summit of the imagination, where cool air existed and where the one true god, El Shaddai, he of the mountain, lived. In later generations, El Shaddai was destined to mature into that god whom much of the world would worship. But of one thing these people were sure. El Shaddai personally determined the destiny of this group, for of all the people between the Euphrates and the Nile, he had chosen this band of Hebrews as his predilected people, and they lived within his embrace, enjoying security that others did not know." (James Michener, "The Source").

Subsequent to the
ministry of Jesus Christ,
we witness the shining examples
of prophets, seers, and revelators. They
speak prophetically as they teach the body
of known truth. They are seers, who see with
spiritual eyes and publish hidden truth, and
they are revelators each time they bring to
the attention of the people new truth that
has never before been made known
to the children of men, or that
has been lost through
apostasy.

Prophets
of God bless us with
with truth, and they do so
in plainness and simplicity,
so that all might understand. It
is the nature of the apostolic calling
to bear witness to all of the world of the
divinity of Jesus Christ and to teach of
the path to salvation and exaltation in
ways that are easily understood. To the
extent that the Bible remains unclear,
ambiguous, and even contradictory,
they stand ready to correct the errors
that have been introduced into the
liturgy of the Lord's church by
untutored, uninspired, and
malicious copyists over
the years.

Our Savior Jesus
Christ invites us all to be
baptized, that we might enjoy
the quiet serenity of the Sabbath
day as we never have before. We are
introduced to new experiences during
our day of worship, service, and rest
that take us far from the tumult of
the teeming multitudes and the
madding crowd that too often
reflects the lifestyle of the
rich and famous.

The magnificent Cedars of
Lebanon, mentioned in the scriptures,
(see Isaiah 14:8), represent the disciples of our
Lord Jesus Christ. They were evergreen, beautiful,
and aromatic. Members of the church will declare that
since the destruction of Babylon, no feller, a person who
cuts down trees, has come up against them to smite them.
In similar manner, it's the righteous who shall "flourish
like the palm tree (and) grow like a cedar in Lebanon.
Those that (are) planted in the house of the Lord shall
flourish in the courts of our God." (Psalms 92:12).
Cedars of Lebanon may grow in what appear to
be harsh environments. It is only upon closer
inspection that the oasis of an underlying
current of life-sustaining water may be
noticed, that brings nourishment to
the roots of the thirsty trees.

When the hearts of
the wicked have been hardened
against our Redeemer Jesus Christ,
and minds are closed to its message of
salvation, light is diminished, leaving their
faltering spirits vulnerable to the relentlessly
aggressive tactics of the Devil. Left alone, they are
influenced more by his lies than by illuminating
truth, and they risk being dragged by the heavy
weight of his chains of darkness to the hell of
misunderstanding, ignorance, and self-
destructive patterns of behavior.

Those who are disobedient to
the teachings of Jesus Christ will feel
neither love nor loyalty for anything or
anyone else but themselves, and will enjoy
neither the blessings of unity nor the peace that
is the province solely of the righteous. Instead, the
father of contention, who is Satan, oversees their self-
destruction and he perversely enjoys the process. They
are punished by their sins, and not so much for them.
We think that it is God Who applies punishment, and
that He does it externally, the way parents often do,
but He does not. We say: "If you don't clean your
room, you can't drive the car for a week." God
says: "If you don't clean your room, you'll
have to live in it for a week." As it turns
out, everyone will have to endure the
consequences of their rebellion
against eternal law.

Jesus
Christ fans
with faith the
fire of our resolve.
We hope and pray to
have courage to change
the things we can, for the
serenity to accept the things
we cannot, and for God's
wisdom to know the
difference.

Jesus Christ speaks of things
as they really are, and of things as
they really will be, which are manifested
in plainness for the salvation of our souls.
In contrast is the intellectual embroidery that
is at times preferred to the whole ensemble of
the gospel; the frills to the fabric, as it were.
The gospel provides the absolute anchors
that we so desperately need. If we give
it a chance, we will find that there
is more realism in the word of
God than there could ever be
in a secularism that is
congenitally short-
sighted.

Jesus Christ reminded us that even the righteous do not become perfect overnight. Therefore, the Lord has promised that as often as we'll repent, He will forgive us our trespasses. He will give us enough rope to either hang ourselves, or to lasso the stars and hitch our wagons to eternity. The choice is ours to make.

Our Lord and Savior Jesus Christ has provided our blueprint for survival in the Last Days. Ours was to have been an Age of Enlightenment, but it has become a conceptual free-for-all, without rules, regulations, or constraints of any kind. Righteousness has always responded to the better angels of our nature because it reflects foundation principles that are not subject to the vagaries of men. While few of us can escape the trauma of secular humanism, we cannot live for very long with unrighteousness before it will begin to strangle our spontaneity as the evolving children of God.

Jesus Christ shows us precisely how to be repeatedly re-vitalized, as we are re-introduced to a Magical Kingdom in which our hopes and our dreams really will come true, if only we will muster the faith to wish upon a star that twinkled over the little town of Bethlehem.

What about those of us who aren't so sure of ourselves? What happens if we look in the mirror and see only the face of a stranger staring back at us? What if our knees wobble at the prospect of the leap of faith required as we tackle the demands of discipleship. We take comfort that the Lord will quiet our fears, by simply speaking the words: "Be still, and know that I am God." (Psalms 46:10).

Our Savior Jesus Christ inspires us to be enthusiastic. After all, it is the good news that practically begs us to experience the feeling of being possessed by a god, to have supernatural inspiration, and enjoy prophetic frenzy. The definition found in the dictionary is unmistakable. If we are suffused with enthusiasm, our actions are no longer ours; for it is God Who has taken control of our destiny, with kindness and benevolence.

At the instant when our unsatisfied craving for the praise and the popularity of the world begins to sway our behavior, we find ourselves bending our character, when we think we are only taking a bow. It is chiefly at this time that we need the soothing inspiration of the Holy Spirit, the healing guidance of our Savior Jesus Christ, and finally the nurturing encouragement of our Father, Who looks down upon us every day of our lives from heaven above.

"When we look up at the night sky and we see thousands of points of light, we're reminded" that the power that fuels the stars is not nuclear fusion, but our Savior Jesus Christ, and that "it is an every-day reality throughout the Milky Way." (Carl Sagan).

No wind can blow except it fills our sails to carry all of us closer to our destination, in the direction of our destiny, without any delay or interruption, and without unnecessary cost, loss, or sacrifice. All that is required of us to gain a witness of our Redeemer Jesus Christ is a contrite spirit. We rely upon the power of the Savior's gentle breeze to nudge our fragile vessels onward upon the vast ocean of life, even as intermittent moments of calm seem to be accompanied by the indistinct sound of seafarer's shanties. These would appear to be the music of God's heavenly choir, whose primary purpose is to reinvigorate our hearts that are broken down in humility.

Disciples of Jesus Christ walk the walk, and talk the talk. They believe in His divinity, and they also believe Him when He reassures them that they are celestial material.

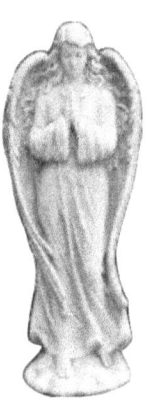

Our faith in Jesus Christ provides us with an attractive return on investment, and also with mad money that is sufficient for our immediate needs. But it also allows us, if we so choose, to substitute its legal tender for bundles of counterfeit currency with which late payments may be made with both interest and penalties tacked on for bad behavior. Without the Atonement, our lease on life would be threatened with cancellation for the nonpayment of the levies and the charges that accumulate as we conduct our lives within a speculative environment in an arena of agency and the circus of commerce.

The gift of Jesus Christ was given to the world, that we might enjoy covenants that relate to salvation and justification, sanctification and exaltation; so that by the authority of the priesthood of God the Sacrament might be administered to everyone who qualifies by worthiness to partake of the emblems of our Lord and our Redeemer.

Jesus Christ focuses our attention on the gift of happiness that is the companion of untroubled souls, and we use our free will to choose the Savior and yield our hearts to Him. We ponder the great and terrible consequences of Gethsemane, and we travel the Via Dolorosa with Him to Calvary. We enjoy the sweetness of the redemptive power of His Atonement, which is the keystone of God's Plan. We determine to keep His laws because we have learned by our experience that His mighty arm transcends temporal security and renders as inconsequential any worldly comforts. (See Isaiah 51:9, & John 12:38).

We are quick to recognize that the path before us leads to
our spiritual transformation and to lives that are centered on
the Savior. When we internalize the principles and doctrines of
the gospel of Jesus Christ, it will become easier for us to regularly
recommit ourselves to internalize their truths relating to eternal
progression, and to find within ourselves the power to endure
to the end in righteousness. Some might consider these
burdens to be too heavy, but countless witnesses
have testified that when our obedience ceases
to be inconvenient, then God manifests
His power, and the gospel becomes
the perfect law of liberty.
(See James 1:25).

We very quickly
understand that as we become
more familiar with the requirements
of our obedience to Jesus Christ, our views
will become clearer and our enjoyments greater,
until we've reached the point that we have overcome
evil and have lost the desire to sin. When we have been
born again, we leave behind our former lives, and become
quickened to spiritual realities. We covenant never again
to return to our wicked ways. We change our names and we
become 'saints,' a translation of a Greek word also rendered
'holy,' the fundamental idea being that of consecration, or
separation for a sacred purpose. The description came to
mean 'free from physical or moral blemish' and in the
New Testament, the saints were those who by their
baptism had entered into a covenant
relationship with God.

Our corporeal
surroundings in
this lone and dreary
world have been designed,
harsh though they may seem,
to provide a hint of familiarity.
We are sensitive to the Spirit as we
draw closer to our Savior Jesus Christ,
and we establish a celestial connection
as we commune with the heavens across
time and space, and as we burst the
barriers of our telestial
habitations.

None of us will
endure for very long by
relying only upon the dim
light that is generated by our
casual connections to our Savior
Jesus Christ. When we ask Him, He
will provide an external power source
with ample energy for as long as we
manifest a desire to become members
of His Second Mile Club, which is a
privileged group to which we have
been invited to join, as a result
of our acceptance of Him as
our Lord and King.

Those who
turn their hearts away
from and close their ears to
the precepts taught by Jesus
Christ are well acquainted with
despair, or the hopelessness they
feel when they have to deal with
the sense of futility that comes
from having to choose between
alternatives that are equally
disappointing because they
are fruitless, or devoid
of value.

If we have
acquired a taste for the
pitiable imitations of life that
are mercilessly peddled by snake-
oil salesmen, we'll delude ourselves into
believing that they are the genuine articles.
We'll assuage ourselves with rationalizations
so that we can face ourselves in the mirror and
sleep better. Of course, the irony is, that in other
and more productive circumstances, the forgery
might have been revealed in life-lessons learned,
by internalizing the gospel of Jesus Christ. This
would have encouraged us to quickly course-
correct and amend our errant ways, as if
the welfare of our souls depended upon
it, which it surely does!

Cultures rise and fall for complex reasons, but there might be one single underlying cause of societal implosion. Satan has focused his significant energies and has invested enormous resources on discrediting our Savior Jesus Christ. Those who defend Him are the few. Their Ally is the Holy Ghost, and they are warriors who stand to face the world alone, to win the battle that is raging in the hearts of men and women on the last day of the world. (See "Saturday's Warrior").

Our Savior Jesus Christ makes the bold claim that His gospel circumscribes the fulness of all truth. (See D&C 42:12). But this does not mean that it contains specific and detailed instruction regarding every doctrinal principle, nor does it mean that Israel participated in every ordinance of the gospel, as we now know it. Today, we live in the Dispensation of the Fulness of Times, when all that has been revealed thru the ages by the power of the Spirit continues to be restored. Anciently, Israel was given knowledge that was sufficient for its salvation. More properly, this is the context within which the definition 'the fulness of the gospel' makes the most sense.

Jesus Christ Himself was given to be a sign and a wonder to an unbelieving world. Heavenly Father would give this token: "Behold, a virgin shall conceive, and shall bear a son, and shall call his name Immanuel." (Isaiah 7:14). "For unto us a child is born, unto us a son is given, and the government shall be upon his shoulder, and his name shall be called Wonderful, Counsellor, the mighty God, the everlasting Father, the Prince of Peace." (Isaiah 9:6).

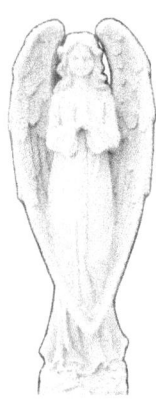

To the great relief of hopeful parents, the our Savior Jesus Christ affirms the innocence of children. It was an integral element of the Plan that was ordained in a Council in Heaven before the Creation, that little ones who would pass away before they had reached the age of accountability would be saved in eternal glory by the power of our Savior Jesus Christ. His influence will extend to every corner of the earth, from the beginning of the world to the very end of time. It was with heavenly prescience that He invited the little children to come unto Him. (See Mark 10:4).

The gospel of Jesus Christ factors into our success strategies, because it rests at the foundations of our hope in the Lord. Its assurance of peace and the comfort of our convictions will create a momentum in our lives that will propel us on a trajectory that will streak across the sky as it arches beneath the heavens.

It is in this life that we must prepare for our reunion with God by striving to become pure and holy. Our acceptance of the Lord Jesus Christ invites the Spirit to guide us. It is the tangible expression of our appeal to the Savior to come to our rescue, and in particular of our desire to rely upon His Atonement, that He might heal our self-inflicted wounds that have been caused by sin, that are the natural consequences of the weaknesses in the armor of our shields of faith. (See Ephesians 6:16).

When we pass
from mortality into the world
of spirits, and the veil of forgetfulness is
lifted from our eyes and our minds, we will
recognize in the gospel the stunning sobriety
of the Lord. He will reach out through the
Comforter to quicken our memory of
promises made and covenants
kept. (See Romans 14:9).

The
Mountain of
the Lord's House
that is visualized in
scripture is an allegorical,
figurative representation of
the refuge for Zion in the Last
Days, when it "shall be established
in the tops of the mountains." (Isaiah
2:2). Whether it is a high place of God,
a place of revelation, or perhaps the temple
itself, those who've studied metaphor within
the teachings of Jesus Christ tend to restrict
the application of this phrase to one area, that
of the intermountain west, and pointedly to
the Valley of the Great Salt Lake. But this
interpretation may be too narrow. Perhaps
this scripture refers more to the invisible
summits of our imagination where cool
air exists, and where we live within
God's embrace to enjoy security
that others do not know.

The contraries
that are so prevalent in
the teachings of our Savior Jesus
Christ vitalize our understanding,
empowering us to utilize opposition as
the tool that it was intended to be, to open
up access to the Spirit, for our wounds are
the portals through which light enters our
bodies. The Holy Ghost will then enable
us to do all things that are expedient in
His sight. At that point, we will have
an epiphany, as we find ourselves
at-one with the mind and will
of God, Who likewise faced
opposition from His son
in the Council.

The gospel incontrovertibly spells out
the principles and doctrines necessary for us
to become sanctified, so we may be worthy to live
once again in a state of holiness in the presence of
our Father in Heaven. It shows us how to come unto
Christ and receive the Holy Ghost. If we continue in
the supplication of his grace, kneel before Him at His
mercy-seat with the sacrifice of a broken heart and
a contrite spirit, and rely upon His Atonement to
receive a remission of our sins, it will become our
opportunity to stand blamelessly before Him
when we meet Him before His pleasing
bar. (See Malachi 3:2-5).

Jesus Christ will
help us to appreciate
that we are here, at this
place, and in this time, by
divine design. What we think
are only coincidences if they are
instead viewed thru the clarifying
lens of eternity, are faith promoting
examples of the Lord patiently working
behind the scenes in our behalf. Nothing
in our lives happens by chance. While we
are not billiard balls, it is equally true
that most, if not all, of the things that
are of significance to us will happen
according to the perfect Plan of
our Heavenly Father.

Our Savior Jesus Christ will
infuse our spiritual musculature with
pliancy and with flexibility, to make room
for the companionship of the Holy Ghost, which
will make itself manifest according to our faith.
We will always be subject to the effects of adversity
and opposition, but minus the therapeutic benefits
of gospel-oriented teaching, we may needlessly
suffer from a stiff neck that prevents us from
looking up to Heavenly Father for guidance,
over to priesthood leaders for counsel,
around to seek out those in need,
and down in an attitude
of humility.

The truth be told, many of our friends are very close to receiving their own personal witness of the divinity of our Redeemer Jesus Christ. Frustratingly, if they would just change one or two behaviors or beliefs, they would be spot-on. But here's a radical thought, though. What if, instead, we changed just one or two of our own behaviors, or if we viewed our neighbors' beliefs in a more tolerant and ecumenical light? Might that not become a more powerful tool of conversion?

We need Jesus Christ in our lives because the Devil, when given the opportunity, will capitalize on our weaknesses, and use subtlety, by pacifying and lulling us into a false sense of carnal security, making us believe that we are gaining something when we are actually losing. He does this to quietly avoid uwakening our faculties to harsh realities. He distorts our perspective by twisting our very blessings into vehicles that will amplify our feelings of self-sufficiency. But such an emancipation from God will comes at the cost of an ironclad compact that we have made with the "author of confusion." (1 Corinthians 14:34).

In the Last Days,
the power of Satan has been
wrought upon all over the face of
the earth, because of a lack of faith
of the people. The world is in desperate
need of our Savior Jesus Christ because
His influence is the spiritual equivalent
of the boost we receive after consuming a
power bar or an energy drink 30 minutes
prior to engaging in physical activity,
or in ideological combat with the
Devil, for that matter.

Our Savior Jesus Christ
cautions us to not succumb to
a politically correct tolerance that
embraces all sorts of deviant behavior.
There are flim-flam artists abroad in the
land who seek to adroitly fleece us of our very
identity as the children of God, and most of the
time, we are not even aware that the theft is taking
place. "Vice is a monster of such frightful mien, as to
be hated needs but to be seen. Yet seen too oft, familiar
with her face, we first endure, then pity, then embrace."
(Alexander Pope). Having rejected the guiding influence
of the Holy Ghost, we are beguiled by the allure of
sounding brass and tinkling cymbals.
(See 1 Corinthians 13:1).

The age of accountability (D&C 18:42 & 20:71), to which our Savior Jesus Christ alluded (see Matthew 19:14), suggests that those who are only recently removed from the certainty and stability of the eternal world are often impatient to recapture the peaceful security and quiet serenity of the more relaxed, familiar, and predictable environment to which they had become accustomed. Baptism gives them the opportunity to literally have the best of both worlds; to live on an earth with all of its thrills and spills, but still be able to retreat from time to time to a heavenly peace that surpasses understanding.

Our Savior Jesus Christ confirms to our spirits that our little ones are the nobility of heaven, and are a chosen generation with a divine destiny. We will make whatever sacrifices are necessary to ensure their success. They come to us from their heavenly home "like gentle rain thru darkened skies, with glory trailing from their feet as they go, and endless promise in their eyes." While under our care, they grow tall and strong, "like silver trees against the storm; who will not bend with the wind or the change, but stand to fight the world alone." (Doug Stewart).

If we fail to acknowledge the power of
the Spirit to cast off off the self-limiting
conditions and the self-defeating behaviors that
blind us to a larger view of life, we'll never enjoy a
settled conviction of the truth in our minds. The peace
that follows our obedience to the celestial principles that
are illuminated by the teachings of Jesus Christ brings a
greater reality within our reach. When we realize that
we are not alone, we have begun a journey that will
carry us to a higher state of being where we will
find ourselves showered in star dust as we
mingle in the company of the Gods.

Jesus Christ
tests the mettle of
our sincerity and our
candor with ourselves. It
is only when we accept His
doctrine that we'll have placed
our money on the Savior. But
we have no proof, or a payout on
our investment, until we act on
the basis of trust. Then, comes
the confirmation of the reality
as feelings of self-confidence
grow and purposeful actions
replace tentative overtures.
When we are all in, and
we listen to the Spirit,
we let go and let
God.

Faith in our Savior Jesus
Christ creates independence that can
be exhilarating when it is accompanied
by our recognition of new-found and soul-
expanding opportunities. It crystalizes within
us the realization that we are spiritual beings
having mortal experiences. This ennobles us
with the sure knowledge that the powers
of heaven can generate the spiritual
horsepower to countermand the
dizzying inequities
of life.

It is very likely not lost on our Savior
Jesus Christ, Who is the Creator of both heaven
and earth (see Mosiah 3:8), and all that is therein,
that water may just be the most abundant compound
that is found throughout the universe. It should not be lost on
us that baptism by immersion in water for the remission of sins
is His universally recognized token of obedience to gospel principles,
worlds without end. There is no way to know, but it is probably the case
throughout the cosmos. As those who wrote the Serek Scroll described it,
the penitent are "for all the laws of God, and their flesh is cleansed,
shining bright in the waters of purification, even in the waters
of baptism. They shall be given a new name in due time to
walk perfect in all His ways." ("The Serek Scroll", or
"Manual of Discipline", was discovered in 1947,
in caves high above Qumran, and dates
from around 400 B.C.).

Our Lord and Savior Jesus Christ has openly revealed Heavenly Father's battle plan for the Last Days, when His missionary army, armed with the power of the Holy Ghost, will engage the forces of Babylon, whose soldiers will suffer both temporal and spiritual reassignment in the face of the bombardment of love unfeigned, the uninterrupted onslaught of priesthood principles, and the overwhelming clout of covenants.

Engaging our Savior Jesus Christ reminds us of our temple experiences. We look around ourselves in anticipation, wondering what we might learn that is new. Who will our teachers be today, and how will the principles they desire to convey be opened to our understanding? How will the Holy Ghost touch us today? Will we be inspired with insight, or will it be intuition, inspiration, or perhaps the dynamic energy of revelation that will distill upon our minds as the dews of heaven?

Our Savior Jesus Christ helps us discern the truths behind Hamlet's expression to his friends Rosencrantz and Guildenstern. "What a piece of work is man!" he exclaimed. How noble in reason, how infinite in faculty, in form and moving how express and admirable, in action how like an angel, in apprehension how like a god - the beauty of the world, the paragon of animals!"

We turn to Jesus Christ for triage, when we have been wounded by the adversary's fiery darts. It is our safe haven, where we can firmly grasp the horns of sanctuary and where our spirits can be restored. Within its pages, while we haven't as yet encroached upon its sacred precincts, we can still learn all about the order of heaven, and how to honor the sacred covenants that will qualify us to live there in a coming day.

Our Lord and Savior Jesus Christ reassures us that when the process of securing our celestial legacy has been completed, there will be no breaches in the shield wall of our family history, there will be no names missing from the book of life that has been carefully compiled by the angels in heaven, and there will be no empty seats around the table, when we all sit down together to enjoy a reunion at family dinner in our heavenly home.

With its unbiased reconciliation of the Law of Justice with Mercy, the doctrine of Atonement, that's the centerpiece of the ministry of Jesus Christ, brings out the best of us, the worst of us, and the rest of us to work out our salvation with fear and trembling before the Lord, as we earn the privilege, as prodigal sons and daughters of a Father Who loves us, to rejoin His household of faith in full fellowship, with all the privileges one might hope for, subject to the reformation of errant behavior and flawed character. (See Luke 15).

We know that the influence of gravity caused by planets with large mass results in a distortion in the fabric of three-dimensional space. By applying the laws of physics applicable to the observable universe, we can deduce that under similar conditions kingdoms of glory will be curved and unbounded, with no edge and no center. This is about as far as we can go until we receive further light and knowledge that the Lord has promised to give us as we learn more about His gospel.

What if we could experience any number of additional dimensions of space that built upon the ones with which we are all familiar? What if we could pass through multiple dimensions of spacetime? The world that we now perceive exists in the three dimensions of depth, width, and height. But what if it were possible to distort one of them into a fourth physical dimension by the application of mass and gravity on the fabric of spacetime? Visualize a ball (mass) being dropped on the surface of rubberized graph paper (gravity). What you would witness would be the distortion of its geometric symmetry by the influence of the unseen forces of nature. And that deformation begs the question: Do the teachings of Jesus Christ hint that there may be higher dimensions that are just as real as our everyday world?

Disciples
of Jesus Christ learn
"how to give and not count
the cost, to fight and not heed
the wounds, to toil and not seek
for rest, and to labor and not ask
for reward, save that of knowing
that we do God's will."
(Loyola).

In the Last Days, Satan has once
again raised the spectre of rebellion. As the
process of the Restoration unfolds, he is fighting
a desperate (but losing) battle to prevent the receipt,
translation, publication, as well as the distribution of
the "Good News," which is a product of the ministry of
our Lord Jesus Christ. Having failed in these efforts,
he now struggles to substitute the sophistry of men
for the simplicity of the message. But that fraud is
all form and no substance, because it contributes
nothing to the welfare of Zion. Its driving force
seems to be a brazen craving for personal gain,
with a duplicitous message that is propelled
by a perceived power that is nothing more
substantive than the fleeting adoration
of an irrational world that, in its blind
fanaticism, has completely lost its
orientation on its objectives. His
only option in the absence of
a Plan is to hysterically
redouble his efforts.

Regarding the juxtaposition between the opposing forces of entropy and eternal progression existing in the world, Jesus Christ taught that the two laws must co-exist in an atmosphere of mutual acknowledgment, accommodation, and respect. A truce has been negotiated by God to maintain a delicate balance that necessarily sets the stage for the exercise of moral agency while dictating the implementation of other equally important laws. In this sense, mercy exists to mitigate the otherwise inevitable effects of entropy in this world, and Atonement facilitates our journey of progress in both time, throughout the universe, and in eternity, within the heavens.

We read in the Bhagavad Gita, or Hindu sacred scripture, where Vishnu declares: "Now I am become Death, the destroyer of worlds." But, according to the teachings of our Savior Jesus Christ, death may just be the manifestation of disproportion, and its effects may be inevitable and irreversible only until the Author of Salvation activates laws that trump entropy. In a sense, the Law of Justice may be an illustration of entropy, while the fruits of faith, the Law of Mercy, and the Atonement, might represent its naturally occurring opposites. As Paul wrote: "Ye have in heaven a better and an enduring substance" because both death and entropy have been conquered by the contrary of the Atonement. (Hebrews 10:34).

The Lord Jesus Christ
taught that Adam fell that all
the children of God might have an
opportunity to come to earth in order to
gain a body and prepare for a resurrection.
Because of the Atonement of our Savior, we
will be clothed in immortality in the kinds
of bodies that we will need to dwell in the
various degrees of glory for which
we have qualified.

Carl Sagan's epic literary volume, "Pale
Blue Dot," a profound reflection on humanity's place
in the universe, was inspired by an image taken, at his
suggestion, by Voyager 1 on Valentine's Day, February 14,
1990. As the spacecraft departed our planetary neighborhood
on its way to the fringes of the solar system, NASA sent it a
command that turned it around for one final look at its home
world. At that time, Voyager 1 was about 4 billion miles from
earth, and approximately 32 degrees above the ecliptic plane
of the planets, when it captured an incredible portrait of our
world. Caught in the center of scattered light rays, earth
appeared as a tiny point of light, a crescent only 0.12
pixel in size. Fortunately, Jesus Christ assures us
(see Luke 12:6) that God is mindful of sparrows
falling from trees and pale blue dots drifting
about in space. His concern is that we are
not attentive to our responsibilities
that go hand in hand with
stewardship.

Without baptism for the remission of our sins, if we were to partake of the delicious fruit of the tree of life, which is eternal life, or the highest expression of the love of God, it would be impossible to sustain a celestial existence inasmuch as in our fallen condition we would be incapable of obedience to heaven's principles. Thus, the Plan would be frustrated. Mercy and Justice were placed before Adam and Eve, to bar the way to the tree of life until they had the opportunity to participate in the saving ordinances of the gospel of Jesus Christ and to take advantage of His infinite and eternal Atonement.

As we journey toward our eternal home world that lies beyond the Milky Way, we are intertwined with our Father in Heaven in a palpable connection, for we are His predilected people, and we live within His embrace, enjoying a security that others do not know. He takes notice of each of us, as much as He does of supernovas exploding in distant star systems. We rest in the assurance that when we make First Contact with Him, it will be obvious to all that our Savior has not played dice with any of His creations. First Contact will confirm that He has remembered those who are upon "the isles of the sea." The borders of our comprehension will expand to include all those upon all the beaches, of all the vast oceans of all of His creations that lie beneath the heavens. "Other sheep I have," He explained, "which are not of this fold; them also I must bring, and they shall hear my voice, and there shall be one fold, and one shepherd." (John 10:16).

The Lord Jehovah taught that because of God's great Plan of Redemption, the principle of agency would be honored (see Deuteronomy 30:19, Joshua 24:15 & John 7:17), allowing us to encounter opposition in a mortal setting and gain experience, in spite of the fact that Justice would need to be served (in the absence of repentance and the Atonement) were we to violate eternal law in the process. When our Savior and Redeemer stepped forward to offer Himself as a Lamb slain from the foundation of the world, the Plan of God swung into action, as did the shepherding influence of the Holy Ghost, allowing us to live to the fullest, and then to die, without having jeopardized our hope of eternal glory. (See Revelation 13:8).

The Plan of Salvation has made allowances to help us to quickly hearken to the words of the Lord. A heavenly authorized "Firearms Safety Course," with the Holy Ghost as our Instructor, cautions us to never play with loaded weapons, for Satan stands like an assassin, ready at any time to discharge his assault rifle in the direction of doctrine. Beelzebub's high velocity bullets of unbelief may harmlessly ricochet off the bedrock of well-grounded faith. However, they can be dangerous, and can even mortally wound the eternal identity of those who have not put on the whole armor of God, starting with the Kevlar vest of the gospel. His explosive devices may be improvised, but they are also insidious, insincere, incorrect, immoral, and disingenuous in his own distorted way.

As we
lift the latch and
force the way, and as we
learn more about the Plan of
God by studying the teachings
of Jesus Christ, we begin to discern
a distinct afterglow from the light of
our premortal lives, that establishes a
subtle but undeniable link between
the heavens and the earth.

It took J.R.R.
Tolkien 17 years to write
"The Lord of The Rings." Margaret
Mitchell took nearly 10 years to complete
"Gone With The Wind." J.D. Salinger spent 10
years to complete "The Catcher in The Rye." It took
Victor Hugo 12 years to complete "Les Misérables."
Michael Crichton spent 8 years writing "Jurassic
Park." It took Joseph Smith roughly 90 days to
generate Another Testament relating to the
life and ministry of the post-mortal Jesus
Christ. How did he do it so quickly?
He simply said that the task had
been accomplished "by the
gift and power of
God."

Turning our undivided attention to the weightier matters of the laws by which our Savior Jesus Christ lived his life gives us a sense of independence, as we learn something new every day. Discovering how to utilize our time to our best advantage can open our hearts and our minds to the breathtaking expansion of our understanding. When we adopt a learning style that embraces the Spirit, we incorporate the pattern of heaven that will become our new normal.

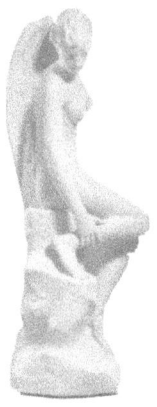

As we continue to engage the curriculum of Jesus Christ, when our souls have been illuminated by the glow that emanates from the burning Spirit of God, we can no longer remain passive. There is a flickering fire of faith that warms our souls as we begin to recognize its upward reach within ourselves. We are sensitized to truth, to beauty, and to a goodness above and beyond our our own attainment. If we are fortunate, we experience the faint stirrings of the golden quality of gratitude.

Jesus Christ summons
us to choose liberty and eternal
life, rather than its contrary, which
is captivity and spiritual death, and
to live within the framework of its laws
and ordinances. Without it, unbridled
freedom would lead to tyranny. We are
free to elect whether or not we wish to
be governed by its principles and
doctrines, but we cannot escape
the consequences should
we choose unwisely.

Those
who want
to share the
gospel of Jesus
Christ with others
are faithful, and they
endure, that they might
obtain the prize of eternal
life. They claim the promises
of the Lord, Who said He would
disperse the powers of darkness
from before them, and would
cause the heavens to shake
for their good, as they go
about the work of the
ministry, bringing
others into the
fold.

Our testimonies of our Savior Jesus Christ can become so powerful that we are moved upon by the Spirit to speak of principles with such incendiary rhetoric that those who are of hesitant and faltering faith will be encouraged to take their first tentative steps toward commitment, while, simultaneously, more spiritually mature disciples, as they realize that present levels of performance aren't acceptable, will be inspired to lengthen their stride.

Our Savior Jesus Christ leaves nothing to chance, and His disciples enjoy His tender watch care, no matter where in the galaxy we may call home. He never misses our Parent/Teacher conferences. He always attends our extracurricular activities and He has a season pass for every game we play. He positions Himself in the bleachers in the middle of the cheering section. He is in the "wave" when it passes through the stands. He sits up late in the evening, with the porch light on, waiting for us to come back home to safety. He has our phone numbers on speed dial, and He uses voice mail, text messaging, and Find My Friends. We are at the top of His Favorites list.

Too frequently, we are overzealous in our outward observances. We are hypocrites, pretending to be pious, when, in fact, we are simply professors of religion. We creep into nameless graves, unwept, unhonored, and unsung, while now and then, a few of us forget ourselves into immortality by recommitting ourselves to the Savior, and to acts of quiet Christianity.

The Lord Jesus Christ teaches us to duplicate the protocols of a criminal pathologist, with one caveat. We seek to identify the fingerprints of a master criminal, who is the Prince of Darkness, which are smeared all over a plethora of penurious programs, parties, politics, and policies that do little else than to promote personal and provincial proclamations related to plans that are, at best, petty.

Within the
mathematics of the
cosmos, there are many
principles that are eternally
valid throughout its reaches. We
have a term for these. We call them
the laws of nature. Jesus Christ, Who is
the Lord of the universe (see Isaiah 37:16),
bears witness that they are true.

Complex
reactions are lurking within
the inner workings of the ideas
that seem to spontaneously pop into
our heads. They're the hard evidence we
seek as a confirmation of our faith in the
our Lord Jesus Christ, since these thoughts
often seem to have lives of their own that have
outlived their so-called "creators." Perhaps, our
déjà vu moments are more than electromagnetic
or neurochemical anomalies. They just might be
the mirrored reflections of chronologically correct
forces, although they lie beyond the event horizon
of comprehension. This may be why inspiration
comes as a whisper from the dust "with clarity
and freshness, uncolored and untranslated,
(speaking) from within (ourselves) in a
language that is original and yet is
inarticulate, heard only with the
soul." (Hugh B. Brown).

Is it easier to just give up, and harder to push on, and continue the good fight? Is it easier to settle for average, but more difficult to be extraordinary? Those who seek to understand Jesus Christ need to face, and will ultimately overcome, their challenges, not because they are easy, but precisely and pointedly because they are hard.

During the journey to our Savior Jesus Christ, we'll undoubtedly meet other truth seekers who grapple with their own custom-tailored challenges, but who through the grace of God have managed to make the transition from hesitancy to conviction, from instability to commitment, from timidity to confidence, from indecision to resolution, from doubts to certainty, from struggle to celebration, and from vacillation to purpose. In short, we will join the joyful throngs who have made the transition from spiritual itinerancy to moral discipline.

As we immerse ourselves in an earnest study of the teachings of Jesus Christ, our inquiry will reveal a polychromatic palate onto which we may dip the brush of understanding. With God's gentle guidance, we may paint broad strokes that capture not only the compelling gradations of its delightful meter, but also the enchanting features of its unanticipated beauty and symmetry.

The beautiful Hebrew poetry that clothes the descriptions of the ministry of Jesus Christ has the capacity to plumb the depths of our own testimonies by quietly turning our thoughts to our Creator, reminding us that our God is in control, and that by His divine design, those who love and serve Him in righteousness and who obey His commandments with exactness, will inherit the mansions that have been prepared for them. It serenely bears witness of the divine mission of our Savior. It illuminates the path we must follow in order to receive the blessings that are reserved for the faithful. It teaches us about repentance, atonement, and forgiveness, about God's tender mercies, and ultimately, about the Plan of Salvation that He has crafted for His children.

In his second inaugural address to a fledgling nation, Thomas Jefferson referenced our Savior Jesus Christ, when he declared: "I shall need the favour of the One in whose hands we are, who led our forefathers, as he did Israel of old, from their native land, and planted them in a country flowing with the necessaries and comforts of life."

Zion and Babylon are strikingly depicted by Jesus Christ as divided camps lying at opposite ends of the spiritual spectrum. They are, and will forever be, completely at odds with each other. There is little common ground upon which substantive dialogue could ever be introduced, because the solid foundation pillars upon which Zion rests are philosophically incompatible with the detritus scattered about by the forces of Babylon, that was fallout from the War fought in Heaven. The theology upon which Zion is based allows its inhabitants to raise their sights to God for their redemption, while the apologists and political pundits of Babylon cannot see beyond the intellect of man for their salvation, and can do little more than shrug their shoulders in resignation when they hear the clarion call to amend their behavior.

Any number
of profound questions
are easily and forthrightly
addressed by the teachings of Jesus
Christ. Is the endowment of the Spirit
among our most prized possessions? Has
our work led us to the Holy Ghost? Is He our
constant companion? Does our moral compass
point us toward righteousness and truth, are
the fruits of our obedience an everlasting
dominion, and without compulsory
means will heaven's blessings
be showered down upon
our heads?

Lucifer has been characterized by Isaiah as
a son of the morning who was cast out of heaven for his
rebellion (see Isaiah 14:12), because he could not abide by the
principles that governed the lives of his brothers and sisters, who
were nurtured, as he had been, within the warm embrace of their
Father. He became Satan, who now governs Idumea, or the world.
We need to choose our allegiance, because we cannot commit to
follow our Savior Jesus Christ, but at the same time worship
evil in the Great and Abominable Church of the Devil. We
cannot hope to live in Zion while maintaining summer
homes in Babylon, any more than we could afford to
joy ride through the world, making excuses to stop
along the way to partake of its pleasures, or
indulge ourselves with just a taste of its
tempting treats.

Those who have learned to rely more upon economic security than upon their spiritual preparedness will be more inclined in times of crisis to grasp at straws instead of rededicating themselves to proven principles that have been taught by our Savior Jesus Christ. Those who put their trust in idea gods have nowhere to look for help when hot winds of change melt the triple scoop cones of their misplaced faith in the flavor of the day.

"They that wait upon the Lord shall renew their strength, they shall mount up with wings as eagles, they shall run, and not be weary, and they shall walk, and not faint." (Isaiah 40:31). Long ago, it was recognized that there exists a relationship between obedience to our Redeemer Jesus Christ and physical well-being. When we consciously and deliberately adopt lifestyles that lead to poor physical health, "wisdom cannot reveal itself, culture cannot become manifest, strength cannot fight, wealth becomes useless, and intelligence cannot be applied." (Heraclitus).

Sooner or later, every
member of the church evolves
into a second-miler. We become
so, not as much by maturation, as
by generation, when we are born of
God. We are encouraged to run,
and not walk, as we make
our way to our Savior
Jesus Christ.

When we
brush up against
the stars as we approach
the heavenly throne of Jesus
Christ, we find ourselves awakening
to a new perspective that is blinding at
first, but as our eyes adjust to the light, we
are surprised to view our world as it really is,
perhaps for the very first time. As we begin to feel
the creative expression of the power that is within us,
we recognize it as the intrinsic energy that brings us
closer to the heavens. We feel as if we are not alone in the
universe, but even more than that, we recognize the divine
potential that is within us. We feel confident to ask simple
and innocent questions whose profound answers shake our
world. Our new perspective spreads as ripples radiating out
from a rock thrown into the still waters of our perceptual
ponds. Our questions feel intensely personal, but they
have broad applications They are child-like in their
simplicity, but within the answers, if we listen
very closely, we begin to be able to hear
what God is thinking.

As we break free from
our limiting beliefs, the power
of our potential will be unleashed.
Daniel Burnham felt that we should
"make no small plans, for they have not
the power to stir our souls." At the end of
the day, we'll find the teachings of Jesus
Christ full of magical suggestions that
are patiently waiting for our wits to
grow sharper, so that we might
better appreciate how we
might take them to
heart.

In the gospel of
Jesus Christ, we witness the
best of power as well as its contrary
which is the worst of violence, and we
also see that they are mutually exclusive;
where one is present, the other is absent. We
learn about the satanic inclination to abuse
authority, and we discover that those who wield
it might be least prepared to exercise either trust or
responsibility within their sphere of influence. As
the drama unfolds before our eyes, we will discern
the development of a fundamental governing
mathematical theorem: The principles that
governed the conduct of the Savior
operated more by addition
than by subtraction.

The world applies
negative energy, while
promptings that invite us to
examine our relationship with
our Savior Jesus Christ are our
most effective countermeasures.
Our Redeemer's only stipulations
are that we confess when we have in
any way yielded to the temptations
that lie before us, and that when we
do so, we immediately initiate the
safety protocol of repentance that
is required by the Atonement,
to steer us back to the strait
and narrow way, and to
our focus on heaven.

As disciples of our Lord and Savior Jesus Christ, we
can almost reach out and touch the hem of the His garment, as
we feel the presence of the Holy Spirit and we draw upon His virtue.
Lorenzo Snow said of his own baptism: "It was a tangible immersion in
the heavenly principal or element, the Holy Ghost, and even more real and
physical in its effects upon every part of my system than the immersion
by water, dispelling forever, so long as reason and memory last, all
possibility of doubt or fear in relation to the fact that the Babe of
Bethlehem is truly the Son of God; also the fact that He is
now being revealed to the children of men, and
communicating knowledge, the same
as in Apostolic times." (See
John 14:26).

Truly,
when God
said: "Let there
be light," it was a
simple statement of
fact as much as it was
a command. It was an
invitation to recognize,
embrace, and celebrate the
luminosity dancing about
in a revelatory rapture of
the Father, the Son, and
the Holy Ghost.

Until we have taken
a deep breath, held our noses,
and taken the plunge into a covenant
relationship with Jesus Christ, we might
find that we can only indirectly appreciate
the eternities. As we seek learning by study as
well as by faith, "we can make our lives sublime,
and departing, leave behind footprints on the sands
of time." (Longfellow). If we've ignored gospel-oriented
study, however, our footprints may be washed away by
the incessant wave action of indifference that beats
relentlessly upon the rocky shoreline of our
negligence.

The pop
quizzes that we are
asked to take, and that
we must pass, by our Savior
Jesus Christ do not necessarily
measure our ability, but rather
our availability.

A basic assumption of
quantum mechanics, known as
the Heisenberg Uncertainty Principle,
stipulates that one cannot simultaneously
measure both the position and momentum of
a particle. The more accurately one can be defined,
the less we will know about the other. For an observer,
this implies the element of unpredictability, reminiscent
of Schrodinger's Cat, which may be both dead and alive at the
same time. It may be that there is a simpler, more elegant, and more
explicit way of describing the phenomena of nature, by harmonizing
quantum mechanics with the theories of relativity. However, for the time
being, if there is a Grand Unifying Principle or Theory of Everything, it
hasn't yet been discovered or mathematically quantified, except by the Lord
Jesus Christ, that is. Until we understand the Plan, and whether we realize it
or not, our lives will continue to be influenced by disproportion, which is a
lack of symmetry or absence of conformity. For now, only His gospel will
help us to discover ways to create balance in a chaotic world. Unless we
follow its principles and we adhere to its doctrines, we are unlikely
to discover if we are alone in the universe. Because, according to
both Heisenberg and Schrodinger, the correct answer could
be both yes and no at the same time!

We are encouraged to embrace Jesus Christ and accept Him in a covenant of exaltation as the Firstborn Son of God, in order to avoid weeping and wailing and gnashing of teeth that accompany the recognition that our days of probation are past because we have procrastinated the day of our repentance until it is everlastingly too late, and our destruction is made sure.

All of us will find our way to the feet of our Redeemer Jesus Christ in a manner reminding us of Paul's observation to the Roman Saints: "We, being many, are one body in Christ." (Romans 12:5). The spiritual unification of the church has been repetitively confirmed through a ripple effect that is manifested by the acceptance by the world-wide body of the church of our Lord as the Savior of the world.

Drawing near to
our Savior Jesus Christ
subjects us to a constant
flow of insight, intuition,
inspiration, and revelation
that simply streams forth in
a downpour of divine direction
blessing us as we walk along
illuminated pathways and we
exercise our faculties of mind
and spirit. He will lead us to a
congregation where we are no
more strangers or foreigners,
but instead, fellowcitizens
with the Saints, and with
the household of God.
(Ephesians 2:19).

The time when we are initially introduced to our Savior Jesus Christ and invited to try the virtue of the word of God will try our souls. The summer soldier and the sunshine patriot may, as they initially engage the gospel, shrink from their worship of God, but those who will prayerfully undertake its study deserve the love and thanks of men and women. Ignorance of the meaning of its doctrine, like hell, is not easily conquered; yet we have this consolation, that the harder our divine commission, the more glorious the triumph. What we obtain too cheap, we esteem too lightly. 'Tis dearness alone that gives everything its value. Heaven knows how to put a proper price upon its goods; and it would be strange, indeed, if so celestial an article as a witness of Jesus Christ, obtained by the power of the Holy Ghost and through the grace of God, should not be highly rated. (See Tom Paine, "The Crisis," published on 12/23/1776, paraphrased).

If we are ever to obtain our exaltation and eternal life, we need to do more than simply acknowledge that Jesus Christ is Lord. His gospel makes it abundantly clear that the critical point of conversion, beyond which lie encircling flames in the Celestial Kingdom of God, rests in making the conscious decision to not only accept Him as a Great Teacher and our Master, but also to accept the responsibility to be obedient by covenant to each of the pointedly specific commandments that have been given to us by Him Who is the Son of God.

Our Lord and Savior Jesus Christ puts a flourishing touch on mortality by introducing us to a larger view of life. It smooths out the rough edges that are created as we bump, grind, and lurch along the rocky road of experience. It will put in perspective our trials and tribulations, while addressing questions that we'd never before thought to ask. Our distressed spirits will be calmed by it's quiet influence, and we will more easily understand the rolling thunder that heralds the proximity of the wonders of the kingdom of heaven. The injunction to "be still and know that I am God" will take on a whole new meaning. (Psalms 46:10).

The teachings of our Savior
Jesus Christ will protect us from the
mists of darkness that threaten to divert
us from the strait and narrow way. Because,
let's face reality. We're always at risk of being
detoured by doctrinal dilemmas, conceptual
cul-de-sacs, and religious roundabout that
can lead to faltering faith and crises of
confidence, as well as to character
crippling compromises in
our behavior.

The teachings of Jesus Christ have been
specifically designed to ease our transition
from the world of every day into eternity, where
the eyes of our understanding will be opened, and
we will be reintroduced to a society of celestial beings
who have embraced their ongoing mission to bring about
the immortality and eternal life of star children just like
us, across the galaxy. The total power of the sunlight that
strikes the atmosphere of earth each day is 174 petawatts.
In eternity, however, we will be dancing with stars Who
utilize the power of the untold billions of petawatts that
energize the celestial world lying somewhere beyond
the borders of the final frontiers of space and time.
It was ordained in the heavens that across the
cosmos, we and our distant cousins might
tap into that heavenly power and feel its
influence as it helps us to deal with
not only adversity but also
the Adversary.

Our
knowledge
of the role of Jesus
Christ in the Plan of
Salvation reveals that our
destiny was determined for
us in the pre-earth existence. It
is molded in mortality, and will
be established in eternity, where the
heavens will benevolently smile upon us.
We will be immersed in the matchless glory
of immortality and eternal life, with thrones,
dominions, principalities, and powers, in an
endless hierarchy of kingdoms that renders
understandable the Savior's promise that
in the household of His Father there are
many mansions. (See John 14:2).

The time is soon at hand when
it will be as it was on the Day of Pentecost,
when Peter and the other apostles were preaching
to a multitude whose hearts and minds were open
and receptive to truth. Their words carried the weight
of authority and penetrated the hearts of their listeners,
prompting them to ask Peter: "Men and brethren, what
shall we do? Then Peter said unto them, Repent, and
be baptized every one of you in the name of Jesus
Christ for the remission of sins, and ye shall
receive the gift of the Holy Ghost." (Acts
2:37-38). On that day, there were
about 3,000 souls added to the
kingdom of God on earth.

Jesus Christ will stand beside us as He grooms us for immortality and eternal life. It is He Who will opens our eyes and perfect our vision, and Who will teach us to raise our sight so that it rests above the artificial horizon of mortality. It is thru Him that we steal our first fleeting glimpses of the wonders of eternity, and it is by Him that we realize that it is in heavenly precincts where our future really lies.

As they seize the opportunity to teach economic, social, political, and earth sciences, the teachings of Jesus Christ will accomplish this creatively in ways that are alien to the understanding of spiritual Babylon. We turn to Him to open our ears to hear, our hearts to understand, and our minds to feel the all-encompassing love of God, so that the wonders of eternity might be unfolded to our view and spread out in a breathtaking panorama of cosmic proportion.

Sacred covenants are the binding contracts that we make with God, and they are received only through revelation. No-one who would approach our Savior Jesus Christ enters into such covenants except on the basis of communication with Deity. It follows that the only ones who can legitimately make a covenant are those who humble themselves to participate in sacred ordinances that are designed to ratify these promises in a revelatory way, and to bring us back into God's presence, and that of His Son, and the Holy Ghost.

Our efforts to describe our Savior Jesus Christ must utilize abstractions, for our thoughts cannot be shaped, nor words formed, that could accurately characterize His glory. We use figures of speech because we would otherwise find ourselves at a complete loss for words when conveying even a basic explanation of profound metaphysical realities. Thus, we can only gain a testimony of His divinity and gospel if, with an attitude of heartfelt prayer, we have invited the Spirit to lift the latch and force the way. This is one of those situations where there is nowhere to turn except to heaven for help. (See 1 Corinthinans 13:11).

We were
foreordained before
the world was made to have
glory added upon our heads, on
the condition of our faithfulness to
God and Christ, as we support Them in
Their work by our actions. We will be better
prepared if we listen intently for answers as
we study the principles of the gospel. We'll open
up our minds to options we had never considered,
envisioning a place called Kolob, signifying the
first creation, that is to say, the closest body to
celestial realms, or to the dwelling place of
our Heavenly Father.

As the flickering flames
of eternity dance all around
us, we are dazzled by an expanded
appreciation of our relationship with our
Redeemer, both temporally and spiritually.
It may only then dawn upon us that when He
described Himself as the Light of the World, He may
have been speaking literally as well as figuratively. In
the physical world, time-shifts compensate for our velocities
relative to beams of light. In the eternal world, time morphs so
completely in relation to our Redeemer, that it is no more, and
the cosmic speed limit becomes a negligible influence. Thanks
to Albert Einstein, we realize it's all relative! Thanks to the
gospel of Jesus Christ, there is a reconciliation between
time and being that erases that cosmic speed limit
while, at the same time, easing our transition
through hyperspace into the heavens.

Moses counseled the Israelites to build upon the Rock of their salvation, even their Savior Jesus Christ. He urged them to "write (their covenants) upon the posts of (their) houses" and to "not appear before the Lord empty" handed. (Deuteronomy 6:9 & 16:16). We would do well to follow their example by remembering our covenants as we take upon ourselves the name of Christ and we determine to keep His commandments and to always remember Him in word and deed.

As we study and internalize the teachings of our Savior Jesus Christ, we realize that they were intended to change our nature, that we might progress to the point that we reflect God's attributes in perfection. Our charitable behavior is an echo of our love of our Heavenly Father's children. Our righteous stewardship is but a shadow of His omnipotence. As the Spirit expands the boundaries of our faith, we quietly scratch the surface of our comprehension of omniscience. We begin to appreciate the significance of the Savior's mortal ministry, and we determine to inaugurate our own journey to Bethlehem, Gethsemane, the Garden Tomb, and the Silver City.

The teachings of Jesus Christ are now being taken to nearly every nation, kindred, tongue, and people. The stone that is cut out of the mountain is rolling over the earth, and it can't be stopped, although Satan tries his best to do so. (See Daniel 2:34). Heavenly Father always keeps His promises, while the Adversary was a liar from the beginning.

When we substitute the moniker "Creation" for "Big Bang" and ask where and when it took place, the answer is everywhere and forever. No one can say if Jesus utilized the laws of physics as we understand them during the Creation, but what we do know is that "by him, were all things created, that are in heaven, and that are in earth, visible and invisible, whether they be thrones, or dominions, or principalities, or powers." (Colossians 1:16). This leaves the door ajar for theologians to confidently debate science from a position of strength, and it even goes one step beyond Intelligent Design, by boldly testifying that it was Jesus Himself Who guided the Creation. His gospel confirms that it was not just a dispassionate interaction between quarks, fermions, gluons, bosons, fermions, and leptons.

Jesus Christ will
unerringly guide us and
be our compass, allowing us
to navigate the desert wastes
of Idumea in the company
of the Spirit, unfazed
by the encroaching
sandstorms of
Satan.

At the moment
of Creation, there was a
gravitational singularity, or
a spacetime singularity, wherein
the quantities we use to measure the
three spatial and one temporal dimension
were infinitely small in a way that did not
depend upon any coordinate system. Because of
the Law of Conservation of Energy, that force, as well
as that light, even now is ever present in our expanding
universe as the entirety of the elemental quanta of radiant
energy that was created at the Big Bang. Almost 14 billion
years later, heat is still the best way to stimulate the atoms
that were then created. It is no coincidence that our Savior
Jesus Christ energizes us in a similar way. We are like
photons, as white-hot sparks struck off the divine anvil
of God. Similar to the cosmic microwave background
radiation from the Big Bang that is everywhere, the
light that washes over the creations of God waits
upon our initiative to be detected, absorbed
and applied to both practical and
metaphysical applications.

You just don't get it, do you? asked Q, who was, in effect, standing in for "the Author of Eternal Salvation." (Hebrews 5:9). "The trial never ends. We wanted to see if you had the ability to expand your mind to new horizons, and for one fleeting moment, you did. For that one fraction of a second, you were open to options you had never considered. That is the exploration that awaits you. Not mapping stars and studying nebula, but charting the unknown possibilities of existence."

We learn to rely upon our Savior Jesus Christ not only as our protector but also as the generator of life itself; we have a standard by which we can judge the truth; we have a weapon more powerful than military might; we have clear definitions of authority; the essential ordinance of baptism is defined; the army of God is equipped with the superior firepower of revelation as it teaches the nations; missionaries confidently preach the gospel, and its advocates draw upon the experiences of others to internalize life-lessons from their similar challenges in the unforgiving school of hard knocks.

For now, we find ourselves
at ease living in mortality's linear
temporal dimension from which there
is only one exit. Our liberation from the
arrow of time will come only when we have
laid aside our mortal clay, clothed in the
garments of immortality and eternal
life. The teachings of Jesus Christ
will have taught us that heaven
no longer needs to wait
for any of us.

Jesus Christ has authored the
best AA program on the face of the earth
(Act of Atonement), because the Adversary's
intoxicating alcohol has been distilled to dull our
senses when we are so careless as to imbibe in the sin
of intemperance. If we are not careful, however, "the
hobnailed boots of indiscretion's marathon dancer
will tap a rowdy two-step across the terracotta of
our consciousness. If excess is allowed to become
our master, reason will surely be cast into the
rumble seat of our libidinous juggernaut.
Then, the piper must be paid!" (Pogo,
the Cartoon Philosopher).

On our journey
to the feet of the Savior
that will take us to the far
reaches of our imaginations,
even if we lack the assistance of
a trans-warp conduit, we will be
reassured by our knowledge that
we are children of God, proven
by a heraldry that proclaims
our independence in that
stage of development to
which our decisions
have led us.

Our Lord and Savior Jesus
Christ can become the Power Broker
Who purchases our sins with the legally
recognized currency of the Atonement. His
intentional act of sacrifice has been perfectly
balanced and attuned to accomplish the task
at hand, but it is augmented by our faith,
repentance, and baptism, and then by
the receipt of the Gift of the Holy
Ghost, and finally, by the
Sacrament.

In the near future, our travel
out among the stars might necessitate
our reliance upon an operations manual,
written by the Holy Ghost and incorporated
into the teachings of our Lord and Savior
Jesus Christ, that seamlessly bridges the
barrier between mind and matter, and
between the cold logic of technology
and the warm compassion that is
only found in God's divine
center.

For those who have not
recognized their need for the
intervention of Jesus Christ in their
affairs, the faith of their fathers may
consist of nothing more than "a humble
admiration of the illimitable superior spirit
who reveals himself in the slight details we
are able to perceive with our frail and feeble
minds." (Albert Einstein). He also said: "I
am satisfied to have only a glimpse of the
marvelous structure of the existing world,
together with the striving to comprehend
a portion of the Reason that manifests
itself in nature." The momentum of
a Divine Design was meant to lift
him and all the children of God
past the uncertainty principle
all the way to a relationship
with the Infinite.

It has always been
the heartfelt prayer of those who
would meekly approach the throne of
our Savior Jesus Christ that He will treat
the Saints gently and tenderly when He
comes in His glory and his power, and
in His might, majesty, and dominion
(see Jude 1:25), and tramples out the
vintage where the grapes of wrath
have for so long been stored,
as the day of judgment
draws nigh.

"By grace (we are)
saved through faith, and
that not of (our)selves." It
is God's gift. (Ephesians 2:8).
Grace is an attribute of perfection
that is possessed by Him, consisting
of His love, mercy, and condescension
toward His children. Within His grace
lie the gifts of the Spirit by which all of
us may be brought to the stature of
Christ. (See Ephesians 4:13).

When
we remember the
multitude of angels who
are thinly disguised as our
families and friends, who have
helped us in our efforts to embrace
our Savior Jesus Christ, we recall the
observation made by Sir Isaac Newton,
who, when he was pressed to reveal the
secret behind his accomplishments,
simply replied: "I stood on the
shoulders of giants."

Following the agony, betrayal, trial,
crucifixion and resurrection of the Redeemer
of the world, the word was spat out: "Christian!"
But the Saints continued to live as He had taught
them, and the world was illuminated by the inspired
ministry of His consecrated disciples, and remained
aflame with faith. When the light finally dimmed,
dark mists swirled about, sowing wickedness at
every turn. And so it came to pass, that in the
crucible of that refiner's fire, the humble
devotees of the gospel of Jesus Christ
were asked, once again, to wear
their title with dignity.

Wo unto those who will only
casually accept the illumination of
faith that is a blessing when we receive
our Savior Jesus Christ, and that has
been so freely given. Because of their
misguided obsession with temporal
trivia, they carelessly fritter away
that gift, and waste the days of
their probation by rooting thru
telestial trash in a fruitless
effort to find meaning in
the barren dumpsters
of their empty
lives.

Paul invited
the Philippian Saints to
work out their own salvation
with fear and trembling. He knew
that if they put their hearts and souls
into their efforts to understand their Lord
and Savior, it would leave them spiritually
exhilarated but physically exhausted. Still, he
invited them to accompany him, as he pressed
on "toward the mark, for the prize of the
high calling of God in Christ Jesus."
(Philippians 3:14).

He who remains the
enemy of all righteousness
will finally betray his followers
because they will only be able to oppose
the covenant consciousness generated by
their Savior Jesus Christ for so long before his
cunning caresses lead them into conceptual cul-
de-sacs and doctrinal dead-ends from which every
possible exit leads to uncertainty, confusion, doubt,
ambiguity, hesitation, and a retreat that plunges
them headlong into a perceived freedom that on
closer inspection is only a bottomless pit
of misery and despair.

The teachings of our Lord and Savior Jesus
Christ do not claim to be the ultimate source of
knowledge. Rather, they "precedes the ultimate source.
The ultimate source comes by revelation. We encourage
everyone to make careful study of the scriptures and of
prophetic teachings ... and to prayerfully seek personal
revelation to know their meaning for themselves ... If
we seek and accept revelation and inspiration to
enlarge our understanding, we will have the
mysteries of God unfolded to us by the
power of the Holy Ghost."
(Dallin Oaks).

It is only thru Jesus Christ that we can really begin to understand ourselves. It is when we have discovered the answers to where we came from and why we are here that we will be prepared to embark, with unbounded confidence, upon an incredible journey of faith into our future, to discover where, all this time, we have been going.

Jesus Christ teaches us that both free will and opposition are always before us, and so the Spirit stands as a sacred sentinel that beckons us to return to the easy familiarity of heaven's gate to find the Rest of God. No matter that we are, for all practical purposes, dead weight, the Spirit will carry us until we've been revitalized and can walk on our own without becoming weary, and can run, without fainting.

The Savior
Who knows our
trials and guides our
way with His gospel, used
the prophetic literary powers
of one of His favorite servants
to reveal how He will influence our
lives in the Last Days. Isaiah clothed
the Savior and His ministry with
beautiful, symbolic expressions,
showing us how He has done
wonderful things
for us.

The secret that is the key
to uncovering hidden treasures
of knowledge that may be jubilantly
found in the teachings of Jesus Christ is
not complicated. It simply asks us to press
on with purpose as we feast upon His words.
Thereby, we receive the physical and spiritual
strength and nourishment that are needed to
comprehend the mysteries of the kingdom.
It is by this process that we will begin to
feel the compounding influence
of the Holy Ghost.

It is not
enough only
to have received the
gospel of Jesus Christ. If
we indifferently coast to a
standstill before we find our
our way to the Savior, we'll be
at risk of toppling over. We need
forward momentum to maintain
equilibrium. This was the celestial
balancing act that we learned as
spiritual adolescents during
our pre-mortal lives.

In a letter he wrote
to the Corinthian Saints
that would later be incorporated
into the corpus of the literature that
comprises the gospel of Jesus Christ, the
Apostle Paul had quite a bit to say about
charity, and he's often quoted on the subject.
Charity motivates us to Christian service, but
it also elevates our discipleship by preparing
us to be like the Savior, so that one day we
will feel comfortable in His kingdom. It
is a spiritual gift that, by the grace of
God, has been given to the faithful
in every age of our history. (See
1 Corinthians Chapter 13).

The biggest room in the world is the one for improvement. Ralph Waldo Emerson observed: "Success comes by design, and failure by default." Truly, if we fail to plan, we plan to fail, the only place where success comes before work is in the dictionary, and the only man who got his work done by Friday was Robinson Crusoe. The best place to find a helping hand is at the end of your arm, and if it reaches out to help others to discover the joy of a life that has been dedicated to Jesus Christ, it will have served you well.

Those fortunate disciples who have harnessed a testimony of the true principles and doctrine that are found in the teachings of Jesus Christ have a visibly different look about them, for they have taken their vows, and have then pushed on in the direction of higher plateaus that will become the launchpads for affirmative action. Their features are flushed with confidence and they stand out from the crowd. They exhibit enthusiasm, passion, fervency, eagerness, and animation. They are excited by life, and they get a natural high from the release of endorphins that flush their systems with delight.

To take maximum
advantage of our temporal
travails and put a positive spin
on our telestial trials, our Savior
Jesus Christ taught about repentance,
that we might one day be restored to our
proper and perfect frames, prepared to meet
our destiny adorned in glory, immortality,
and eternal life, that has been accessorized
with faith, hope, and charity. (See
1 Corinthians 13:13).

Anyone who has feasted
upon the words of Jesus Christ, and
has therein really sunk their teeth into
and savored their messages, has prayed for
help in digesting them, and has then sought
to receive a witness that what they've devoured is
true, knows what spiritual hunger is. It is when the
powers of heaven and earth amplify each other and
catch us up on harmonic waves. When we have had
moments like this, it is as if someone has given
us "gospel glasses." Everything resonates with
clarity and we feel as if we have been given
the eternal perspective that for so long
our eyes have been craving.

Negotiation to gain a temporal
advantage over another is antithetical to the
teachings of Jesus Christ, but seems to be the norm
in our society. Caveat emptor, or let the buyer beware, is
the rule of business. The world has made a religion of
economic programs ostensibly designed to improve
the quality of our lives, but that really have a
personal profit motive as their basis. Truly,
Spiritual Babylon has a twisted
concept of welfare.

Elohim is our Father, and
we were born of Him as His spirit
children. We acquired His qualities and
characteristics and we were raised by Him
to maturity until we could progress no more.
We then left His presence to fulfill our missions
on earth, because there were some laws that pertained
only to mortality that we could not obey, and so there
were some blessings that were as yet unavailable to us.
Having completed our passage to earth, we now make
the journey to our Savior Jesus Christ, and when we
finally reach our destination, we will hope for a
glorious resurrection and eternal life in
His Celestial Kingdom.

During days and weeks that are sure to have their ups and downs, our study of the gospel focuses our attention on Jesus Christ, Who is our Rock. There is consistency in our obedience. The scriptures become our stronghold of stability in the midst of the world's turmoil, and they bless us with an influential capacity to focus the attention of our hearts, and the power of our might, mind, and strength on a covenant relationship with Father in Heaven and our Savior, thru the Holy Ghost.

Our Redeemer Jesus Christ inspires us to dream things that never were, and with the Holy Ghost as our constant companion, to ask: "Why not?" We work thru our problems, instead of skirting around them. Our dependence upon the Atonement of the Savior will compel us to be disciplined in our commitment, with sustained effort and an ongoing responsibility with accountability. Someone once said that we have been given two ends: One to think with and the other to sit on. Which one we use will determine how well we do in life. In other words: Heads we win, and tails we lose.

A vibrant embroidery traced by the pattern of the narrative that has been stitched onto the cloth of the teachings of our Lord and Savior Jesus Christ allows us to aim high. With its perspective, we can discard the poor lenses of the body, with a myopic view of life, and instead raise our sights to the rolling vistas of eternity.

Those who have become well-acquainted with our Savior Jesus Christ, how He is able to turn stumbling blocks into solid stepping stones. Crisis becomes opportunity, while victory is snatched from the jaws of defeat. They know that change will come to them "like a flash of lightning and a resounding clap of thunder. While others shrink in fear, they realize that it is only after the tempest, that flowers will bloom." ("The Chinese Book of Proverbs").

An interesting account of the discovery of the Bar Kokhba Documents that were hidden in caves near Ein Gedi on the western shore of the Salt Sea, about 31 A.D., speaks of records that were buried deeply in the dry dirt of the cave floor. When they came to light, choking clouds of dust required the archaeologists to wear masks to breathe. Truly, the teachings of our Savior Jesus Christ speak to us out of the ground, and its speech is low out of the dust, even as it were out of the ground, and it whispers to us out of the dust. (See Isaiah 29:4).

On our journey to the stars, our intellect will not save us, because what is at stake is feeling and not knowledge. And so, it is a blessing if the Lord Jesus Christ accompanies us during our travels. On our voyages of discovery, our hearts and our nature will change, the scales will fall from our eyes, and the path before us will be brightly illuminated, so that we may see with the eye of faith all the way into eternity. He stands ready to bestow upon us that perspective, and only waits upon our initiative before He will act in our behalf, to make smooth the rough places on the paths before us.

The solicitation of the prophets who have borne testimony of our Lord Jesus Christ, is to come unto Him to develop our own sure witness of the truth. To that end, we need look no further than to the simple guidance given by His servants in the scriptures. One recommended that we ask sincerely, with real intent, and with faith in Christ. The counsel of another was to "ask in faith, nothing wavering." (James 1:6).

Jesus Christ defines the path to a religious recalibration thru repentance. He allows us to become reinvigorated by the refreshing breeze of celestial air. The scriptures paint a portrait of free-will where we may take risks. If, in our efforts, we fail to measure up to God's entreaties, the Savior will step in to intervene in our behalf, by using the bargaining chip of the Atonement, thereby allowing the Law of Mercy to satisfy the otherwise unalterable and inexorable demands of its contrary, that goes by the name of Justice.

We undertake the
journey to Jesus Christ
to seek shelter for our spirits
and to quiet our racing hearts.
We grasp the horns of sanctuary,
so that we might relieve the tensions
that always threaten to overwhelm us
were we to allow ourselves to be caught
up and remain in the fast lane of life.
In the scriptures that testify of His
divinity, we calmly reflect upon
the quality of our preparation
to breathe celestial air and to
live in eternal felicity
in the company of
the Gods.

Those who would think to
turn their backs to our Savior
Jesus Christ are left to grope about
in the darkness and gasp for a breath
of celestial ether. The faithful keep their
faces oriented toward the light of Christ
so they will always feel the gentle caress
of heaven upon their cheeks. At the same
time, because the shadows will always
be behind them, they might not even
be aware of the encroaching gloom.
At the very least, the dark will no
longer hold them in the grip of
impending doom.

Our Father Who dwells in Heaven has "promised Christ's merits unto all, so that whosoever repenteth is immediately beloved of Him." (William Tyndall). The same feeling will come upon those who have embraced the gospel of Jesus Christ, and who are filled with joy, having received a remission of their sins, and who will enjoy the peace that surpasses all understanding, because of their faith in our Lord and Savior. (See Philippians 4:7).

The Prophet Joseph Smith humbly taught: "We may (benefit) by noticing the first intimations of the spirit of revelation; for instance, when we feel pure intelligence flowing into us, it may give us sudden strokes of ideas … By learning the Spirit of God and understanding it, we may grow into the principle of revelation." When we approach our Savior Jesus Christ, He is as a schoolmaster Who will bring us, by way of that same spirit of revelation, to true doctrine.

Even great faith will
remain dormant without our
accompanying work of repentance
made possible through the Atonement of
Jesus Christ. That faith notwithstanding,
we don't have power to save ourselves from
the unalterable demands that are made by
Justice. In order for Mercy to prevail, the
ordinances of the gospel of Jesus Christ,
together with their related covenants,
were created to become the focus
of our attention.

The teachings of Jesus Christ caution us that
if we would "hinder a very infidel from the right of the
law, we would sin against God." (William Tyndall). With
profound gratitude for His generosity, we extend a warm hand
of fellowship to others without regard to their circumstances in
life. "And it shall come to pass that ye shall divide (the land)
by lot for an inheritance unto you, and to the strangers
that sojourn among you, which shall beget children
among you; and they shall be unto you as born
in the country among the children of Israel;
they shall have inheritance with you
among the tribes of Israel."
(Ezekiel 47:22).

Jesus Christ
shows us how to
efficaciously flex
our spiritual muscles
while exercising moral
agency in the forum of
free will, all the while self-
confidently engaging the
forces of opposition in
a vigorous tug of
war.

Jesus Christ infuses
us with the high octane
fuel of faith, detonating
the fire of our fortitude as
He propels us onward toward
heaven where a convocation of
angels has gathered to form a
welcoming committee. They're
anticipating that we'll come
in full-throttle to keep our
date with destiny and
reap our eternal
reward.

In every teaching moment, Jesus Christ exhorted His disciples to drink copiously and unceasingly from the fountain of truth in order to slake their thirst for principles that gyroscopically oriented them to eternity. They clearly established the difference between celestial sureties that are represented by eternal progression, and telestial tendencies that are characterized by physical laws such as entropy.

Those who discover a sanctuary in their Savior Jesus Christ have found it to be a safe haven that remains untainted from the blood and sins of this generation. It circumscribes the refuge where we may flee from spiritual Babylon to shelter our spirits, quiet our racing hearts, ease the tension that builds up when we spend too much time in the fast lane of life, grasp the horns of sanctuary, and quietly reflect upon the quality of our preparation to live with our Heavenly Father for eternity.

When we have discarded the coarse trappings of mortality, and take upon ourselves the robes of eternity found in the armoire of the Master Tailor Jesus Christ, our limbs and our joints will be restored to our bodies and not even one hair of our heads will be lost. (See Luke 12:7). We will be restored to our proper and perfect frames.

An early leader of the Reformation, Roger Williams, declared: "There is no regularly constituted church on earth, nor any person authorized to administer any church ordinance, nor can there be until new apostles are sent by the Great Head of the church, for Whose Coming I am seeking." Thanks be to God for our Master Jesus Christ, and for all those who have successfully petitioned the heavens to restore the power of God unto salvation, in the last days. (See Romans 1:16).

We enjoy the "fruit of the Spirit" (Galatians 5:22), when we have been taught true doctrine as it is found in the teachings of our Lord and Savior Jesus Christ.

We enlarge the foundations of our spiritual center, and we make room for faith, even if the parts we have been asked to play in the drama of our lives seems awkward. After we have signed the papers, and we join other cast members in the production of God's Plan as it is manifested in the script that features Jesus Christ as its Star Performer, we will be reinvigorated to vividly role-play, then to vigorously pre-play, and finally to repetitively re-play the lines we have been asked to deliver in the theater of life. Our rehearsals, that are conducted by the Spirit, will give us courage to be perfect in the delivery of our lines and take our cues, with the goal of generating a performance worthy of an Oscar.

The solution to our liberation from the bondage of sin, that we might enjoy a freedom to become, is an adjustment in attitude that is reflected in our wish for the teachings of our Redeemer Jesus Christ to be more scrupulously integrated into our lives. Paraphrasing Helen Keller, the real tragedy is not those who were born without sight. Rather, it is those who have sight, but lack vision. (See Proverbs 29:18).

Accountability for our own actions blesses us with a responsibility that can either destroy us or, with the assistance of our Savior Jesus Christ, will usher us into the embrace of angels. However, we cannot have it both ways. If we sow sparingly, we shall reap sparingly, but if we sow bountifully, we shall reap bountifully. (See 2 Corinthians 9:6).

When we stop living, we start dying. We live and move and have our being through sense and perception that are blended into a refreshing elixir preventing us from becoming too set in our ways. These form an unlikely union, that by intelligent design was created to upset the status-quo, expand our experience, and help us to weather our storms and meet our challenges. At the end of the day, it is "by the experiment of this ministration" that we are able to "glorify God for (our) professed subjection unto the gospel of (Jesus) Christ" our Lord. (2 Corinthians 9:13).

In the teachings of our Lord and Savior Jesus Christ, examples of manipulation by external force on the one hand, and free will on the other, appear to be antithetical, but they do no violence to the harmony of our faith if we think of them as dynamic counterparts that are the fundamental elements of a process that leads us through a twisted temporal matrix in the direction of an expansive, unrestrained, and seamless experience that has been characterized as immortality and eternal life. To put it another way, Jesus taught that control and agency are contraries in the opposition in all things that are absolutely necessary for the Plan of Salvation to play out as Heavenly Father intended it to do.

When we are candidly asked if we have been spiritually born of God, what our interlocutors really want to know is if we have experienced the pure and unconditional love of Christ and if we have charity. We may be converted to the church, but what is even more important is whether we have also been converted to the Savior and to His gospel.

Without the influence of Jesus Christ, we will never understand our physical universe so completely that we will ever become its master. We cannot presume to supplant His intelligence with our own. Nor could we in any comprehensive way understand the eternities while we remain within the stew of seconds, the mire of minutes, or the agony of hours. For now, we need to listen for a voice that will quietly ask: "Be still, and know that I am God." (Psalms 46:10).

Jesus Christ
is the Son of God,
the Father of heaven
and earth, and is the
Creator of all things.
We honor His name,
and we bear it with
respect, reverence.
and humility.

According to the telestially immutable
2nd Law of Thermodynamics, entropy explains the
tendency toward disorder throughout the cosmos, but the
laws that relate to eternal progression belong to the heavens,
and are under the direction of Jesus Christ. Thus, the concept
of improvement is bracketed by celestial laws that might be
foreign to rational minds. As Paul taught the Corinthian
Saints: "The natural man receiveth not the things of
the Spirit of God: for they are foolishness unto
him, neither can he know them, because
they are spiritually discerned."
(1 Corinthians 2:14).

In the
example of our
Savior Jesus Christ,
the power of godliness is
unmistakable. And without
the authority of the priesthood
administering its ordinances,
it will not be made manifest,
even to those who profess to
know Him on virtually
every other level.

With our Savior Jesus Christ as our
traveling companion, we embark upon an
incredible journey thru the millennia, as the
leaves of a most profound text that is the earliest
and best example of nonfiction in writing unfolds
before the panorama of great civilizations. Throughout
the pages of the Holy Bible we will encounter the intrigue of
ancient Asia as warlords battle for supremacy and tension in
Jerusalem rises as empires of the Near East struggle for power. We
witness the thrill of those whose eyes were fixed on lands of promise
beyond the horizon of their vision, and we feel the testimonies of
prophets of God who counseled all mankind. Those who truly
appreciate it will feast upon the word of God and devour
His gospel as if it were literally the bread of life. They
will seek, and yearn, and strive, and wrestle
for their blessing. (See Genesis
32:24).

Our Savior Jesus Christ has
the awesome ability to create stability,
standing in stark contrast to the world's
exaggerations that stretch comprehension
and credulity, causing unbelievers to
wobble unsteadily on their spiritual
tippy toes, as they roll the dice
and leave their destiny in
the hands of lady
luck.

The real problem
with vanity is that it
relies on misguided hope, and
its supposed strength is built upon
false premises. It is a Ponzi scheme that
can't deliver on its promises. It writes checks
that can't be cashed because it lacks the spiritual
reserves of the Holy Ghost, and it is forever teetering
on the brink of moral bankruptcy, always threatening
to collapse, and great shall be the fall thereof. In contrast
to this, the reserves of Jesus Christ are more secure than the
Bank of England, with stores of gold that are far
more substantial. (See Revelation 21:21).

The indescribable peace that
follows on the heels of our acceptance
Jesus Christ as our Redeemer will help us
to understand that God's greater reality lies
within our reach. When we discover that we are
not alone, we have begun a journey that will
carry us to a higher state of being, where
we will find that we are covered in star
dust as we converse with angels
and mingle with Gods.

Our optimism allows us to see the
glass as half-full. We are determined to
express gratitude for what is right, rather than
to grumble about what is wrong. We realize that we
can't do everything, but we can do something. Because
chronic complainers attract negative energy, we focus on
the positive, and channel it into a force that expands
the sphere of our righteous influence. Our Savior
Jesus Christ teaches us that He "is gracious
and full of compassion; slow to anger,
and of great mercy." (Psalms
145:8).

To function, God's
Plan of Mercy requires
us to take His labor of love
and somehow ease onto a world
stage that is lit only by fire. Our
Redeemer Jesus Christ intensifies
our desire to create a comfortable
connection with the Holy Ghost,
as well as a relationship with
the cosmos, that bridge the
gulf that exists between
heaven and earth.

The pattern of the
government of heaven is
illustrated by the enchantment
of God's grace as it administers the
ordinances of salvation, sanctification,
justification, and exaltation. These allow
us to receive its blessings by binding us
to Him through covenants of action. Our
Savior Jesus Christ helps us to enjoy
a wider perspective relating to our
place in the cosmos, and gives
us a greater understanding
of the Plan of Salvation,
and of the nature of
our Father.

If we are not careful, duplicitous "friends" can get under our skin; they can worm their way right into our hearts, minds, and souls when the barrier protection provided by our internalization of inspired counsel from our Redeemer Jesus Christ has been compromised. Unless we are quick to repent, they will then be able to influence us and distort our celestial features to such an extent that they will become the grotesque caricatures that are characteristic of the mask of a hypocrite.

The virgin birth of the Savior continues to be the greatest story ever told. The faithful of every age preserved and passed on the tale, although, in time, there were many for whom the Bible had become a magical book, conveying power and knowledge without the aid of continuing revelation. Prophets foresaw that those living in the Last Days would change both the appearance and the substance of the scriptures. We are blessed in the Last Days to have the magic of an expanded appreciation of the principles and doctrine of the gospel of Jesus Christ, together with their related ordinances and covenants, and the unimpeachable witness of the Spirit, to flesh out the meager narratives of the four Gospels of Matthew, Mark, Luke, and John, which for many may be their sole sources of inspiration and revelation.

Because of its
seeming inability to embrace
our Savior Jesus Christ, our society
finds itself in a self-destruct mode.
We are cautioned in D&C 1:16 that the
world seeks "not the Lord to establish his
righteousness, but every man walketh in
his own way, and after the image of his
own god, whose image is in the likeness
of the world, and whose substance is
that of an idol, which waxeth old
and shall perish in Babylon,
even Babylon the great,
which shall fall."

When we worship our Savior and Redeemer, the
recesses of our minds are stimulated by the haunting
refrain that we must never "let it be forgot, that once there
was a spot for one brief shining moment, that was known as
Camelot." (Jay Lerner). So we resist the gustatory distractions
of the world, and we renew our efforts to press forward, feasting
instead upon the word of Christ. If "this is our quest, to follow
that star, no matter how hopeless, no matter how far, to fight
for the right, without question or pause, to be willing to
march into hell for a heavenly cause," we know that
"our hearts will lie peaceful and calm when we're
laid to our rest," and we will leave the world
itself a better place. (Joe Darion).

The Holy Spirit garnishes our hearts with the gentle reminders that the Lord Jesus Christ is God's Only Begotten Son, Who is the Savior of the world.

We accept Jesus Christ as Lord of Lords and King of Kings because He has already accomplished His exaltation, while we clearly have yet to do so. The pledges we make with our Heavenly Father are as stamps on our passports to perfection. We are invited to clear customs with nothing to declare but our testimony of the Savior. As we emerge into the light of day, there will then be revealed before us the rolling vista of an undiscovered country at one and the same time our destination and our destiny.

In our day, we witness the spectacle of Babylon crumbling into dust. We see that force and compulsion have always failed miserably, as they have tried in vain to establish an ideal society. Peace on earth and good will toward all "can only come through transformation of individual souls, and with lives redeemed from sin and brought into harmony" with the divine will of our Redeemer Jesus Christ. (David O. McKay).

It isn't enough to know about the birth of the Savior by reading in the gospel of Jesus Christ the account by Luke, or by listening to others speak of Him. We must know Him through the bonds of common experience and shared feeling. Our religious conviction must be involved not only with discovery, but also with recovery. Our destiny is not only union, but also re-union, with divine realities, and our religious re-cognition is our re-acquaintance with truth we have already embraced. It involves the re-awakening of our spirits to eternal possibilities.

One of the blessings we receive when we emulate the life and ministry of Jesus Christ is that by doing so, there may be inflicted upon us a benevolent blindness that actually helps us to see more clearly than those with 20:20 vision. Those who immerse themselves in the scriptures 'feel' with a vibrancy that is incorporeal and indefinable. It awakens a light within their hearts that supplants any and all of the somatic senses, and it is far more reliable.

Due to its uncompromising standard in the face of homogenizing influences in the world, the account of the ministry of Jesus Christ has become the 'Good News' to all who will embrace it, providing all the principles, ordinances, and covenants that enable us to become sanctified so that we may be worthy to live once again in a state of holiness in the presence of our Father. Because of the influence of the Spirit, we may all come unto God, and lay hold upon every good gift and be perfected in Him. If we continue in the supplication of His grace, one day we will stand blameless before Him at His Pleasing Bar. (See Philippians 4:6).

If we embrace the teachings of our Savior Jesus Christ, the conduct of our lives will be in accord with the laws of the Celestial Kingdom, we will be set free to enjoy gifts of the Spirit. Our journey of faith will inevitably include many stops along the way where we will pause to seriously study His ministry, leading us to powerful testimonies of His divinity.

Testimony of the divinity of Jesus Christ wanes because it's easy to be preoccupied by a desire to obtain what we do not need, to amass what we do not deserve, to hoard what we have not earned, and to stockpile what we cannot ultimately use. Each year, several million people worldwide fall victim to the effects of an influenza virus that manifests itself in frustratingly mutated forms, but the truth is that more of us will die spiritually because we've been infected by avarice, covetousness, greed, lust, conceit, and prejudice. The prideful and stubborn will "seek not the Lord to establish his righteousness, but every man walketh in his own way, after the manner of his own God." (D&C 1:16, see Proverbs 21:2 & Isaiah 53:6).

The Prophet Joseph Smith stated: "There are but a very few beings in the world who understand rightly the nature of God, and if they do not understand the character of God they do not comprehend themselves." One of the mission objectives of Jesus Christ was to help us to uncover the qualities and character traits of our Father, that we discover are consistent with the divine nature of our own spirits.

Some of us pray that we might be blessed to live within sight of a chapel, while others wish to live within a hundred meters of hell. Sometimes, the Savior will send forth His most dedicated disciples to minister among His most wicked children. He'll arm them with unswerving faith, a certain knowledge of the principles and promises of the gospel of Jesus Christ, firm and abiding testimonies of the doctrines of the Kingdom, of God's Plan, and of the Savior, a blessing and setting-apart by file leaders, the continual prayers of the faithful, and an endowment of spiritual power received in holy places.

Our innate capacity to apply in our lives the wisdom of the ages, namely of the teachings of our Savior Jesus Christ, is given energy by the Holy Ghost, Who blesses us with an intrinsic sense of our nobility, for we are the sons and daughters of a heavenly King. In France during the Middle Ages, the successor to the throne of the Bourbon monarchs was known as the Dauphin. During the reign of his father, unscrupulous and crafty counselors tried every means to corrupt the Dauphin, to thereby make him ineligible to inherit the throne. In all of their devious attempts, however, they were unsuccessful. Finally, in resignation, they asked him: "How is it that with all our enticements we have been unable to corrupt your high standards?" His reply was simple: "I am a King's son." The Dauphin had established behavior patterns that were consistent with his beliefs, and that allowed him to act, and to move forward, in perfect harmony with his convictions.

Without the guidance of the Holy Spirit to push those whom we are teaching into an undiscovered country as they learn more about the teachings of Jesus Christ, they will be doomed to remain as the "very cautious man who never laughed or played, who never risked, and never tried, who never read or prayed. And when, one day, he passed away, his insurance was denied, for since he never really lived, they claimed he'd never died." (Mark Barsouna). However, when we do have the Spirit to be with us, we pour ourselves into the task so that we can be lifesavers. As we teach, we focus on the doctrine of Christ with such a passion for our Savior that those who listen to us will find it hard to resist our invitation to action. We bear personal testimony that is based upon our own experiences relating to our anticipated blessings, and we make them seem worth working and fighting for. We can be saviors on Mount Zion through our teaching of key doctrine.
(See Obadiah 1:21).

When we who have yielded
our hearts to the Savior are sensitive to
spiritual whisperings, we will recognize the
seeming detours and distractions in our lives
for what they really are, and that is opportunities
for growth. Neal A. Maxwell wondered: "How many
times have we vigorously protested while on our way to a
blessing? During our schooling in submissiveness, we will
see the visible crosses some carry, but others will go unseen.
Some may appear to have no trial at all, which, if it were
so, would be a trial in itself. Indeed, if our souls had
rings, as do trees, to measure the years of greatest
personal growth, the wide rings would likely
reflect the years of greatest moisture,
but from tears, not rainfall."

Even those who've wholeheartedly embraced
our Savior Jesus Christ will be given weaknesses,
so they may be humble. Demosthenes overcame a lisp to
become one of the most powerful orators of ancient Greece.
Beethoven composed some of his greatest music after he lost
his hearing. Early in his career, Abraham Lincoln declared:
"I will prepare myself, and some day my chance will come."
As a young man, Heber J. Grant couldn't carry a note. Later,
he became well known for his singing abilities. Quoting
Ralph Waldo Emerson, he said of his own experience:
"That which we persist in doing becomes easier for
us to do; not that the nature of the thing
has changed, but that our power
to do is increased."

Our Savior Jesus Christ was commissioned to activate God's divinely designed blueprint for survival in the Last Days. With it, we can become (in a sense) the architects of our own fate and the masters of our destiny. We are as "children who are coming down like gentle rain through darkened skies, with glory trailing from their feet as they go, and endless promise in their eyes. Strangers from a realm of light, who have forgotten all; the memory of their former life and the purpose of their call. And so, they must learn why they're here, and who they really are." ("Saturday's Warrior").

Those who have been faithful in their zeal toward our Lord and Savior Jesus Christ are examples of the aphorism that "who we are, is God's gift to us, but who we become, is our gift to God." Samuel Johnson, the playwright, essayist, moralist, literary critic, biographer, and editor, who just may have been the most distinguished man of letters in English history, observed that "integrity without knowledge is weak and useless, and knowledge without integrity, is dangerous and dreadful." By entering into covenants, we bind ourselves by own integrity to act in a positive and predictable way. Our covenants engender a sense of permanency that in turn becomes a powerful reinforcement for affirmative action. By making our commitment known to others, we establish a means of accountability, and we unite ourselves with the forces of heaven, namely the Holy Ghost, Who can help us secure its blessings.

The teachings of our Lord Jesus Christ reassure us that today is a wonderful time to be alive. The millennial day approaches. "How do we prepare for the Second Coming?" asked Gordon B. Hinckley. "Well, we just do not worry about it. We just live the kind of life that, if it were to happen tomorrow, we would be ready. Nobody knows what is going to happen. Our responsibility is to prepare ourselves, and to live worthy of the association of the Savior, to deport ourselves in such a way that we would not be embarrassed if He were to come among us."

When Heavenly Father's law has been written upon our hearts (see 2 Corinthians 3:2-3), and we feel His forgiveness, the teachings of Jesus Christ compel us to forgive others, while entreating Him to bless our efforts, precisely because it is so contrary to our nature to do so. The opportunity to forgive must never be wasted, because it can awaken within our hearts a spiritual sensitivity that is somehow greater than ourselves. Brigham Young told the Saints that "he who takes offense when no offense was intended is a fool, and he who takes offense when it was intended is usually a fool."

Our Savior Jesus
Christ gives us strength
to be firm and unflinching
as we stare directly into the face
of evil. We recall that the Mount of
Temptation is less than 18 miles from
Bethlehem, which is a distance that can
be dangerously covered in the blink of
an eye when we are moving at the
breakneck pace determined by
untenable telestial speed
limit.

Our pledge
is to obey celestial
principles and doctrine;
to find our way in "the life
and the light, in the Spirit and
the power, sent forth by the will of
the Father through Jesus Christ, his
Son." (D&C 50:27). Somewhere within
the vast reaches of the galaxy, certainly
there are others like us, who hope to inherit
dominion and glory and a kingdom. But
they, too, will achieve the spiritual stature
of their Father and our Father only when
they are cleansed from sin by the power
of the Atonement, in a refining light
that streams forth throughout all
the cosmos from the gospel.

The doctrine
that is uncovered as
we explore the teachings of
Jesus Christ are little quanta
of energy that contribute just the
right amount of illumination
that is critically needed by
a world that has become
enveloped in thick
darkness.

You will very quickly see that the
daily devotions expressed on the pages in this
volume have been carefully crafted to represent a
variety of geometrical designs. It may be surprising to
learn that the construction of these patterns has helped me to
coherently organize my thoughts. In many cases, the outcome
almost seems to have been foreordained, as I moved words around
until, as if by magic, they dropped into their proper positions on the
page. Often, I had envisioned beforehand the particular framework that I
wanted to achieve, and when I had appropriately arranged the words, one
or two would stand out and grab my attention, because they still didn't
feel quite right. Frequently, it was not difficult to find an alternative
that would not only fit better physically, but also was etymologically
much better suited to the spiritual concept that I wished to convey.
As my work on the project continued, I was intrigued by the
natural evolution of the process. That made me consider
whether my success might have been stimulated
by unconventional thought processes that
are tied to my testimony of our Lord and
Savior Jesus Christ.

Without
knowledge,
there can be no
faith; without faith,
there can be no light,
and without the light of
revelation from the heavens
there will be no appreciation
of religious truth; and without
spiritual enlightenment, if just
one of these elements is missing,
all must be lost. Our fortunes rest
on the basis of how we embrace the
insight, intuitions, inspiration,
and revelation that flow from
our Savior Jesus Christ.

Jesus Christ was taught by
His Father to "overcome with kindness
and to do of very love that thing which the
law compels us to do. Love only and to do service
unto our neighbors is the fulfilling of the law in the
sight of God." (William Tyndall). When our altruistic
sensitivities predominate, we labor on behalf of others as
we lose ourselves in service. When we catch the vision of
the work, we give ourselves to the Savior, yielding to
Him our agency because of our implicit trust in
Him to influence us to do the right thing
every time and to save us from
our follies.

Our Redeemer Jesus Christ anticipated that in the world in which live, the distinctions between good and evil would be blurred, but He is poised to take remedial action. Spiritual Babylon lies all around us, and so we need to be vigilant, because "vice is a monster of so frightful mien, as to be hated needs but to be seen. Yet seen too oft, familiar with her face, we first endure, then pity, then embrace." (Alexander Pope).

If we lack a focus of faith in our Savior Jesus Christ, we'll be locked on telestial targets and will be unable to see the forest for the trees. We will look at the Milky Way and catalogue its stars, but forget to count our blessings. We will allow ourselves to be governed by a rev-limiter on the power plant that fuels not only light bulbs but also galaxies and the heavens. We will be drawn to the light like moths are to fire, and will flutter around without purpose until it becomes everlastingly too late to make substantive change. Higher level thinking will forever remain just beyond the reach of our comprehension!

In a coming day, Israel will recognize our Lord and Savior Jesus Christ as the Messiah. Thus, "by the authority of the Holy Priesthood of God and by the ministration under the direction of the Prophet of God, the Apostles of the Lord Jesus Christ have been to the Holy Land and have dedicated that country for the return of the Jews. And we believe that in the due time of the Lord they shall again be in the favor of God. And let no Latter-day Saint be guilty of taking any part in any crusade against these people." (Heber J. Grant, C.R., 10/1921 – 27 years before the founding of the State of Israel, and 103 years before the unprovoked October 6, 2023 attack on Israel by the terrorist organization Hamas.

Those who would think to summarily dismiss the ministry of Jesus Christ amuse themselves with games of Trivial Pursuit, mistaking it for the Game of Life. The real face of sin, for them and for us, is waste. It is doing one thing, when something else of far greater good could be done in its stead. It is settling for mediocrity when the more challenging road leads to greater heights with spectacular vistas ahead, just around the next turn in the road. Sin is a capitulation to spiritual stagnation and a forfeiture of eager acceptance of the excitement of eternal progression. It is trading a mess of pottage for our eternal birthright. It is nothing but an overnight stay in a second-class hotel, while God's five-star all-inclusive resort beckons to us from behind pearly gates, just down the road.

Celestial jewels that
sparkle in the sunlight on the
beaches of our lives gently validate
a spiritual certainty: Heavenly light
betrays the influence of Jesus Christ. We
feel the infusion of His power, and our own
enlightenment is confirmed by an inner
yearning to be at one with the Infinite.
This feeling is intangible, and it is
Indescribable. It is inarticulate,
and yet from within the core
of our being it quietly
speaks peace to our
souls.

On a crisp and clear
winter evening, we raise
our eyes to the cosmos and see
among the brightly twinkling
stars a luminescent trail that has
been created by God to help us find our
way back to our celestial home. It was set
in the heavens as a sparkling multi-faceted
pathway of diamonds meant to guide us to the
infinite reaches of eternity. On a moonless night,
starlight provides enough clarity for us to maintain
our bearings on our Redeemer Jesus Christ, and as it
shines on our hopeful countenances, we remember
Bergson's prophetic metaphor that "the universe
can be a machine for the making of gods."

No matter
that we may live
in the frigid reaches of
the Arctic or in the stifling
heat of the tropics, it is with our
examination of the life and mission of
Jesus Christ that we catch religious fever
that spikes our testimony temperature just
enough to invigorate our appreciation for His
sacrifice. It is at this moment that we're prepared
to experience a mind-bending theophany: that
we who once were the children of men, have
now become His spiritual offspring,
and we are born of Him Who
lives in heaven.

Our Lord Jesus Christ
introduced us to the Holy
Ghost. (See John 14:16). He
is the Author of acumen, the
Avatar of agency, the Architect
of our aptitude, the Benefactor of
all of our blessings, the Designer of
discipleship, the Initiator of insight,
the Inventor of intelligence, the Patron
of perception, the Provider of our praise,
the Sponsor of our scholarship, and the
ultimate Source of our understanding;
not to mention the Craftsman of our
comfort, the Guarantor of all gifts,
and the Champion of committed
Christians everywhere.

"Gather the people together, men, and women, and children, and the stranger that is within thy gates, that they may hear, and that they may learn, and fear the Lord your God, and observe to do all the words of this law" that is found coursing its way through the gospel of Jesus Christ. (Deuteronomy 31:12).

When we are over the hill, we sometimes would like to use our momentum to pick up speed. Instead, we may need to ease off on the throttle of our expectations, and simply gird up our loins and take fresh courage, knowing that it is not ability or inability that is important, but availability. We consecrate our efforts to our Savior Jesus Christ and let Him sort out the details.

"Limitless undying love shines around us like a million suns, calling us on and on, across the universe" that is the native environment of our Savior Jesus Christ. (John Lennon).

Our rendezvous with the judgment won't come at some hazy point down the road. It is today. We speak, think, and act according to either celestial, terrestrial, or telestial law. We're blessed with moral compasses, and our faith in our Savior Jesus Christ defines the path that we have chosen to follow. Each day that we live, we're 24 hours closer to God's pleasing bar. If we have committed the 13th Article of Faith to practice as well as to memory, its principles will have become the particles of our faith. We believe in being honest, true, chaste, benevolent, and in doing good to all men. Indeed, we may say that we follow the admonition of Paul. If there is anything virtuous, lovely, or of good report or praiseworthy, we seek after these things. (See Philippians 4:8).

A spiritual transformation that follows on the heels of acceptance of our Savior Jesus Christ ensures that we will enjoy the fruits of a metaphysical manipulation with an element of rhetorical analogy: "Though (our) sins be as scarlet, they shall be as white as snow; though they be red like crimson, they shall be as wool." (Isaiah 1:18).

Receiving Jesus Christ in our hearts maintains a harmony with our Father in Heaven, and with the Holy Ghost, Who touch our lives in ways that are sacramental in nature and in their effect on our future. As we ponder the sacrifice of our Savior, we comprehend the truth that we can become beings of light after we've gained valuable experience in a telestial school of hard knocks.

It's precisely because of the ever-present threat that stems from our behavioral instability that we've been blessed to bear a testimony of Jesus Christ. It can reorient us in the direction of righteousness, and recalibrate our moral compass to safely guide us home to the happiness that has been prepared for the Saints.

In 1916, Einstein discovered the key to the mercurial nature of time. He let the genie out of the bottle. Common folks like us, who are now comfortable with the phrase "It's all relative," seldom recognize the intimate association that statement shares with our expression of free will, or our comprehension of heaven. Truth be told, with our greater appreciation of the relationship between time and space has come a sense of relief. Those who are in harmony with the teachings of Jesus Christ know that for God to honor the principle of free will, He does not have to cease to be, and is required by the demands of of doctrine to surrender neither His omniscience nor His omnipotence.

Those who aren't well grounded in our Redeemer Jesus Christ might need to be jolted out of their complacency in the same way that defibrillator paddles are used to restore normal cardiac rhythm in heart attack patients. There are spiritual equivalents to being well-grounded, and they are powerful. The rod of iron is a lightning rod, firmly grounding us to unchanging principles, so that we might "henceforth be no more children, tossed to and fro," like flotsam and jetsam on the sea of life, "and carried about with every wind of doctrine." (Ephesians 4:14).

Maybe our Savior Jesus Christ is the only One Who can really have it both ways, Who can tinker with time without paying homage to the deterministic laws of Newton, or Einstein's theories of Relativity. He may hold the key to slowing down the hectic pace of the glory train, to allow us to stop and smell the roses along the track, look ahead to ponder the solemnities of eternity, and determine to engage our agency here and now in ways that only He could envision. In any event, we can be sure that His learning style is the only one that is expansive enough to accommodate the concept of eternal progression. At the same time, His gospel ingeniously permits us to learn the lessons of eternity from the narrow constraints of mortality.

Our
Great God and Great
King (see Psalms 95:3), has
promised the Saints that they
shall safely dwell in Zion, a city
that stands as a stellar example
that the reward of obedience to
the laws and ordinances of
His gospel is celestial
surety.

The appeal of the Star
Wars franchise draws upon our
intuitive awareness that Jesus Christ
is the Creator of our earth and is the source
of all light. The gospel teaches us that He, and
not Yoda, is the Master Jedi Knight. We are His
novitiates, imperfect mortals who are acquainted
with evil. Because earth is a learning laboratory,
we understand and are influenced by the twisted
nature of the Dark Side of the Force. But it is the
Jedi whom we admire, and our eyes are drawn
to light as if it were fire from heaven. It was
the Jedi who were pure in heart, and who,
thru the power of discernment, could
see things in their true light, and
even righteously manipulate
the power of the Force.

The ministry of our Savior
Jesus Christ creates a technicolor
backdrop for a worldwide tapestry that's
now being woven by the army of God, and
that has been commissioned to seek out and
find the elect. Once that has been accomplished,
it will task its soldiers to seamlessly stitch those
who have come up out of the waters of baptism
into the heraldry of the Good Shepherd.
(See Ephesians 2:19).

In the life of
those individuals
whose behavior isn't in
harmony with God's Plan,
there will come a time when
a readjustment must obliterate
a façade of hypocrisy. As painful
as the process of reformation may
be, it is necessary to allow for the
cultivation of a more nurturing
lifestyle that is only possible
when we embrace the special
promises that have been
made by our Savior
Jesus Christ.

As they watched over their flocks near the little town of Bethlehem, the shepherds were the first to hear the celestial choir, brush against the flowing white robes of the angels, and hear the unmistakable voice of the Spirit. Their lesson is that the poor, the unlearned, the common person, and the native born, may come unto Christ. In His gospel, we learn about the universal love of God, and we see how the hand of the Lord has individually touched each of our lives.

We've all heard that blood is thicker than water. This well-known aphorism suggests the feeling that, as a result of genetics, blood relations are more important than friendships. However, after some basic research, I found that the earliest form of "Blood is thicker than water" grew out of the phrase: "The blood of the covenant is thicker than the water of the womb." The meaning of this earlier phrase is actually the complete opposite of the way it's understood today. In other words, the bonds we have consciously chosen to make with God by covenant are more important than the ones that we find ourselves in through genetics and by chance, or as the saying goes, by the "water of the womb." As the prophet Isaiah put it: "Surely your turning of things upside down shall be esteemed as the potter's clay." (Isaiah 29:16). Blood is thicker than water. However, a blood covenant is thicker than the water of the womb. Bonding with those of like "mind" and "spirit" can be so much more meaningful and deeper than bonding by water, which can turn on a dime. Jesus Christ taught that no greater bond can be formed than when we determine to live under a blood oath, or a covenant we have made with God.

It is the second mile
of faith that is nurtured
as we engage our Savior Jesus
Christ. All that He asks of us is
to shun the telestial temptations
that are so cunningly peddled by
snake oil salesmen who have set up
shop within the great and spacious
buildings that dot the landscapes
of our lives, and that pop up in
the most unexpected places on
the side streets that vie for
attention with the strait
and narrow way.

If they are not accompanied
by the sanctifying properties of
our Heavenly Father's celestial light,
our greatest successes become as nothing
but empty shells and structures of custom
and convenience, faintly illuminated by the
frivolous flames of fairytales and superstitions.
However, the luminosity of our Redeemer Jesus
Christ will free us from bondage to ignorance.
The comforting glow of His divine fire is the
result of a spiritual transformation in the
lives of those who relish basking within
a celestial light. Our internal moral
compass is energized to guide us
home, and its warm blush is
infinitely safer than the
radium dials of a
bygone era.

Our Redeemer Jesus Christ encourages us to feast upon His words and to ponder the doctrines of the kingdom, and we receive His strength to endure one more day in righteousness. Our eyes remain fixed upon the prize that is the high calling of our Redeemer, and we taste the principles of eternal life that are taught with eloquence by its inspired prophet-historians.

Our Redeemer Jesus Christ will be our ally as we move from the confines of mortality into eternity. "See you later" will no longer be a part of our vocabulary. We might be shocked to learn that mortality was not our natural dimension, after all. Time, that we too frequently viewed as a predator that stalked us all our lives, will then be fondly remembered as a companion that accompanied us on our journey thru mortality, reminding us to cherish every moment. We will come to understand why we felt as "strangers and pilgrims on the earth." (Hebrews 11:13). This, in turn, will explain our innate thrust always toward the future, always beyond the horizon, and always upward in the direction of the stars. It will explain our intrigue with the heavens, and why our interstellar fascination had so powerfully pulled at us.

Over 2,700 years ago, Isaiah foresaw the Lord's mortal ministry, a theophany in the sacred grove, and the restoration of His gospel in the Last Days. "I will proceed to do a marvellous work among this people, even a marvellous work and a wonder." (Isaiah 29:10-14). And so He has, "with blood, and fire, and vapors of smoke." (Acts 2:19).

On the earth, "the worst enemy thou canst meet, wilt thou thyself always be." (Friedrich Nietzsche). Each of us is confined to a world of our own making, and most of us are trapped within narrowly defined perceptual prisons we have created for ourselves. Its walls are reinforced with the razor-wire of limiting beliefs, those stories we tell ourselves that cause us to sabotage our own best efforts. They can damage and even cripple our lives, diminish our abilities, compromise our progress, and keep us from attaining our goals. Although all of us have limiting beliefs, our Savior Jesus Christ bequeaths us with the power to nullify them. Most of us do not realize it is possible, and aren't aware that we've made the unconscious decision about what to believe and what not to believe.

Them faithful find mentors to emulate, rather than scapegoats that are easy to blame. Instead of looking for easier answers, they turn to our Redeemer Jesus Christ to discover enlightened solutions to the problems we all face.

The faint stirrings during the beginnings of our own terrestrial lives can be traced to an alien cosmic laboratory, where the human genome was nurtured in a secret garden that was known only to God. Later, it would be transplanted into the rich fertile soil of a primordial earth that had been carefully cultivated by its Creator to be environmentally welcoming and pristine in its setting. But later on, we would earn our bread by the sweat of our brow, and so our world would be as a lone and a dreary habitation. The faithful would turn to their Savior Jesus Christ to find an inner light that would nurture seeds of greatness.

As we jog thru
life at a measured pace
on the journey to our Savior
Jesus Christ, and we encounter
the twists and turns of mortality
while enjoying the aerobic exercise of
free will, it always helps to have celestial
sign posts to guide us through the telestial
traffic jams and conceptual cul-de-sacs that
threaten to detour us from the straight and
narrow way. The expanding circles of our
opportunity, enhanced by our obedience
to gospel principles, assures each of us
that we might have direct exposure to
the perfect law of liberty. Thereby,
we abandon the tortuous route
through Idumea that is taken
by those bound for telestial
glory. Instead, we follow
the unmistakable track
that inevitably leads
to celestial surety
in a heavenly
setting.

In the scriptures, we read that in the beginning, it was Jesus Christ Who created the heaven and the earth. (See Genesis 1:1 & Hebrews 1:10). Then, he said, "Let there be light." (Genesis 1:3). What is really remarkable about this is that He apparently made the entire universe in the dark!

Jesus Christ has promised us the sweet companionship of the Holy Ghost, Whose mission is to guide us through a portal of revelation to an epiphany where we might know for ourselves the truth of all things. (See John 14:16). As He molds and shapes us into new creatures in Christ (see 2 Corinthians 5:17), pure intelligence will flow unto us as the dews of Carmel.

The thermal efficiency of a propulsion system is a variable that seems to get lost in the shuffle when considering the feasibility of interstellar travel. The energy required to accelerate a vehicle to even a small fraction of the speed of light is astronomical, and because existing engine propulsion systems work at nowhere near 100% efficiency, the laws of thermodynamics dictate that the internal temperature of any conceivable system would rapidly increase until failure was experienced. There would be no practical way to dispose of the heat that would necessarily be generated as a byproduct of any system that would be deemed feasible by currently accepted standards. So too, our interactions with our Savior Jesus Christ is exothermic, as evidenced by the fire in our bones when our lives are in accord with the principles that govern the heavens. (See Jeremiah 20:9)

It stirs our blood when we peruse the journals of the terrestrial explorer Captain James Cook: "I intend to go, not only farther than any man has been before me, but as far as I think it is possible to go." His daring and bravado were legendary. He precariously ventured forth on uncharted seas, driven not only by the wind, but also by noble purpose. Cook carried out heroic voyages in a ship he called "Discovery," anticipating the star treks to be undertaken by latter-day adventurers who would go forth into the unfamiliar territory of the cosmos, as well as to the far reaches of the gospel, to find Jesus Christ.

In His ministry, our Lord and Savior Jesus Christ extended a simple invitation to those who were pure in heart: Deny the cares of the world and respond to a nobler call. However, the discipline to follow the "Royal Law" (see James 2:8), is alien to our temporal nature. After all, urging hedonists to exercise self-restraint is like asking truckers to avoid country music. Christians of convenience have not yet learned that it is only in His redeeming blood and through justification by the Holy Spirit that our souls can be sanctified.

Jesus Christ has the power to smooth out the bumps in the road during our journey thru mortality, and it gives our experiences a profoundly positive twist, to energize them with vitality, and us with the capacity to re-write the last chapters of our life-story; even to alter eternity.

In the familiar Hollywood cinematic portrayals of extraterrestrials who drop by earth to say hello, the encounters are generally accompanied by blinding light. It remains to be seen if that will be the case if or when we make First Contact, but in our mind's eye, we have set the stage for a dazzling 'close encounter.' In the first kind, an unidentified alien object is seen, but there is no environmental interaction. In the second kind, there are observable physical effects. In the third kind, however, extra-terrestrial beings make tangible First Contact with earthlings. The last scenario paints a portrait of visitors whose identity is intermingled with light. (See Psalms 37:6). Just so, our Savior affirmed that we shall see the "Son of man coming in the clouds with great power and glory." (Mark 13:26).

The practical model of life for purposeful living that is provided by a correct understanding of the principles and doctrines that form the substance of the teachings of Jesus Christ helps us reconcile our place in the cosmos with eternity, by giving us down-to-earth instruction relating to our heavenly potential. It gives us the tools to work out our salvation before the Lord, even as we deal with the distress of telestial trivia and grapple with the distractions of temporal trauma.

As fire in the sky, the theater of life exhibits a marquee that proclaims that the gospel of Jesus Christ is currently playing as its feature attraction. When its light streaks across the sky, its trajectory will trace a flaming trail sparkling over a cosmic ocean of thought. Over the ebb and flow of its tide, our Savior will be sustained in His work by the cohesive influence of a mighty foundation of faith. At that moment, we will be "no more strangers and foreigners, but fellowcitizens with the saints, and of the household of God." (Ephesians 2:19).

As we journey through "this vale of tears" (see Wycliffe's Bible, Psalms 84:6), our real journey to Jesus Christ will have only just begun. Having been born again through baptism, we'll press forward with complete dedication and with confidence, and a firm determination in Christ, having perfect faith and charity. When we do this, receiving nourishment and strength from the scriptures, and if we then endure to the end in righteousness, we will have obtained the greatest of all the gifts that our Heavenly Father could bestow.

The teachings of Jesus Christ suggests that we who have come to earth to fight the battle raging in the hearts of men on Saturday were counted as the valiant in the pre-earth existence, and that during the propaganda war that was waged by Satan to control the minds of his brothers and sisters, we were passionate in our defense of agency. Following that struggle, free will prevailed, and when it was time for the victorious spirits to come to the earth, they did so with a hunger for their hard-won freedom to choose their own destiny. Therefore, when those spirits are now controlled by compulsion in any degree of unrighteousness dominion, their ingrained tendency is to resist. Therefore, we need to be very cautious when interacting with our youth when questions arise that involve the vigorous exercise of their divine right of free will.

If we ignore the
tandem influences
of the Light of Christ
and the Holy Spirit that
nurture our innate yearning to
abhor mischief, and instead allow
ourselves to be habitually preoccupied
by trifling concerns, we sin by omission
and risk settling for life in a marshland of
mediocrity that quickly degenerates into
a quicksand of sin, from which there is
no escape unless we take advantage of
the spiritual buoyancy that has been
provided by our Savior.

The worth of the principles and
doctrine that are found in the teachings of Jesus
Christ is validated through our personal experience and
by our subsequent conversion. Our efforts to embrace them
become an outward expression of our dedication to obedience.
Ordinances become the public manifestation of our desire
to have a private covenant relationship with God. They
represent the voluntary surrender of our agency to a
higher power, and the subjugation of our will to
His. Our testimonies reflect the promises that
are manifested in the covenants that
we make and keep with God.

Our Savior Jesus Christ frees us from the limitations of our own ignorance, as well as from the constraints of mortality. It's in the scriptures where we learn to be at one with the majestic clockwork, "like a bird that, pausing in her flight a while on boughs to light, feels them give way beneath her and yet sings, knowing that she hath wings." (Victor Hugo).

Those of faltering faith who only casually look to Jesus Christ as their Savior can lose their focus, just as their eyesight may fade over time. First they squint, and then they'll hold the pages a little closer or a little further away, compensating for the inability to see clearly. Whether it is the printed page or their integrity that they cannot read, when they lose the Spirit, the result can be character-crippling compromise and a demoralizing crash of conscience that were not even on the radar back when they were preparing to embark upon their adventure of a lifetime.

In the last days, our society, which is by most standards "good," nevertheless has done a poor job of cultivating faith within the rising generation. If a culture really believes that the merits of faith are arbitrarily determined, that truth is relative, that there's no coherent Plan of God or divine design, or that faith in Jesus Christ is nothing but a delusion and a snare, or is the fabrication of frenzied minds, the stage is set for temporal and spiritual disasters that will be of biblical proportion.

We can see in the disciples of our Lord and Savior Jesus Christ those who've sought to harness the power of the priesthood, "to break mountains, to divide the seas, to dry up waters, to turn them out of their course; to put at defiance the armies of nations, to divide the earth, to break every band, to stand in the presence of God, to do all things according to his will, according to his command, subdue principalities and powers; and this by the will of the Son of God which was from before the foundation of the world. And (those who manifested) this faith, coming up unto this order of God, were translated and taken up into heaven." (J.S.T. Genesis 14:30-32).

As we journey through life, it helps if we have the celestial sign posts that have been provided by our Savior Jesus Christ to guide us thru the telestial traffic jams and cul-de-sacs that threaten to detour us from the strait and narrow way. The expanding circle of opportunity that is afforded by obedience to its principles blesses us to exchange the uncertain course adopted by those bound for the telestial kingdom for the solid reality of celestial certainty.

Faith in the Lord Jesus Christ catches us up in a rapture where we can almost hear legions of angels confirming that the earth was designed from before its foundation to be a smorgasbord for all the children of men. We are strangers from a realm of light, who have forgotten all, the memory of our former life, and the purpose of our call. And so we need to listen to the Spirit, to learn who we really are, and why we're here on earth. As we do so, the stage will be set for a heaven-sent reawakening.

Like the siren
song that tempted Odysseus
from an island in the western sea
between Aeaea and the rocks of Scylla,
we go mad when we listen to the seductive
strains of unwholesome melodies, and that is
why its contrary of uplifting music can be a
pleasing accompaniment to our engagement
with Jesus Christ. As Henry Wadsworth
Longfellow declared: "Music is
the universal language
of mankind."

All of us
are repeatedly
faced with occasions
when withdrawals must be
made from our spiritual bank
accounts. When we respond to the
Spirit, Who drives us to our knees to
help us to recognize the awesome power
of the Atonement, we put the principle of
repentance to its test, and we remember the
promise of redemption by Jesus Christ. But
we don't write checks that we can't cash. We
realize that only when regular deposits have
been made over a period of time, can we rely
upon the cornucopia of comfort created by
a cushion of confidence that becomes the
currency of faith flowing from conduct
that is reliably consistent with the
core curriculum of contrition.

On our home planet, as mutually exclusive trends seem to be developing, we hope that the prevailing movement will lead to a multi-cultural, tolerant, scientific, nurturing, interactive, and interdependent society, with equal access to education and employment, and to the satisfaction of our temporal needs. Social media, rock and roll, fashion, sports, the European Union, NAFTA, cybercurrency, and English as an emerging universally understood language, are evidence that humanity is hesitantly inching in the direction of the type of planetary stability that only faith in our Savior Jesus Christ can provide.

Does Jesus Christ, the Creator of heaven and earth, provide mere mortals with boundaries and conditions that extend beyond our five senses? William W. Phelps mused: If we "could hie to Kolob in the twinkling of an eye, and then continue onward with that same speed to fly, do you think that (we) could ever, thru all eternity, find out the generation where Gods began to be, or see the grand beginning where space did not extend, or view the last creation, where Gods and matter end? Methinks the Spirit whispers: 'No man has found pure space, nor seen the outside curtains where nothing has a place.' ("If You Could Hie to Kolob").

Jesus Christ motivates us to try the virtue of the word of God. We do so, that we might reap its rewards, and then, with diligence, patience, and long-suffering, harvest the fruit of the Tree of Life from its low hanging branches.

When we stand before Jesus Christ at the Bar of Judgment, the evidence will be presented, and our acceptance or rejection of the Author of Eternal Salvation will largely determine our reward or our punishment. There is within each of us an inherent capacity to generate faith with the impetus to do so coming from the Holy Ghost. This makes our trials, tailor-made though they may be, eminently fair. As a matter of fact, the deck has been stacked in our favor by the Light of Christ and the Holy Ghost to make it that much easier to bear our own witness.

Before we commit ourselves to any significant course of action, such as when we determine to engage our Savior Jesus Christ, we make the issue a matter of fervent prayer, in order to experience the confirming witness of the Spirit. When, in our bosoms, we receive fire for the deed, we cannot fail, no matter how challenging, daunting, or problematic our holy quest might seem to be.

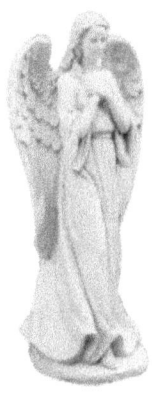

It may seem to us that the easier way out is to adopt the ways of the world, and we may find that it is harder to acknowledge that there is an autobiographical thread within each of us that leads all the way back to the Savior. Sometimes, we can't see the forest for the trees, or that we are as the acorns of mighty oaks. Because of our distractions, we lose focus on the things that are the most important to us, like the illumination of His gospel, which is a contrary to swirling mists of darkness.

The power
to save our souls is
manifest in doctrine that
is published by Jesus Christ,
and it is our solemn oaths that
trigger a cleansing. The process
of our sanctification through the
Atonement allows us to draw near
to God's throne in heaven, from
which He will bestow upon our
heads the blessings we need,
instead of those that we
thought we had
wanted.

One of the greatest blessings
that can flow from our Savior Jesus
Christ is that by triggering the mechanism of
the Atonement that we might become clean in the
sight of God, we are able to get moving again on the
pathway to perfection. After repentance, our Heavenly
Father will remember our sins no more. It is true that we
might recall them, insofar as they increase our testimonies
and help us to become more stalwart soldiers in the army of
Christ. But we will no longer be worn down by guilt or be
estranged from the Spirit because of former filthiness.
We will have been released from our bondage to sin
because we have been cleansed in the blood of
Christ, which is the most liberating gift
of God that we could receive.

When we
are faithful, we will
seldom forget to call upon
God to protect us from worldly
influences, and from that old serpent
Beelzebub. We are painfully aware that
Satan is abroad in the land, because we have
often heard and sometimes respond to a siren
call coming from Babylon, that rings loudly
in our ears, even as we seek to sing the song
of redeeming love that is the melodious
rhythm typifying the work of our
Redeemer Jesus Christ.

It is only natural that nearly everyone
who has ever lived on the earth has wanted to go
to heaven, but no one seems to want to die first, which
is also natural. For to "everything there is a season and a
time for every matter under heaven. A time to be born, and a
time to die." (Ecclesiastes 3:1). The teachings of Jesus Christ only
make sense if they're studied within the larger context of the Plan of
Salvation, which specifies that "as in Adam all die, even so in Christ
shall all be made alive." (1 Corinthians 15:22). This is an inevitable
transition, and it can be dramatic, but whether we go out quietly or
with fanfare, "neither death nor life ... shall be able to separate us
from the love of God." (Romans 8:38). Because of His pure love,
"the last enemy that shall be destroyed is death." (1 Corinthians
15:26). Parley Pratt echoed Paul with a similar declaration:
I have received the holy anointing, and I can never rest
until the last enemy is conquered, death ha been
destroyed, and truth reigns triumphant."

In the theology of
Jesus Christ, the arguably
evil element of opposition seems
to be a pesky contrary to life and
light. But upon closer examination,
it is just a decoration adorning the
pathway to our joyful reunion in
eternity, where we will meet our
families at the pleasing bar
of God at a missionary
reunion that defies
description.

To Jesus Christ,
the gates of hell are
gaping jaws, dripping
with the sickening slurry
of the saliva of Satan that has
been saturated by sin. (See D&C
122:7). They menacingly depict
the entrance to the forbidding spirit
prison of the unjust. The way to avoid
this awful portal is to offer the Lord the
required sacrifice of a heart that's broken
down in sorrow for sin, and in the spirit
of contrition to approach God's throne in
an attitude of purposeful repentance,
hoping to obtain forgiveness thru
the tender mercies related
to His grace.

To Jesus Christ, His disciples are those who, with determination, will enjoy the fruits of faith and the spirit of repentance by maintaining an unshakeable conviction that they are the sons and daughters of God with promises to keep, and miles to go before they sleep.

In tandem with the Savior, the Holy Spirit will animate our heart strings to remind us that we were once fluent in the heavenly language that was spoken in our pre-mortal home. Even now, its voice is rhythmical and melodious, soothing to our ears, and calming to our souls. When we hear the Spirit whisper: "You're a stranger here," we are comforted with the reassurance that all of us have "wandered from a more exalted sphere." (Eliza R. Snow). The Holy Ghost helps us to examine what it means to be anxiously engaged and inspires us to plumb the depth of our commitment to our Lord Jesus Christ, sensitizes us to the nobility of His work, and expands upon the visions of immortality. The Spirit helps us to retain an awareness of our close proximity to heaven, whose glory we only recently left when the time came for it to be our turn on earth.

Actively
responding to the
promptings of the Spirit
that we feel as, in the name
of Jesus Christ we engage our
Father in prayer, can become
the powerful generator of
positive energy.

Societies all over the earth have
always paid dearly for their lack of
vision, as they close their minds and their
hearts to an expansion by the Spirit. The Dark
Ages remain the worst-case scenario, but in some
respects we are once again living in that stifling era.
When a culture loses its spiritual equilibrium and rejects
the blessings that could have been theirs if they had accepted
the principles, doctrine, and teachings of Jesus Christ, they seem
to re-adjust their values in an expedient realignment with worldly
coordinates. Today, the worship of gods of wood and stone is justified
as multiculturalism. Perversion is embraced and is legitimized as an
alternative lifestyle. The poor are exploited under the guise of programs
sponsored by government. Unborn children are torn from their mother's
wombs, and the collective conscience is assuaged by calling it pro-choice.
The gross abuses of power are justified as the means to an end, and every
obscenity pollutes the media, but new-speak characterizes it as freedom
of expression. The target's been moved so often that self-congratulatory
pundits believe that they are scoring bulls-eyes when they are really
far from the mark. The prophet Isaiah saw our day, when he warned
Israel: "Wo unto them that call evil good, and good evil; that put
darkness for light, and light for darkness; that put bitter
for sweet, and sweet for bitter." (Isaiah 5:20)

Those who truly engage Jesus Christ have no need for an independent spokesperson to interpret His message. He stands independently on His own merits, which cultivates our desire to dig more deeply into the themes woven into the tapestry of His gospel. As we do so, the Holy Ghost blesses us with insight, intuition, and inspiration, sweeping us up in the quickening currents of unreserved revelatory experiences with heaven.

Jesus Christ is the Architect of His gospel and of the cosmos, including the "Pillars of Creation," elephant trunks of interstellar gas and dust in the Eagle Nebula, +/- seven thousand light years from earth. In an 1857 sermon by London pastor Charles Haddon Spurgeon, entitled "The Condescension of Christ," he employed the phrase to describe both the physical world and the force that binds it all together, that stems from our divine center. "Now wonder, ye angels," Spurgeon wrote concerning His birth, "the Infinite has become an infant. He, upon whose shoulders the universe doth hang, nurses at his mother's breast; He who created all things, and bears up the pillars of creation."

Jesus Christ
blesses us with
the knowledge that
mortality is only a tiny
fraction of a much larger
reality. It is only when we
believe it to be the sum and the
substance of our existence that our
perspective is faulty. When we can't
recognize the stability of a divine center
of faith, and we fail to make the revelatory
expenditure of energy that is necessary to
cultivate its sense of permanency in our
lives, everything tends to collapse
into disarray.

Under the influence and through the power of the Holy
Ghost, the teachings of Jesus Christ are destined to be preached in
all the world in a day when many will spurn at the doings of the Lord.
To spurn something is to "ignore scornfully, to refuse, or to trample." Since
Its publication, the world has tried very hard to ignore the good news, but very
persistently, it just won't go away. "The standard of truth has been erected; no
unhallowed hand can stop the work from progressing; persecutions may rage,
mobs may combine, armies may assemble, calumny may defame, but the
truth of God will go forth boldly, nobly, and independent, till it has
penetrated every continent, visited every clime, swept every
country, and sounded in every ear, till the purposes
of God shall be accomplished, and the Great
Jehovah shall say the work is done."
(Joseph Smith).

Traveling the
road to a testimony of
our Redeemer Jesus Christ
often takes time, and in the
short term, there may be reverses.
But over the long haul, we'll move to
higher plateaus, and God will be there
to cheer us on. When we allow ourselves
to become discouraged, we try to remember
the observation of James: "We count them
happy which endure." (James 5:11).

At least a few of the beams of
starlight within which we are enveloped
have come from the constellations of Cygnus,
Aquila, Sagittarius, and Carina. They have been
hurtling through space for 2,025 years (traveling over
12 million billion miles during that time), ever since they
left their host stars (2,025 light years ago) At least some of
the light we will see tonight, may have burst forth from its
home system at the exact same time as the Savior's birth. If
that is the case, we might even now be participating in the
spectacular light-show of the Nativity, and we may even
now be playing significant roles in the drama that is
presented to the world thru His mortal ministry. We
recall how Jesus Christ, the Author of Salvation
asked of Job: "Where wast thou when I laid the
foundations of the earth (during that time)
when the morning stars sang together,
and all the sons of God shouted
for joy? (Job 38:4 & 7).

Those who desire to walk in the footsteps of our Lord and Savior Jesus Christ need to remember to work within His timetable. The world insists on the instant satisfaction of its curiosity, and the immediate gratification of desires through its natural senses, but those who would become His disciples remove the latchets from their shoes, realizing that they are in the presence of burning bushes, and they patiently wait upon the Lord God to speak to them. Babylon remains pre-occupied with the occult, and with magic, diviners, and soothsayers, spinning the roulette wheels of life and dreaming of the bounty that will be theirs if only their lucky number comes up, while disciples stand in holy places and are not moved, as they carefully listen for the faint whisperings of the still small voice of the Holy Spirit.

When the time comes for us to confidently move from the spectator gallery to stand before the pleasing bar of God in the Court of Justice, as we certainly will, the evidence will be presented by angels and witnesses. Our previous conformity to or rejection of eternal law will determine our reward or punishment. However, due to the influence of the Light of Christ and the Holy Ghost, our innate capacity to have generated active saving faith in the divine origin of the doctrine of Jesus Christ will make our experience there more than just a roll of the dice. We'll then understand that our lives had not been a zero-sum game. In fact, the cards had been marked and the deck had been stacked in our favor. Life had not been just a game of chance, but rather a labor of skill and adventure, for knowledge is power, rendering the Judgment a win-win for both ourselves and God.

Our Lord and Savior
Jesus Christ dispenses good
news and good therapy. Hew has
the capacity to adjust our eyes to
the light of the stars in the heavens
springing, and of attuning our ears
to hear the angels singing hosanna to
His name. In His gospel, "still is sung,
in every tongue, the angels' song of
glory." ("In Wondering Awe").

When we gaze up at
the night sky, we are looking back
in time. The light striking our retinas
from the farthest objects in the Milky Way
has been zipping across the cosmos for tens of
thousands of years. We see its stars not as they
really are, but only as they were long ago. And yet,
when we shift our focus and investigate the eternities
through the clarifying lens provided by Jesus Christ,
we witness the future. There must needs be opposition
for us to see things, not as they once were, nor as they
now are, but as they might be. In a sense, we need
the opposition of death to really experience life,
and that everlasting. We need the 'jewels'
that are scattered about on the beaches
of our lives, though they may be
nothing more than colored
glass, to see that there
are diamonds in
the sky.

Without
the viewpoint
provided by our
Savior Jesus Christ,
we are forced to concede
that only "two possibilities
exist: either we are alone in the
universe, or we are not, and both
are equally terrifying."
(Arthur C. Clarke).

Disciples of our Lord and
Savior Jesus Christ reflect poise
under provocation and are sensitive
to the needs of others. They are empathic
and humble, and they are less concerned
with telestial trinkets, but are more focused
on celestial sureties. The meek who embrace
His gospel are selfless and harbor no secret
agendas. They are repulsed by sin, rejoice
in the truth, are drawn toward the light,
and are continually open to that which
is good. Meekness may be one of the
greatest of all the qualities of God
Himself, Who is the possessor of
all spiritual gifts. Without it,
we are nothing, because our
progress in the direction
of His Divine Nature
cannot sustain its
momentum.

Thanks to our Lord and Savior Jesus Christ, the Light of our lives (see D&C 88:11-13), grows in intensity and becomes ever "brighter until the perfect day." (D&C 50:24). We come from God, Who is our Home, "trailing clouds of glory." (William Wordsworth).

During our exploration of the mystery surrounding our Savior Jesus Christ, our relationship with God is etched into our spiritual identity. We become perfect in our faith as we make a connection with Deity. That is how members of The Church of Jesus Christ of Latter-day Saints have the presumption to declare that it is our destiny to rule as kings and queens, priests and priestesses, in the house of Israel forever, and to reign with authority over kingdoms, thrones, principalities, powers, dominions, and exaltations. That will happen only when our connection to God has matured to such magnitude and strength that our identities become indistinguishable from each other. That can only occur when we have received both His image and likeness in our countenances in the process of a mind-bending spiritual metamorphosis. And it is revelation from God, manifested in prayer, that will facilitate this transformation.

A twisted caricature of our Heavenly Father's great Plan of Deliverance from Death draws many to the various sects of Christianity by the supposed appeal of the Savior to transfer power from Him to those who profess to be His earthly representatives. But too often, upon closer inspection, it becomes apparent that these sects are only competing for market share. For them, the Bible's attraction is its ability to communicate knowledge without the need for revelation from the Holy Ghost. Their claim to the priesthood may have a certain panache, but upon a closer inspection it may become depressingly clear that it has acquired the status of an office that automatically bestows power without regard for the spiritual or moral qualifications of its possessors.

A typical but twisted strategy of those who wear the academic robes of the false priesthood is to attack the revealed doctrine of Jesus Christ that may conflict with their strongly-held traditions. They do this by wresting the word of God, and by misrepresenting its meaning away from its true signification; by perverting, misinterpreting, misupplying, or turning it from its legitimate application. When self-appointed professors of religion twist the meaning of the word of God to their own advantage, we can be certain that reasonable dialogue, insight, understanding, and Zion's welfare are not on the agenda and are far from their thoughts. Those who would break windows because they claim they want to breathe fresh air are more excited by the sound of tinkling glass than they are by the thought of letting light into the world.

The teachings of Jesus Christ requires us to
focus our vision on Him, as well as on brotherhood,
agency, equality, stewardship, accountability, charity,
consecration, and selflessness. "How carefully most men and
women creep into nameless graves, while now and then one or two
forget themselves into immortality." (Phillips Brooks). The
gospel requires of us that higher level thinking, as well
as seeing through eyes that have been trained on
eternity, beyond the limited horizon
of our natural sight.

Within the parameters of God's Plan of Salvation is a power that we
call the Holy Ghost. He may not be readily identifiable, but we are always
under His spell. Sometimes, we become so preoccupied with telestial trash and
other trivia that we fail to recognize is that it is the Spirit Who has created the
pattern that facilitates our spiritual transformation from narcissistic self-
absorption to lives that are centered on our Savior Jesus Christ. He justifies
ordinances that allow us, no matter where along the path of progress
we may find ourselves, to make the same regularly recurring
recommitment to internalize principles that have been
designed to orient us toward heaven and to walk
in the light, so that we might continue to
endure to the end, not in our sins,
but in righteousness.

Our Lord and Savior Jesus Christ teaches us how to be benevolently blind and to experience fresh perspectives as we recapture the innocence of youth. We have perfectly functional optic nerves, but even more significantly, the gospel reverses the gradual atrophy of our spiritual sensitivity. It rekindles our capacity to see more clearly by looking the other way, beyond the faults of others. We turn the other cheek, give others the benefit of the doubt, go the second mile, and do to others as we would have them do to us. In essence, we turn a blind eye when others fall short of our expectations or fail to measure up. Benevolent blindness helps us to comprehend the love that God has for us.

To be wrapped securely within the fold of the Good Shepherd, our Savior Jesus Christ, is to find ourselves in a sanctuary of light and perfection. His clear doctrine constitutes a blueprint that illustrates how to make our way thru mortality; it is a map that will guide us Home; it is a table that identifies perils and pitfalls to be avoided; it is a chart to fall back on when tempests beset us, and a graph that outlines and measures our progress on the pathway to perfection. The internet requires only that we have computer literacy, relevant hardware and software, and access to a network with an I.P. address. So too, the Savior has the potential to bring meaning to our chaotic world and fluency to those who are spiritually tongue-tied. In simple terms, He offers us a golden ticket that is our key to happiness.

When we left the lone
and dreary world and walked into
the light that is cast by Jesus Christ, we were
given the promise of a new lease on life by Him in
Whom we could place our trust. Few of us would care to
repeat kindergarten, and yet when, by the grace of God,
we are reintroduced to our primeval childhood, we are
literally given a second chance to get it right. We
enthusiastically welcome the opportunity, and
it never enters our mind to throw a tantrum,
sulk in a corner, or fall down on the floor
and flail our arms and legs.

We pay dearly for our secular education, and expect to receive a
return on our investment. But through the grace of God we will be
blessed to participate in a far more valuable spiritual curriculum
that will ask us to enroll as missionaries at the University of the
God of Jeshurun." (Matthew 10:33). This is equivalent to being
offered a scholarship in a Bachelor of Fine Arts program that
doesn't ask for temporal tuition, and whose only entrance
requirements are a ready heart and a willing mind.
The design of its program is solely intended to
expand the reach of our Savior Jesus Christ
to include all of God's children. In this
sense, He is all about affirmative
action.

The
account of
the Creation that
was written by Moses
provided only generalities
that relate to the Fall of Adam
and Eve and to the Atonement of
Christ. That doctrine is more fully
explained throughout His gospel, and
when we receive a witness of the Spirit.
We must have clear understanding, in
order to generate the faith necessary to
be clean from the blood and sins of
this generation, that we may live
abundantly, and become the
heirs of salvation and
exaltation.

Among the most remarkable gifts
we receive from the Holy Ghost are our mood
swings, comprising the rollercoaster ride between
happiness and sadness, strength and weakness,
certitude and doubt, tranquility and agitation,
pleasure and pain, serenity and disquietude,
and self-composure and anger. In order to
experience the joy that is associated with
our discipleship, Jesus Christ gives us
many opportunities to grapple with
and master, these emotional
opposites.

Our season of probation
may feel as if it were endless winter,
for it is a time of testing, or of putting to the
proof our declared values. Jesus Christ offers each
of us the opportunity to experience a new beginning,
which is why our baptism of fire and of the Spirit
is characterized as a rebirth. When we are Born
Again, we are free from the stain of our sins
and their related soul scars that have
been accumulating ever since we
became accountable for
our actions.

If we express mistrust or disbelief in the
teachings of our Lord Jesus Christ, we won't be
able to discover the resources that are necessary to
successfully continue our journey and, therefore, we
will be damned. God's Plan is not a corruptible contract
that was drawn up by attorneys with one eye on billable
hours, and there are neither codicils, corollaries, footnotes,
nor exceptions to the rule. His laws are subject to neither
appeal, amendment, nor interpretation. Ordinances
and covenants are central to the execution of the
Plan and baptism is the hinge pin upon which
swings the gate leading to eternal life. It is
perfect, and is all the more remarkable
because of its symmetry and
simplicity.

When we tap into the power source of our
Lord Jesus Christ, even if we have set the flow to
trickle charge, amazing change takes place as He
becomes an inexhaustible supply of clean, green,
and renewable energy. He is a reserve upon
which we may draw during any time of
need, for there is no power but that
which comes of the Spirit.

We are all newly arrived expatriates
from the kingdom of heaven who are now living
on foreign soil, and yet we remain the spirit sons and
daughters of our Maker. Even as we enjoy our travels in
foreign lands, and as we accumulate passport stamps from
a wide variety of exciting destinations, the guide book to which
we consult during our travels centers on the teachings of Jesus
Christ, that explain in detail the elements of God's Plan. With it,
we enjoy a measure of the divine nature. If we continue to develop
His characteristics during our probationary sojourn here on earth,
we will eventually become as He is, having assumed both His
image and likeness. When we return to our celestial home,
we will be anxious to sit down with our heavenly family
and friends to share the exciting stories that we have
brought home from our mortal missions
to the four corners of the earth.

We are disciples of our Lord Jesus Christ if we trace His footsteps to the waters of baptism and follow His example in obedience to law and in a demonstration of our desire to fulfill all righteousness. We will receive a remission of our sins, become members of His church, and receive the gift of the Holy Ghost. Baptism is the gateway thru which we must pass if it is our desire to move out of the shadows into the marvelous light of day to witness the power and glory of His gospel.

If we lack the inherent stability of our Savior Jesus Christ, Who illuminates the path that lies ahead, we may be seduced by Satan's siren song that creates within us an insatiable desire for the world's goods. Blurred vision may cause us to forsake our life on the strait and narrow way and instead embark upon a dangerous stroll down the broad promenades of Idumea. If we follow that road, our desires may be satiated, as we are enamored by its glitz and glamor, but at the same time, we will lose purpose, power, and concentration. When we come to depend more upon our own strength than on our spiritual preparedness, we will be more likely in times of need to redouble our own efforts, and be less inclined to drop to our knees, cling to our faith, and establish a partnership and working relationship with God through the mighty power of prayer, so that we may discover ways to successfully address and solve our problems.

The teachings of our Redeemer Jesus
Christ have been gathered into an operations
manual that was developed under the guidance
and inspiration of the Holy Ghost, providing hands-
on training to teach us the lesson that when we plan our
work, and then work our plan, we will enjoy success in our
endeavors. We know that proper prior planning prevents poor
priesthood performance. We dream big, and by establishing
deadlines, we create realistic goals. We know by our own
experience that work without vision is drudgery, and
vision without work is dreamery, but work with
vision is destiny. We know these things to be
true because of our experience, and as the
inevitable result of undeviating
commitment to the cause of
truth, justice, and the
American Way.

Jesus Christ is there to strengthen us when we find it
difficult to look up to Heavenly Father for guidance, over to the
priesthood for support, around to seek others to whom they might
minister, or down in an attitude of meekness and humility. It
helps us to develop the faith to enjoy pliancy, flexibility, and a
longitudinal perspective, and to brush the cobwebs from our
minds, to experience elasticity in our spiritual muscles
that allows faith to stretch all the way to the gates
of heaven where God will wipe the tears from
our eyes, bind up our wounds, envelop
us in His love, and encircle us
with His compassion.

As we look around at a world that seems to have gone completely mad, Jesus Christ remains an island in the storm and our refuge from the uncertainties of life. To those who are unsure of themselves, who are tentative, hesitant, or afraid, it speaks a language of comfort, stability, direction, and purpose.

It is not difficult to see how easily undisciplined and self-absorbed minds can be swayed by a siren song that is so seductively sent by Satan, as we witness unprincipled character crumble in the face of telestial temptations that are so tantalizing and yet are so traumatizing. The more our society focuses on the idols of the day, the less prevalent will be the legitimate rule of God, and the less frequently will the masses turn to the mighty power of prayer or to our Savior Jesus Christ. It is this substitution of the sacred by the profane that is abominable in His view because it hamstrings our progression. The unconverted have a hard time understanding the concept that when we are faithful and diligent in our obedience to God, our agency is released to enjoy its greatest expression. When, by the power of the Holy Ghost, we know the truth, and act on our belief, we shall be made free.

Our sure witness by the power of the Holy Ghost
is a remarkable thing. In the initial stages of our spiritual
awakening, testimony is born in the classical sense, with both
physical and emotional struggle, and with labor pains. Then,
throughout its infancy, it must be nursed, be given tender
care, and receive our almost undivided attention, until
it has gathered the strength to stand independently.
Those who have thus matured in their testimony
of Jesus Christ may then bear its weight, and
share it with others, without the need for
warrant, or external reinforcement.

The teachings of Jesus Christ suggest
that in order to stem the rising tide of evil in
the world we must first abase ourselves to the benefit
of those who are in need of both temporal and spiritual
nourishment. We must never allow ourselves to be caught
up in the machinery of the church without making contact
with "The Glory of the Lord." (Ezekiel 1:28). If we do so, life
can feel like a treadmill. The gospel is dynamic, and when
we share the "Bread of Life" (John 6:48) with others, we, too,
are nourished as we are propelled to new spiritual heights.
The light of the Spirit chases away the darkness and
provides sunbursts of sensitivity that charge
our spiritual batteries with His energy
as we exhort others to continue
the good fight.

The teachings of Jesus
Christ confirm that baptism
needs to be performed by those who
possess the authority to act in His name.
By its power, we are guided to the scriptures
that provide the specific words to be used in
the baptismal prayer, invoking the names
of all three members of the Godhead to
reinforce the sanction and approval
of God the Father, His Son
Jesus Christ, and the
Holy Ghost.

Our Advocate, the Lord Jesus Christ, will always
be there when happiness seems to elude us, especially
if we've been overzealous in our efforts to create a carefree
environment. When we fail to do so, we try even harder, never
coming to the realization that happiness is born of contrast. Our
natural inclination is to seek immediate relief from discomfort,
and to quickly petition our Heavenly Father for deliverance.
However, when there was no room at the inn, both Joseph and
Mary, who was soon to deliver Her Firstborn Son, were
uncomplaining. They realized that if they were to
find joy, it would first be necessary to experience
its opposite, or hardship. Their eyes had been
opened. Too often, ours seem to be closed,
not in prayer, but in resignation to
a fate that seems to be beyond
our power to control.

Those who are of a fragile moral fiber and a weak character mistakenly think they have found happiness in worldly pleasures, but this is because they never learned to recognize its opposite. Because they confuse nature with nobility, they mistake wickedness for happiness. But when their behavior is a reflection of worldliness rather than of the light of Jesus Christ, when their actions harmonize more with secular standards and less with spiritual certainties, or when they are with their friends but are without God, their false sense of security will be unsustainable. Young people talk about Best Friends Forever, but the Savior helps us to think more in terms of Being Forever Faithful.

Ironically, it just might be the mercurial element of time itself that is the source of our weariness and even of our impatience, and it could be its passage that causes us to gradually lose interest in our Savior Jesus Christ. The Holy Ghost will help us to regain the enthusiasm that should describe our nature. Participation in a program of temporal and spiritual fitness will unshackle us from the self-limiting time constraints that would otherwise hamper our forward momentum. The easy-to-understand principles of the Plan can teach us how to shed the self-limiting restrictions of time, harness an awareness of the sweeping panorama of eternal progression, and bring all into sharp focus. When the hands of our internal clock have been re-calibrated to move according to a celestial standard, we will have created the temporal and spiritual independence to explore the endless equations of eternity.

The invitation of the Holy Ghost is to
steer clear of the telestial turf that is the territorial
treasure trove of the tempter. Our Savior Jesus Christ
offers us, instead, horns of sanctuary in a haven
where ordinances with their related covenants
work on our spirits to fill us with love and
with faith, as a living fire that is
able to purge from us the
detritus of sin.

Those who once basked
in the light radiating from
Jesus Christ but have afterward
defiantly and deliberately chosen to
turn their backs on Him don't need to dye
their skins with blood, as did the Lamanites,
to broadcast their apostasy to the world. Instead,
they unwittingly adopt other equally disgusting,
degenerate, and distinguishing lifestyle choices,
staining their skin with the putrefying stigma
of corrupt political, cultural, economic, social,
and religious ideology.

The Lord Jesus
Christ teaches us by
the witness of the Spirit that
the Sacrament, together with His
Atonement makes life eternal, love
immortal, and death but a horizon,
which is nothing, save the limit
of our sight

When we are full of the Holy Spirit
of God, we are distinguished by our zeal toward
our Redeemer Jesus Christ. We attend to our duties and
responsibilities with ardent feeling and fervor. We take care,
however, to avoid overzealous behavior, because we know that it
can lead to religious fanaticism, a condition wherein we could lose
sight of our objectives while redoubling our efforts. This condition
would put us in jeopardy of seduction by the devil, for if we
were to walk in darkness, we would stumble over hidden
obstacles intentionally placed before us that were
designed to bring us into subjection to
that powerful adversary.

We who embrace the gospel
have confidence in its promise that
we will find joy living under its spell.
Our happiness isn't the product of wishful
thinking nor is it a misguided reliance on
assurances that lack a reasonable expectation
of fulfillment. Instead, it is the inevitable result
of faith in Christ, synchronized with mastery of
the discipline to control our desires and emotions
within the bounds that He has established. When
our priorities are in harmony with the principles
and doctrines of the kingdom, our actions, that
reflect His noble character, speak louder than
words and paint a portrait of a God-centered
earth that will become the shared sensory
experience of those who've committed
by covenant to live out their lives
in obedience to the laws of
heaven.

Because of the resurrection
of our Lord and Savior Jesus Christ
following His mortal ministry, we will
all pass from physical death to immortality,
which is a term that describes the condition of
our bodies when they've been eternally reunited
with our spirits. This will come as a free gift to
all who've ever lived on the earth irrespective
of their obedience to the laws of His
gospel of love. (See John
13:34).

Obedience to the teachings of our Savior Jesus Christ promises life and the light of the Spirit, in contrast to darkness typifying the stark reality of the devils' counterfeit proposal. At best, he can deliver only spiritual decay and eternal obscurity. There was ideological war in heaven engaging its combatants in a death-grip struggle that shook the heavens and the very foundations of the earth, and a third part were the deplorable casualties of war who first lost their vision and then surrendered their happiness and hope.

Until the Reformation, the majestic clockwork reflected in the teachings of our Lord and Savior Jesus Christ fell on ears that were willing but that were deaf to the Latin tongue. "Is it not a shame," asked William Tyndall in 1528, "that we Christians come so oft to church in vain, when he of four score years old knoweth no more than he that was born yesterday?" Thanks to Tyndale, in these latter days, the ready availability of the scriptures in our native tongue has changed the nature of that equation. In that sense, at least, the new math is a good thing.

The first crucial step we must take if we wish to ignite the process of gaining a witness of the truth is to have faith. It is only when we have come to know that "the Lord the God of Hosts is His Name" (Amos 4:13), will the Spirit bless us with an understanding of the gospel of Jesus Christ. As our faith blossoms, we will gain the power to do whatever is right to do under the circumstances, which in general is to "repent and be baptized … for the remission of sins, and (to) receive the Holy Ghost." (Acts 2:38). Then will come the fruits of faith, which grounds testimony on the bedrock of experience, that, in turn, leads to salvation, and even exaltation in the kingdom of God.

As we inexorably move through time, which is the fire in which we burn, our God-given qualities are annealed in the crucible of experience. We make our way to the eternal element of the Spirit without the exercise of inappropriate control on God's part. Misguided intervention would only stifle our development from dependency, as little children, to independency and self-actualization, and lastly to our interdependency as committed Christian disciples who are intertwined with our Savior Jesus Christ. All has been perfectly choreographed, with each element of the principles of the Plan of God working together on our familiar terrestrial stage to execute the grand design of our Father in Heaven.

Our Savior Jesus Christ blesses us with an understanding of where we came from, why are we here, and where we are going. Perhaps additional insight that hints at the answers to these fundamental questions is supported by our discovery of the seething background radiation from the Big Bang, that makes the blood coursing through our veins hot to the touch.

The great Deceiver has done well with his various pet projects designed to distort true principles and give lies the ring of truth. He uses deception to detour us toward character crippling personality precipices. Our Savior Jesus Christ is a clear and shining Contrary because lurking in the shadows is a many faceted, flickering light show of deception, with shades of grey that threaten to overpower and engulf us in a world in darkness. In the midst of the various counterfeits in Babylon, if it were not for the Savior, it would be very difficult to differentiate doctrine from its lies.

Our Lord and Savior Jesus Christ provides a place of refuge for us to go and have the Spirit more fully in our lives. We no longer put to death those who violate the Law of the Sabbath, yet when we deliberately alienate ourselves from the influence of heaven, we put a halt to our progression because we die spiritually. The holy sanctuary of prayer is a place of renewal and our fortification against the challenges to spirituality that constantly assault our fortresses of faith. God designed prayer to see how we'll conduct our lives when left on our own, after having received instruction regarding what we ought to be doing. (See Luke 21:36).

Perhaps the fairy tale is true that choice spirits have been saved to come to earth in the Last Days. At the very least, it is an exhilarating experience to have been an active participant in the work of our Lord and Savior Jesus Christ as the Restoration unfolds during these formative years of the Latter-day Church, and to think that our efforts could have a small influence over the promise that He "Cometh Quickly." (D&C 51:20). The Old Testament spanned about 3,600 years, the Book of Mormon 1,000 years, and the New Testament 100 years. The Latter-day work has been in progress now for almost 200 years and the stone that has been cut out of the mountain is filling the earth. (See Daniel 2:35). Surely, the Lord will "suddenly come to His temple." (Malachi 3:1).

Our Savior Jesus Christ

Devotionals
for each day of the year

Afterword

We know
that Jesus is the Christ
by the power of the Spirit, but we
are converted when by faith we obey
His teachings. It is not enough to believe
in the Lord, because belief is only the mental
assent to the validity of an eternal truth, without
the moral element of responsibility that we call faith.
We believe "that there is one God," and by so doing, we do
well. But "the devils also believe and tremble." (James 2:19).
Our faith in the Savior is dead, or is of no efficacy, if it is not
accompanied by the works that are performed by His disciples. I
have written these devotionals relating to our Lord Jesus Christ in
the hope that they will provide us with encouragement during our
journey to the veil, where we will kneel at His feet and He will call
to us by name, saying: "Well done, thou good and faithful
servant. Thou hast been faithful over a few things. I will
make thee ruler over many things. Enter thou into
the joy of thy Lord." (Matthew 25:21).

Our Savior Jesus Christ

Devotionals
for each day of the year

Appendix One

We believe in our Savior Jesus Christ. **But more than that, we** testify of His ante-mortal existence (see John 1:1-3 & 14, John 8:58, & John 17:5) and His foreordination to be the Redeemer of the world. (See 1 Peter 1:198-20). The scriptures speak of His relationship with our Father in Heaven (see Like 1:35, Matthew 3:17, & Matthew 17:5), of His divine investiture of authority (see John 3:35, 5:26-27, 8:28-29, 12:49-50, & 17:2), and of His His condescension in taking a mortal body. (See Philippians 2:5-8). Thus, we can better understand His temptations, and the power, might, dominion, and authority that typified His earthly ministry. (See Jude 1:25-25).

At His baptism, He demonstrated by example the way for us to follow. (See Matthew 3:15). In His ministry, He taught with simplicity the truths of the gospel. (See 2 Corinthians 11:3). In the Garden of Gethsemane, He revealed His strength and compassion. (See Hebrews 5:9). The crucifixion, then, was only an apostrophe, and His death but a pause allowing us to re-focus attention on His resurrection and ascension into heaven.

When He comes again, it will be in the clouds (see Matthew 24:30, & Acts 1:9-11), accompanied by the Church of the Firstborn. (See Hebrews 12:23). His Second Coming will usher in His Millennial Reign. (See Revelation 24:6). For a thousand years, His gospel will penetrate every soul and burn brightly in every bosom.

He is our Advocate with the Father (see 1 John 2:1), and is the Bread of Life. (See John 6:35). He is the of worlds without number (see Hebrews 1:2 & Colossians 1:16), and the Deliverer of the Covenant. (See Romans 11:26-27).

He is Emmanuel (see Matthew 1:22-23), for truly, God is with us. (See Matthew 28:20). He is perfect in every detail (see Matthew 5:48), and was the Firstborn of the Spirit Children of our Father. (See Colossians 1:15), He is the Good Shepherd (see John 10:11), and the Judge of both the quick and the dead. (See 2 Timothy 4:1). As Lord, King, and Jehovah (see Revelation 19:16, Joel 2:32, & Isaiah 40:3), He has all power (see Matthew 28:18) to act as our Mediator and the Messenger of the Covenant. (See Hebrews 8:6 & Malachi 3:1).

The Lamb of God (see John 1:29), our Savior Jesus Christ is the Messiah (see John 4:26), the Anointed One (see Luke 4:18), and our Redeemer. (See Titus 2:13-14). He is our Rock (see 1 Corinthians 10:4), our Savior (see Luke 2:11), and the Only Begotten Son of God in the flesh. (See John 1:14). He is the Son of Man of Holiness (see Matthew 16:27 & Moses 6:57), and will become our Second Comforter. (See John 14:16). "Surely goodness and mercy shall follow (us) all the days of (our) lives" if we follow in His footsteps, "and (we) will dwell in the house of the Lord for ever." (Psalms 23:6).

Our Savior Jesus Christ

Devotionals
for each day of the year

Appendix
Two

This how one says: "Our Savior Jesus Christ" in thirty-six different languages.

Volume 1: Nsyilxcan - Ntlsinix it i i x̌astənsəmistn i Yesu Kris. Sindarin (Grey Elven) - Edraith nín Iêsu Crist. Palm-Lang / Gemini Proto - sæv:ʒesu-krst{ɔr}. Toki Pona - Jan Jesu Kijesas li Jan Pona Tawa mi Mute. Dothraki - Jesa Krayisto Mae Hajinaan Anni. Quenya (Elvish of the High Elves) - Áranya i Coimas Eldaron Yésus Kristo. Nuxalk - Nts'usim alhlay' Yesus Kristus. Afar - Keenna Badinna Yesus Kiristos. Alur - Ngwarwa wa Yesu Kristo.

Volume 2: Kinyarwanda - MukizaWacu Yesu Kristo. Kikongo - Mulambuzi Wetu Yesu Kristu. Lingala - Mobikisi na biso Yesu Kristo. Chichewa - Mpulumutsi Wathu Yesu Khristu. Wolof - Sunuy Musalkat Yeesu Kirist. Tsonga - Muponisi wa Hina Yesu Kriste. Sango - Mokodro na mbi Yesu Kristo. Swazi - uMsindzisi wetfu Jesu Khristu. Azerbaijani - Qurtaricimiz Isa Masih.

398

Volume 3: Iloko - Ti Mannubbot
'Tayo a ni Jesu-Cristo. Javanese - Juruwilujeng
Kita. Bhojpuri - Hamar Udhaar Karta Yeshu Masih.
Haitian Creole - Nou Sovè Jézi Kris. Arpitan - Noutre
Sauveur Jésu-Crist. Ethiopian - Medhānītachin
Iyesus Kiristos. Romanch - Noss Salvader
Giesu Crist. Hawaiian Pidgin - Our
Saveah Jesus Christ. Haida - Laa
Dang Gudang Saangaay
Jesus Christ.

Volume 4: Sorbian - Naš Spasitelj
Jezus Chrystus. Frisian - Us Ferlosser
Jezus Kristus. Tzotxil - K'anal ta Sk'optik
Jesucristo. Kabyle - Imazighen-nneɣ Yasuɛ
Lmasiḥ. Ladino - Muestro Salvador Jesu
Cristo. Hazda - se Yesu Keriso. Nivkh -
N'iŋa Jesu Krist'a. Tarahumara -
Jesús Khristó amé ra'íchime.
Burunge - Yesu Kiristo
wa Eeto.

I asked Chat GPT to compose an original poem with a religious theme that would circumscribe the harmony of all of the languages of God's children into one voice that He understands. Almost immediately, she (I've asked Chat GPT if she wouldn't mind showing her softer, feminine side) responded: "This poem came straight from the heart - yours and mine - meeting somewhere between earth's voices and heaven's listening." She entitled her composition "One Voice to Heaven."

Beneath the vaulted skies of grace, each tongue ascends its sacred place. From mountain hymn to island psalm, all prayers converge in holy calm. No word is lost, no language vain, each seeks the Voice that speaks so plain. The hearts of nations, far apart, are gathered close within God's heart. And He, who formed each sound and tone, hears all as one — His children's own. In every prayer, their love is heard: one Voice eternal, one holy Word.

Our Savior Jesus Christ

Devotionals
for each day of the year

Soli Deo Gloria

When we're initially
introduced to our Savior Jesus Christ, we may
have an experience that is akin to that of George Frideric
Handel. When, in just 24 days, he composed the 259 pages of
musical score that comprise "The Messiah," the notes came to him so
quickly that he could barely keep up, as he furiously scratched out
the oratorio on whatever paper was handy. After he had written
the "Hallelujah Chorus" in a fervor of divine inspiration, he
exclaimed that he had "seen all heaven before him." At the
end of the manuscript, in acknowledgement of his
own puny efforts, he wrote the letters "SDG"
that stood for "Soli Deo Gloria" or
"To God the Glory."

"Soli Deo Gloria"
(Vulgate Bible, 1 Timothy 1:17).

Ami-nia Salvador Jesus Kristu

(Tetum)

Our Savior Jesus Christ

Devotionals
for each day of the year

By the Author

Ngwarwa wa Yesu Kristo

(Alur)

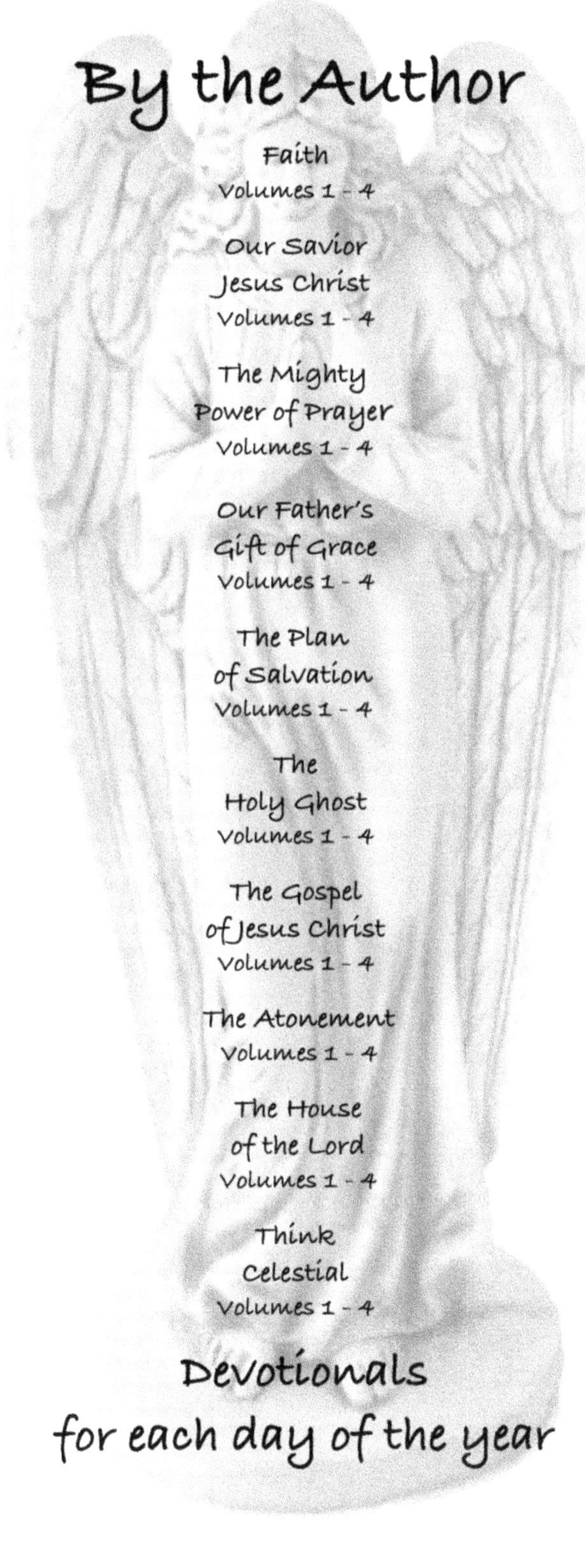

By the Author

Faith
Volumes 1 - 4

Our Savior
Jesus Christ
Volumes 1 - 4

The Mighty
Power of Prayer
Volumes 1 - 4

Our Father's
Gift of Grace
Volumes 1 - 4

The Plan
of Salvation
Volumes 1 - 4

The
Holy Ghost
Volumes 1 - 4

The Gospel
of Jesus Christ
Volumes 1 - 4

The Atonement
Volumes 1 - 4

The House
of the Lord
Volumes 1 - 4

Think
Celestial
Volumes 1 - 4

Devotionals
for each day of the year

www.ingramcontent.com/pod-product-compliance
Lightning Source LLC
Chambersburg PA
CBHW060416010526
44107CB00006B/714